IMAGES
of America

STAMFORD

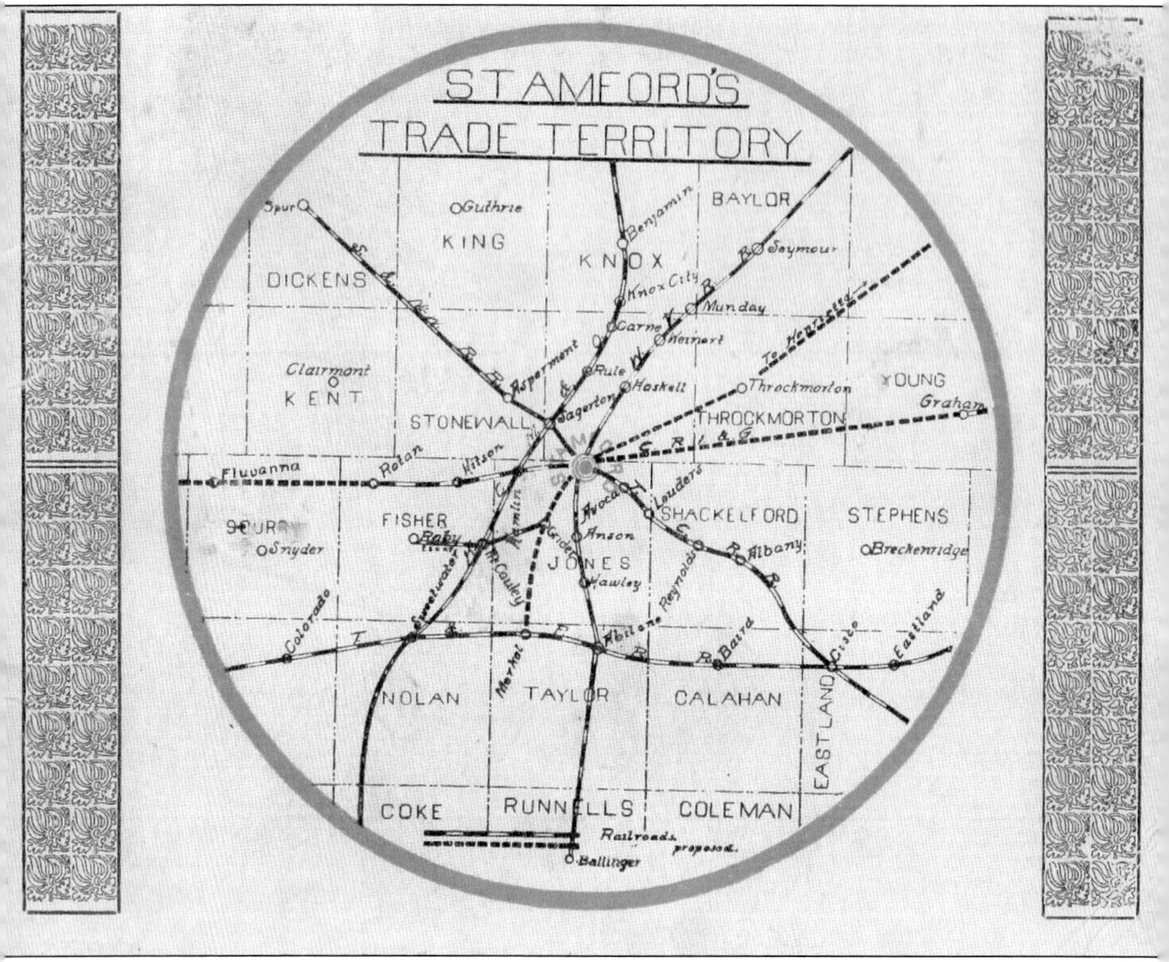

In 1910, the First National Bank of Stamford published a small brochure promoting Stamford as "the paved city of Texas," which included this map. Three railroads—the Texas Central, the Wichita Valley, and the Stamford & Northwestern—linked Stamford's "trade area" to the larger Texas cities and the eastern markets. The map also sketched additional routes for other rail lines that never materialized. (Courtesy of Cowboy Country Museum collection.)

ON THE COVER: In 1930, in the lean early years of the Great Depression, a group of Stamford men created the Texas Cowboy Reunion as an annual event to attract people and money to their community. Each year, they invited pioneer cowboys to bring their wagons and gear and relive the days of the longhorn and the open range with rodeo events, chuck wagon cooking, and an old fiddler's contest. The parades through downtown drew large crowds, including a daring few who climbed atop the Penick-Hughes Building. (Courtesy of Cowboy Country Museum collection.)

IMAGES
of America

STAMFORD

James Collett and the
Cowboy Country Museum

ARCADIA
PUBLISHING

ISBN 978-0-7385-9575-7

Published by Arcadia Publishing
Charleston, South Carolina

Printed in the United States of America

Library of Congress Control Number: 2012950484

For all general information, please contact Arcadia Publishing:
Telephone 843-853-2070
Fax 843-853-0044
E-mail sales@arcadiapublishing.com
For customer service and orders:
Toll-Free 1-888-313-2665

Visit us on the Internet at www.arcadiapublishing.com

For all the Stamford pioneers—of rail and retail, cow pony and plow

Contents

Acknowledgments		6
Introduction		7
1.	Prairie Boom Town	9
2.	Before Stamford	37
3.	Land and Cattle	43
4.	Good Times, Tough Times	67
5.	A Changing World	103
6.	Legacies	123

ACKNOWLEDGMENTS

Since 1975, the Cowboy Country Museum has worked to preserve the rich history of Stamford and the surrounding area. The museum contains a collection of artifacts large and small from Stamford's past, as well as archival records and photographs.

Unless otherwise noted, photographs are from the Cowboy Country Museum collection. The museum board played a significant role in the creation of this book. The 2012 board includes Kelly Williamson, president; Marge Barnet; Donna Sue Anders; Phil Swenson; and Lee Dickerson. Special thanks also to Sandra Rhea, museum curator, and Beverly Bryan for their help locating photographs and records in the museum collection; to Oran Brigham, Jackie Busky, Luci Frazier, Lee Roy Nauert, Tony Selmon, and Don Walker for interviews and photographs; and to Pattie Lay, Cheree Smith, and Megan Gooding for their proofreading assistance.

Introduction

In early 1900, the SMS ranches, owners of several vast tracts of land on the rolling plains of West Texas, partnered with the Texas Central Railroad to improve their connections to cattle markets. Swante Magnus Swenson, the first Swedish immigrant to Texas, who built a fortune in the mercantile business and later became one of the largest landowners in the state, founded the SMS ranches and passed them on to his sons with the charge to make them profitable. Together, the railroad and the Swenson interests established a town site company on a section of SMS land and launched the extension of a rail line 40 miles west from Albany. Texas Central Railroad president Henry McHarg named the community after his Connecticut hometown.

Stamford was officially incorporated on January 8, 1900, and lots began selling almost immediately. Entrepreneurs hauled buildings and supplies from Albany and Anson to erect temporary businesses. Among these was Robert Lee Penick, who established the first bank and became a founding father of the young city. The first train arrived on February 11, 1900. A boxcar served as both the first railroad station and the first post office. Within a month, Stamford's first newspaper, the *Stamford News*, began publication. The Commercial Club held its organizational meeting in a tent.

The youthful city grew rapidly as a shipping point. The Swenson Land and Cattle Company sold large portions of its land to farmers, who rushed to acquire a quarter section of the rich farmland of Jones and Haskell Counties. The prestigious Stamford Inn opened on February 3, 1901. Penick-Hughes, the first mercantile establishment in town, constructed a warehouse with rail facilities to handle the rapidly increasing stock of hardware, implements, and furniture. In 1905, a two-story city hall, also containing a fire station and an opera house, was constructed in the town square.

Within a few years, Stamford had a distribution center for the Armour Packing Company, an iron foundry, a number of wholesale produce houses, and even a piano warehouse. The prosperous community boasted numerous fine brick homes along streets and sidewalks paved with locally produced brick as well as the largest Methodist church between Fort Worth and El Paso. A flour mill was a leading industry from 1906 until its destruction by fire in 1946. A cottonseed oil plant, gins, and brick manufacturers were other significant employers. Stamford College, originally called Stamford Collegiate Institution, was opened by the Methodists in 1907. By 1909, the Stamford & Northwestern Railroad extended 80 miles northwest to the community of Spur, fueling further land sales around that community. Other rail lines reached Stamford, and with its new railroad roundhouse, it became a regional railroad hub.

Over the next decade, Stamford continued to grow and provide regional commercial leadership, including the formation of the West Texas Chamber of Commerce, headquartered in Stamford. The West Texas Utilities Company, which electrified much of western Texas, established a major regional office in the community. In 1910, the 12-bed Stamford Sanitarium opened in a frame building constructed by Dr. Sam Webb and Dr. M.E. Lott, chief surgeons for the Texas Central Railroad. The youthful city even gained a $15,000 Carnegie library, one of the smallest communities to do so.

The Swenson Land and Cattle Company pioneered the mail-order cattle business, with catalogs filled with photographs of its award-winning Hereford stock and images of working cowboys on the SMS ranches, all taken by local photographers like Ray Rector. There were setbacks as well. Due to several adverse circumstances, including a devastating fire in 1918, Stamford College closed in 1920. A more deadly fire destroyed the Stamford Inn on Christmas Eve of that year, claiming four victims. The inn was rebuilt the following year with steel beams and concrete floors and remained a Stamford institution for decades.

Stamford faced challenges during the Great Depression as small farms failed and business declined. In 1930, several local leaders, including Robert Lee Penick, Swenson Land and Cattle Company manager W.G. Swenson, and Flat Top Ranch foreman John Selmon, created an event they hoped would attract visitors and money. The Texas Cowboy Reunion, held around the Fourth of July, was a gathering of and a competition among working cowhands to honor their traditions. From the beginning, the reunion was a major social and economic event that attracted such national figures as Will Rogers. The discovery of oil in the region also helped broaden the local economy.

During World War II, a flying school operated out of Arledge Field, the local airport. Established in 1941, the school provided valuable revenue for the community. Each class of cadets published an edition of the *Plane Wrangler* until the school closed in September 1944.

In the latter half of the 20th century, Stamford dealt with a shrinking agricultural population even as mechanization and larger-scale farming increased the regional agricultural output. Several local manufacturers closed. The growth of oil production in the county provided an economic boost. Lake Stamford, constructed 10 miles northeast of the city, provided new water and recreation resources. The railroad lines declined in revenue and eventually ended service. Transportation shifted to the expanding state and national highway systems. Stamford became the junction of Highway 277 and Highway 6. Local business declined around the town square, as people looked more to larger cities for many resources. A series of small apparel manufacturers came and went, but Stamford continued to be the largest small city in the area, partly due to its excellent medical services. In 1969, a new 50-bed hospital replaced the aging sanitarium, and it later expanded to 74 beds.

By the beginning of the 21st century, Stamford adapted to survive in the face of urbanization and high technology. The large warehouses and mills are gone. Standardization has come in the form of national chain outlets, but local businesses continue to provide critical services. The city, now more than a century old, remains the social, economic, and medical center for a tri-county area of one of the richest agricultural regions of Texas. As it has for decades, the community of Stamford preserves the legacies of the Swenson Land and Cattle Company, the Texas Cowboy Reunion, and the vanished farm communities.

One

Prairie Boom Town

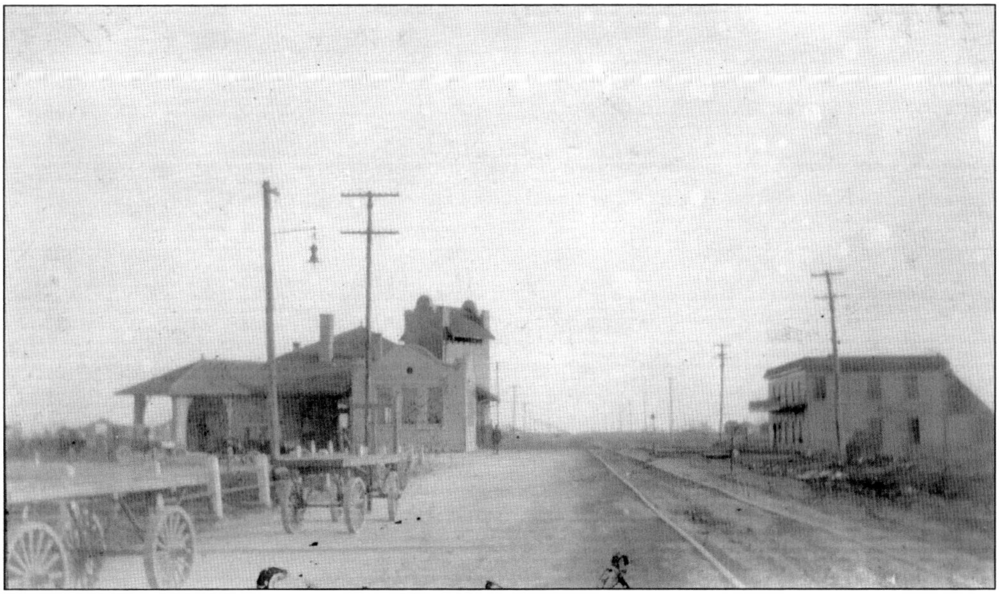

Stamford was created as a real estate partnership between the Swenson brothers and the Texas Central Railroad. The two formed the Stamford Townsite Company in November 1899. The Swensons gave the railroad half the town site section of land in return for making it the new end of track. Several years later, after the construction of Union Station (left), the rich prairie land still dominated the view along the track.

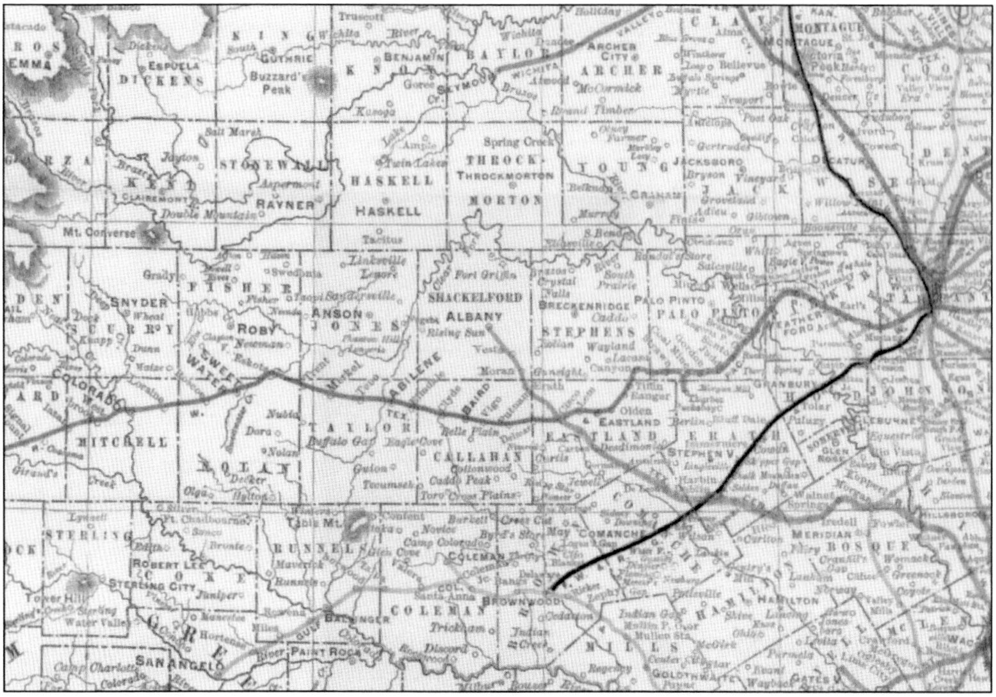

The Texas Central Railroad Company, chartered in 1892, acquired a railroad originating near Waco (lower right corner of this 1893 map) and extending northwest to Albany in Shackelford County. The company ambitiously projected expansion to Las Vegas in the New Mexico Territory. In 1900, construction began on the 40-mile line to the Stamford town site. Two small communities, Linksville and Lenore, appear on this map near the future location of Stamford. (Courtesy of Texas General Land Office.)

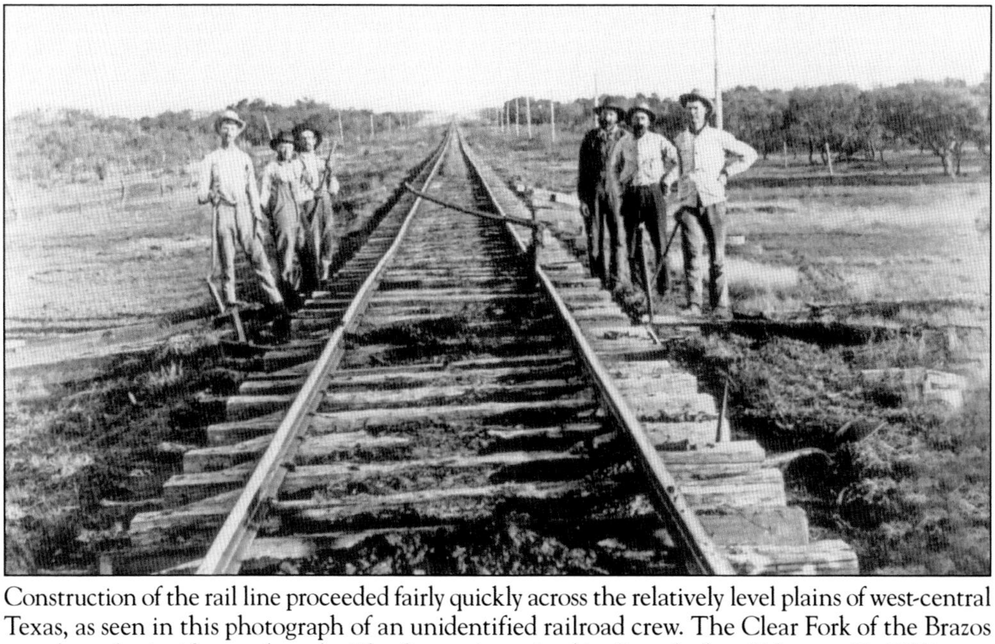

Construction of the rail line proceeded fairly quickly across the relatively level plains of west-central Texas, as seen in this photograph of an unidentified railroad crew. The Clear Fork of the Brazos was the only significant obstacle. The first train arrived in Stamford on February 11, 1900.

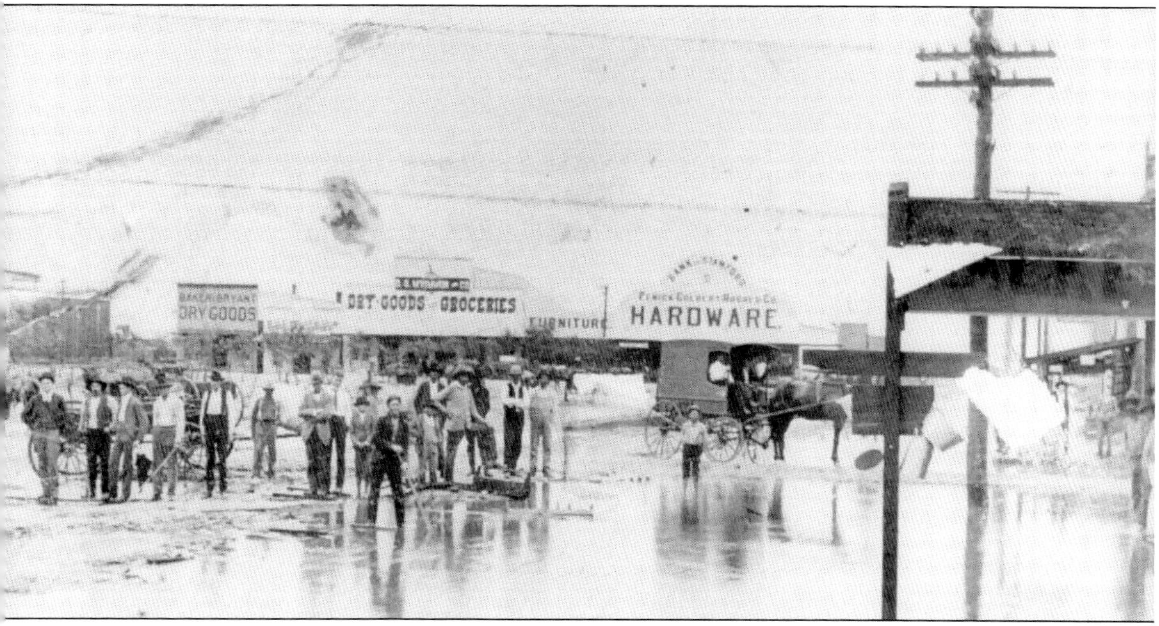

Stamford began before the railroads arrived. The first lots sold on January 15, 1900. However, Robert Lee Penick convinced P.P. Berthelot, the manager of the town site company, to allow him to occupy two lots ahead of sales, even though prices had not yet been established. Penick, a hardware dealer from nearby Anson, decided to stake his fortune on the new town. Partners R.V. Colbert and Ed S. Hughes helped Penick move a small 12-foot-by-20-foot frame structure from Anson. On January 8, the Bank of Stamford became the first business to open in the new city. Nathan Leavitt, later the first postmaster, made the initial deposit of 15¢ on January 15. In this photograph, looking south across what became the city square, residents assess flood damage caused by the remnants of the hurricane that destroyed Galveston a few days earlier. In the background is the Bank of Stamford, which also housed Penick-Colbert-Hughes Co. Hardware. Dry goods, groceries, and furniture stores have joined the bank along Hamilton Street.

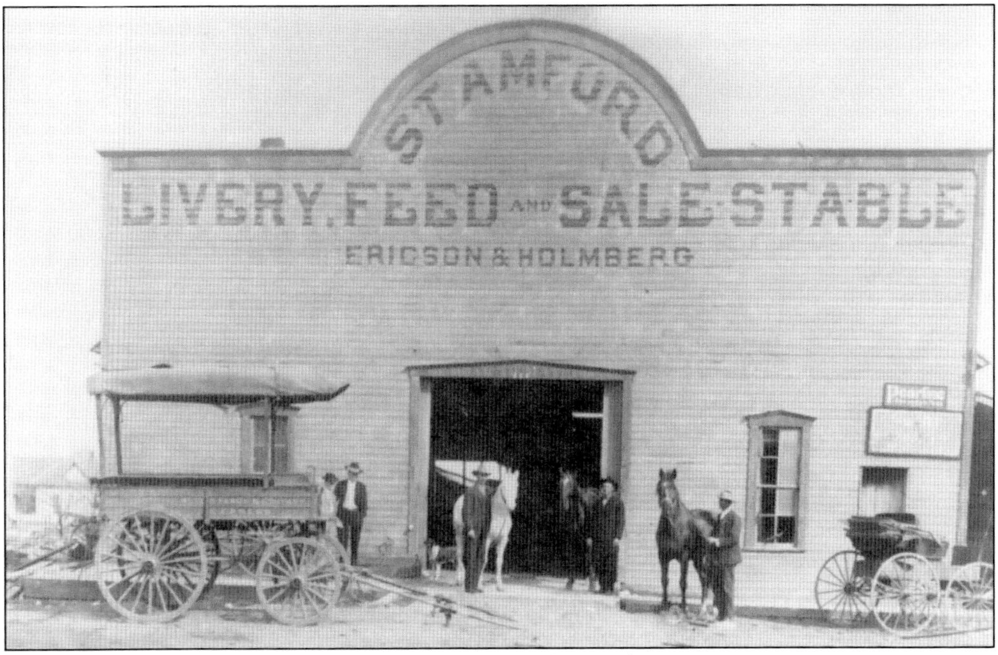

Lots went on sale on January 15 and ranged from $25 to $350. The livery stable, seen here, purchased three lots. P.P. Berthelot kept a staff of salesmen and clerks busy selling business lots. Within a week, more than $6,500 in real estate had sold. Before the trains arrived, construction was rudimentary. The Commercial Club, an early-day chamber of commerce, held its organizational meeting in March 1900 in a tent.

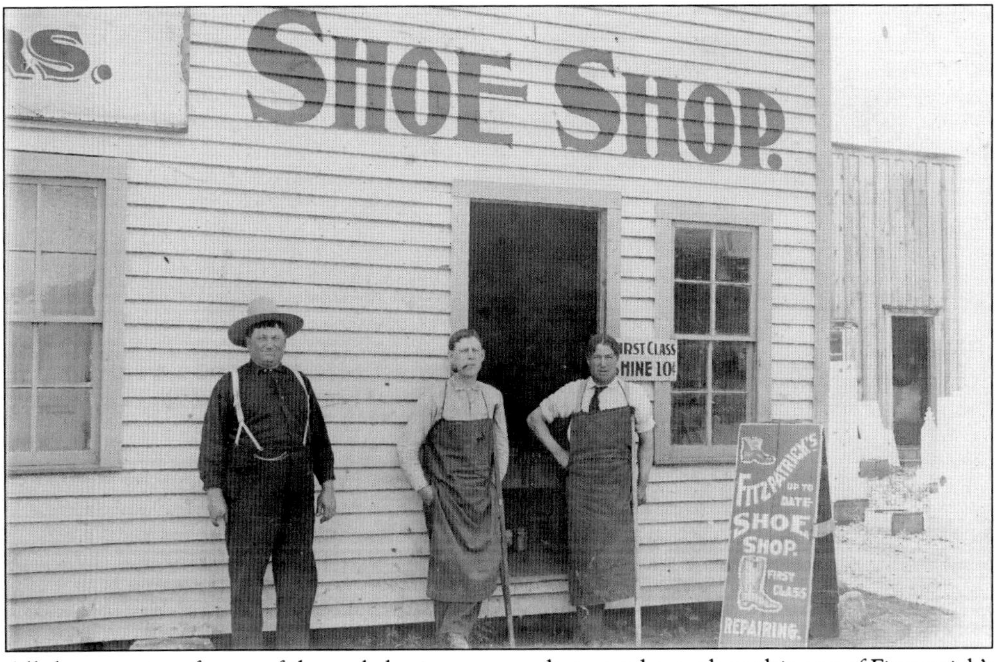

All that remains of some of the early businesses are photographs, such as this one of Fitzpatrick's Shoe Shop. The names of the two shoe repairmen and their visitor are unknown. A cemetery monument workshop is next door.

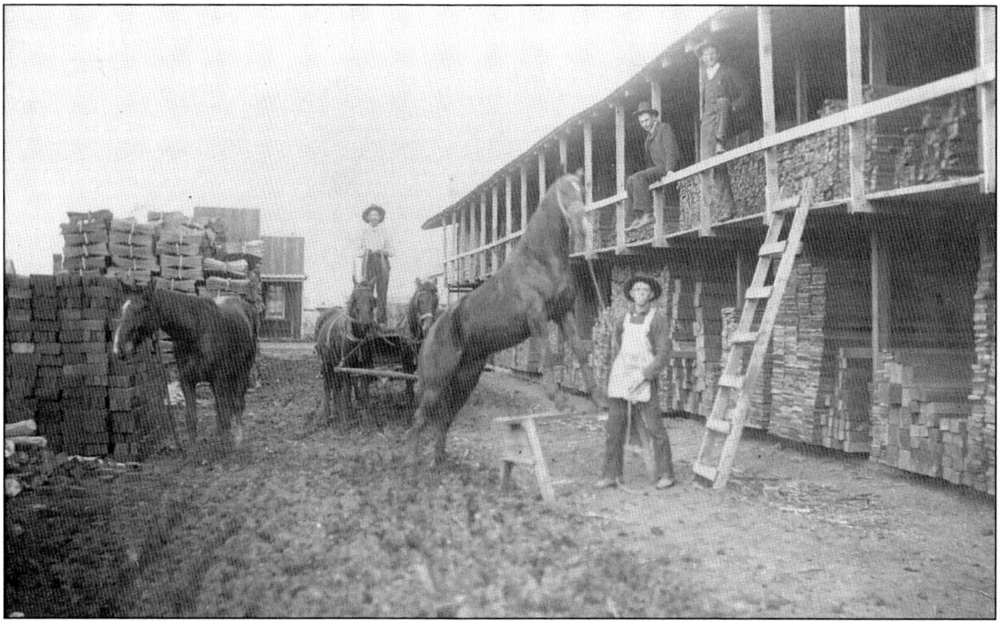

The arrival of train service quickly brought lumber and other construction materials, along with household goods and people eager for a new start. Lumber companies such as Brazelton-Johnson worked hard to meet the demand. In this photograph of an unidentified Stamford lumber company, the trained horse has center stage, but the large yard in the background indicates that business was good. By May 1900, the population had grown to 1,500.

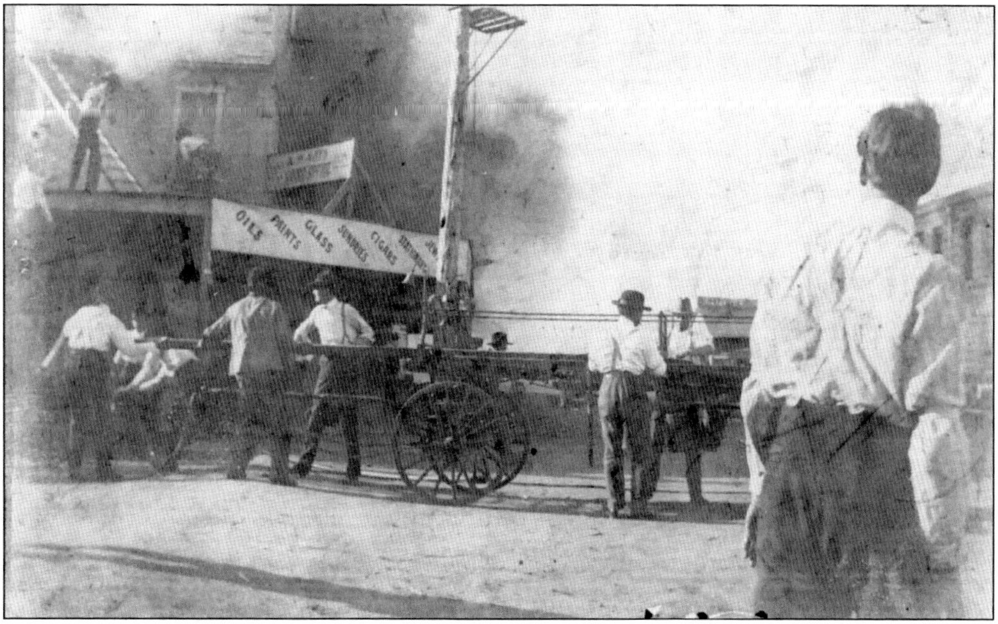

Rapid and sometimes haphazard growth had its dangers, especially fire. John Sledge, a recent arrival from Comanche, Texas, joined R.L. Penick in establishing a volunteer fire department. Their first equipment included a hand-drawn hook-and-ladder truck and 250 feet of hose, which sometimes proved to be inadequate, as in the case of this 1906 fire that destroyed the land office of B.W. Gay.

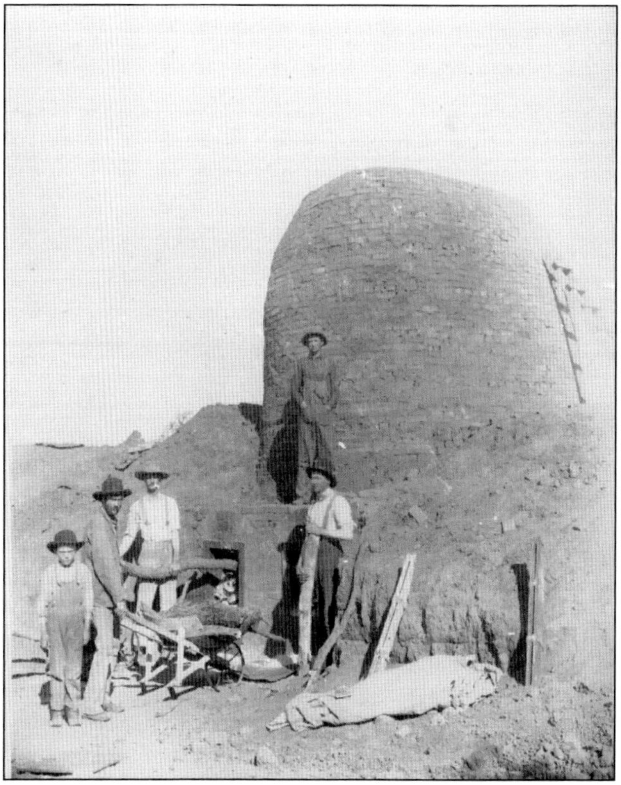

Local brick allowed for more substantial construction. The Brewington Brick Plant, seen here in August 1901, began as a primitive operation. Local red clay deposits were mined and bricks made primarily by muscle. Many early Stamford businesses were constructed from this brick, with Pattillo Hardware being the first. More substantial brickworks operated here in later years.

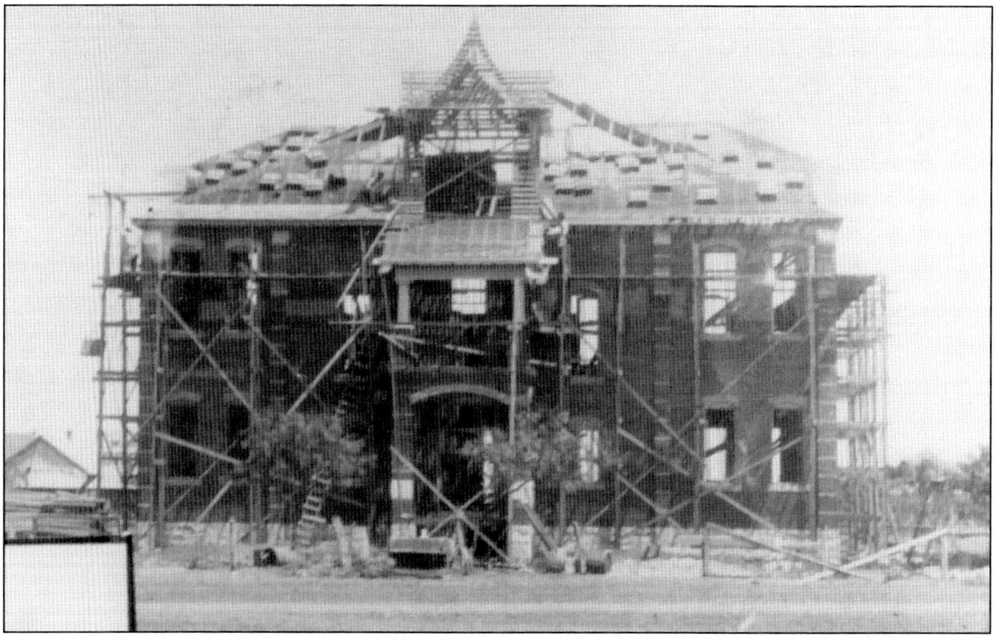

Stamford's first mayor, P.P. Berthelot, was elected in 1901. He was followed in 1903 by R.L. Penick and in 1905 by Dr. John R. Sledge. In 1905, construction of this town hall began in the center of the city square, at the corner of Swenson and McHarg Streets. When completed, the building housed the city government and the firehouse on the lower floor and an opera house upstairs.

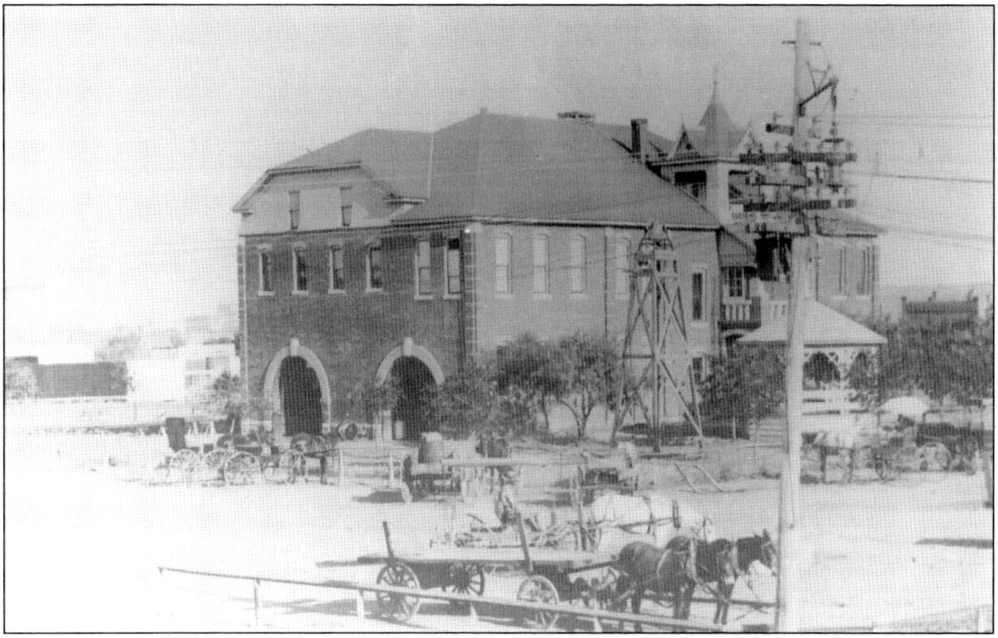

The north end of the town hall had two arched doors, which served as the fire station exits. Harnesses and riggings for the fire horses hung from the ceiling and could quickly be lowered onto the animals to answer a fire. In 1907, the city bought a team of three gray horses and a one-horse hook-and-ladder wagon. The tower beside the gazebo held a large fire bell.

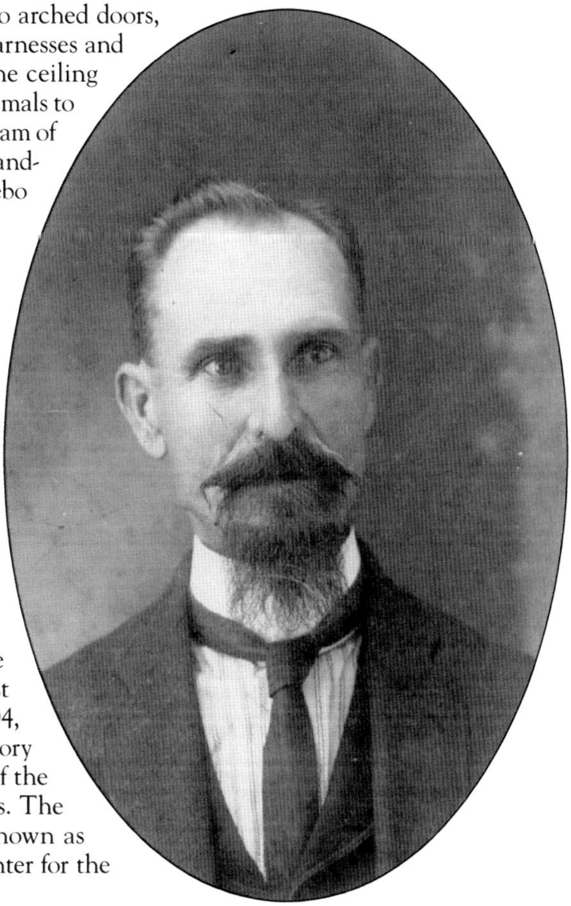

Dr. John Randolph Sledge served as the first fire chief. He was also Stamford's first public health officer, from 1900 to 1904, before becoming mayor. He built a two-story white frame building on the south side of the square. Dr. Sledge's offices were upstairs. The bottom floor was a large auditorium known as Sledge Hall, which served as a social center for the town in the early years.

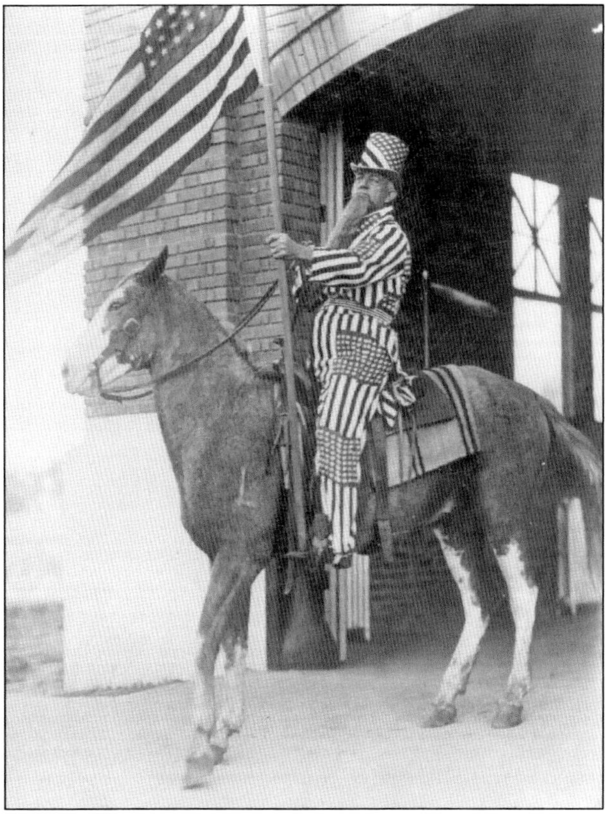

Robert Lee Penick, dressed here as Uncle Sam in front of the firehouse, played a pivotal role in Stamford's history and later became known as "the father of Stamford." Penick led the original Commercial Club, served on the first city council, became the city's second mayor, and helped Dr. Sledge establish the first fire department, serving as president. Penick eventually gained the honorary title of "colonel" and long remained a civic leader.

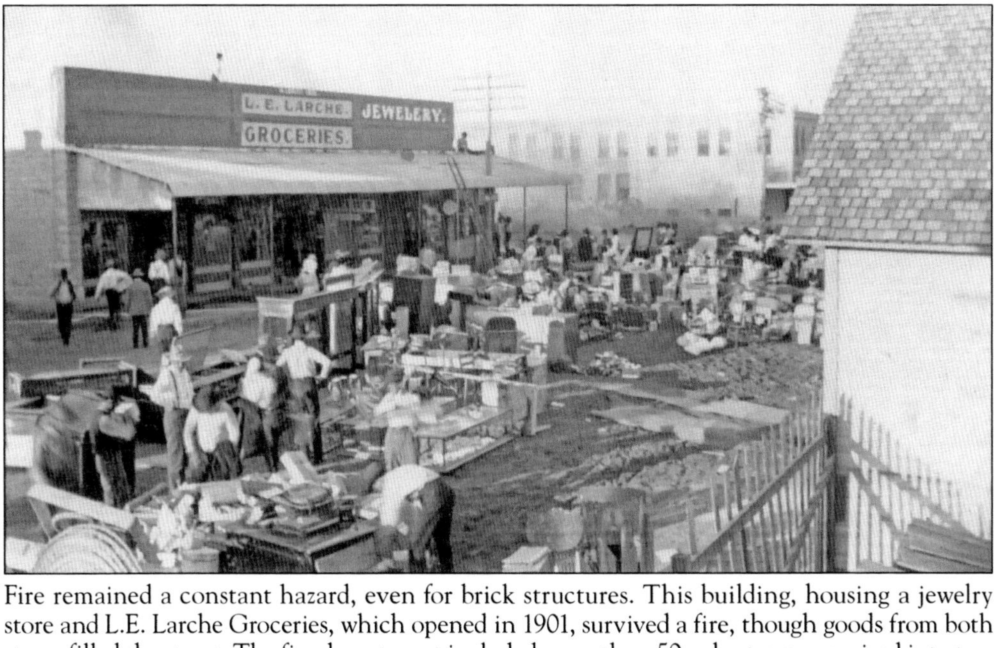

Fire remained a constant hazard, even for brick structures. This building, housing a jewelry store and L.E. Larche Groceries, which opened in 1901, survived a fire, though goods from both stores filled the street. The fire department included more than 50 volunteers organized into two companies. Many fires were devastating due to inadequate water pressure and lack of training by the volunteers.

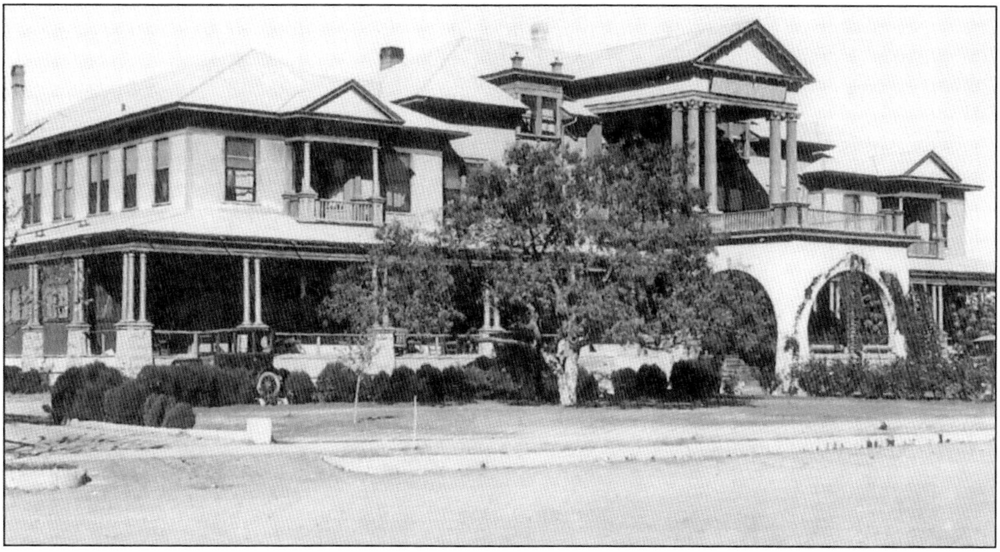

A railroad passenger car served as the Tavern, Stamford's first hotel. In the spring of 1900, the Stamford Townsite Company began construction of the Stamford Inn on McHarg Street, just east of the town square. Built at a cost of $40,000, the inn opened in February 1901 and quickly became a favorite with businessmen and travelers.

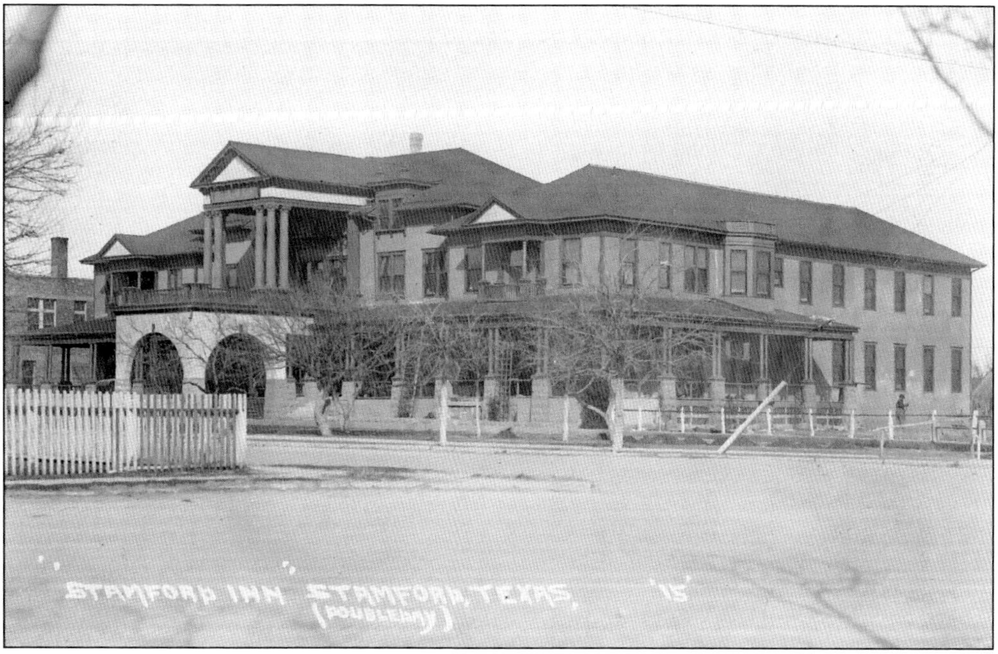

A large veranda extended across the front of the inn and wrapped around the edge of the three-story wood-frame structure. The building could be seen for miles across the flat Texas plains. Locals considered it a mark of distinction to dine at the inn. W.E. Gunning managed the hotel for the company.

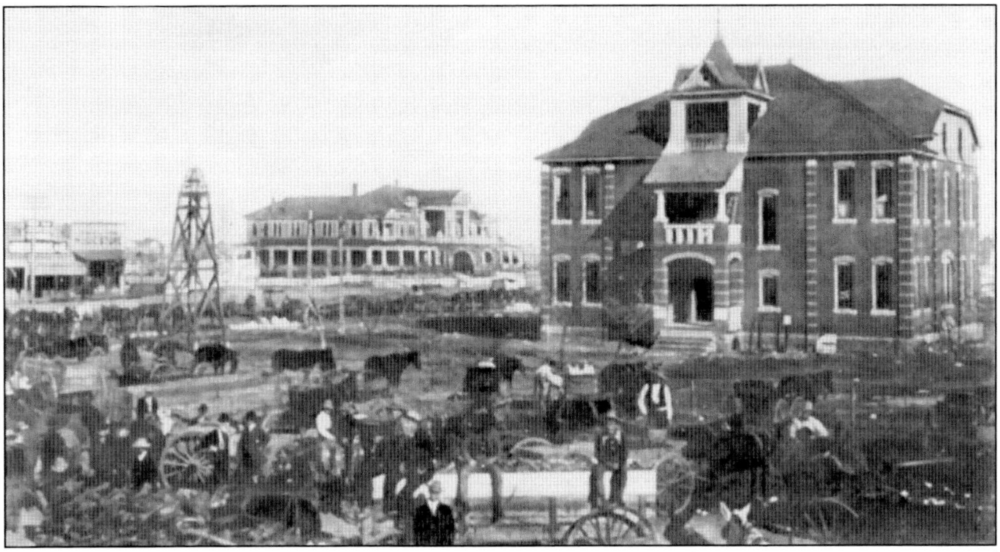

This postcard looks northeast across Stamford's busy square around 1907. Numerous wagons and buggies line the square, some loaded with lumber or other supplies for the surrounding ranches and farms. The gazebo does not appear to have been constructed yet. In the background, the Stamford Inn, Green Brothers, and a music store face the square along McHarg Street.

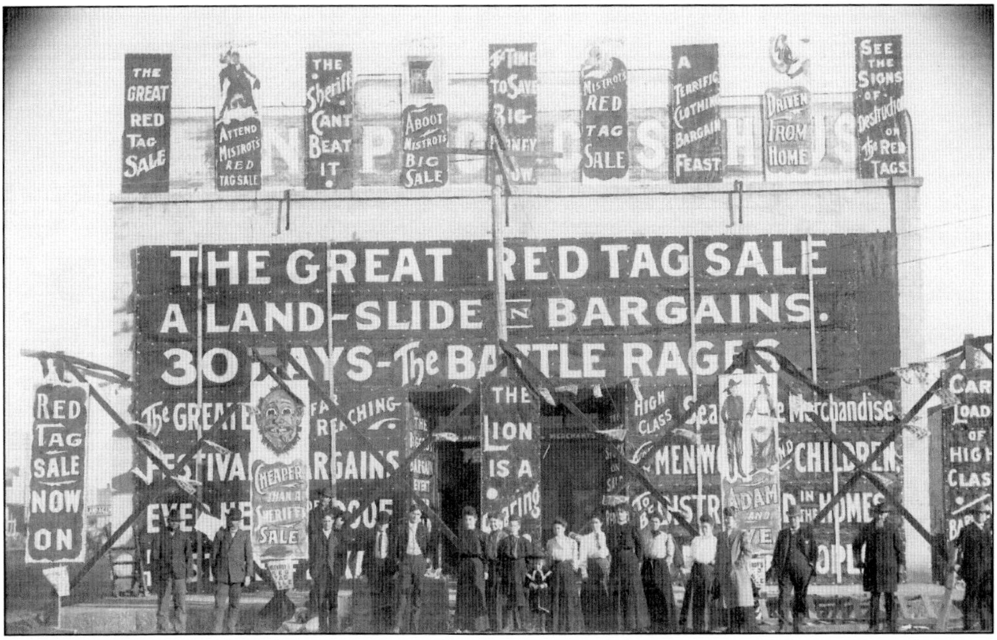

During the early building boom, new merchants competed for customers. Mistrot Bros. became known for its flashy promotional sales. Here, store clerks and potential customers line up outside a Mistrot store advertising "The Great Red Tag Sale," with banners and posters covering most of the building's front. Interesting artwork and claims like "cheaper than sheriff's sale" all aim to entice shoppers into the store.

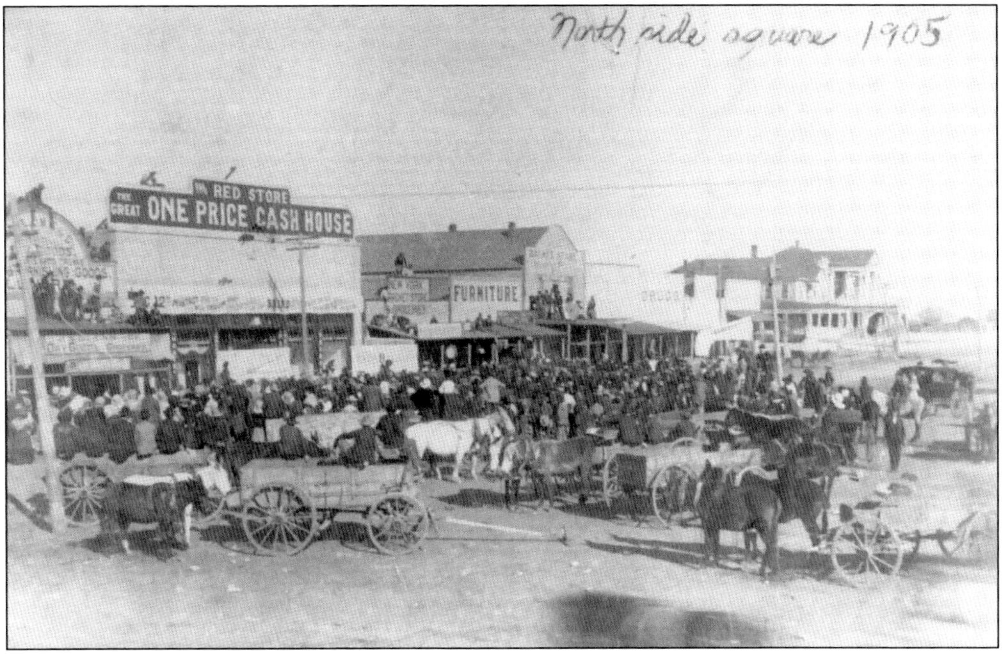

This December 12, 1905, event was sponsored by the Red Store, "the Great One Price Cash House," where, it advertised, "Mistrot Bros. and Co. will throw away the old goods of the Baird Store from the top of the Red Store building" to attract a crowd. "It usually did, too," recalled one old-timer. The Stamford Inn is on the right.

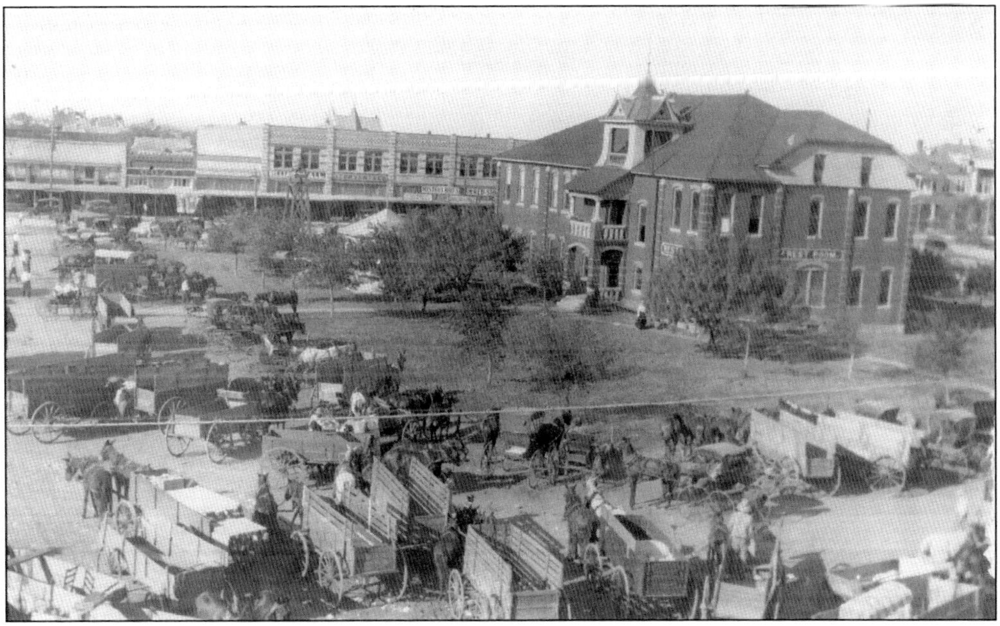

The square changed rapidly after 1905. This photograph's perspective is close to that of the postcard on page 18. The inn is on the far right. Brick buildings line McHarg Street, including, from left to right, the Nickel Store, the Cozy, a billiard hall, J.T. Bryant and Company Dry Goods, Mistrot Bros., and the Red Store. A note on this photograph labels it a typical Saturday.

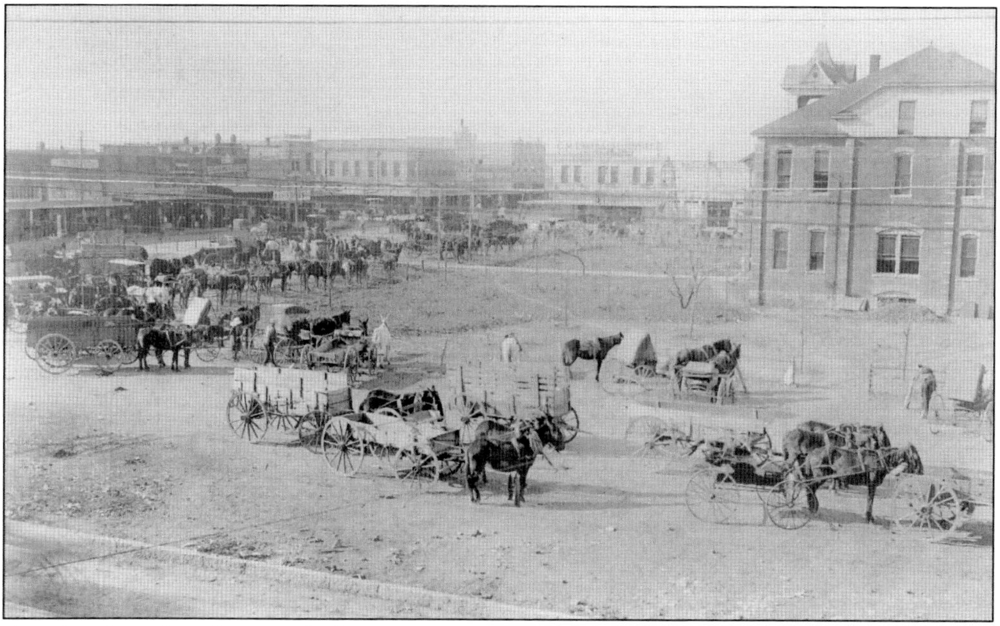

Another Saturday photograph shows even more activity, with a maze of wagons, buggies, and people filling the square and Swenson Avenue. Pattillo Hardware (center) occupies the corner of Swenson and McHarg Streets. Across the street is the First State Bank, organized in 1909. Businesses along South Swenson Street included J.E. Raines Dry Goods, B. Yates Drugs, and the Citizen's National Bank, on the corner.

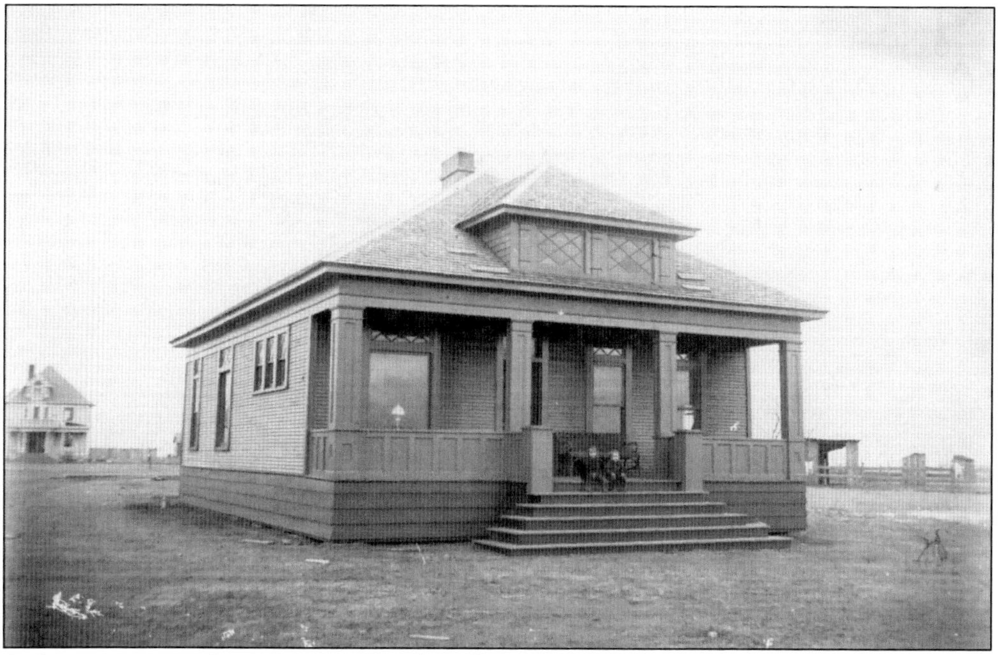

As businessmen and investors prospered in the new city, they erected fine homes. Some, like this house on Moran Street—named for Charles Moran, the largest Texas Central Railroad stockholder—were built when streets were little more than lines on a map. These unidentified children watched a city growing faster than they were.

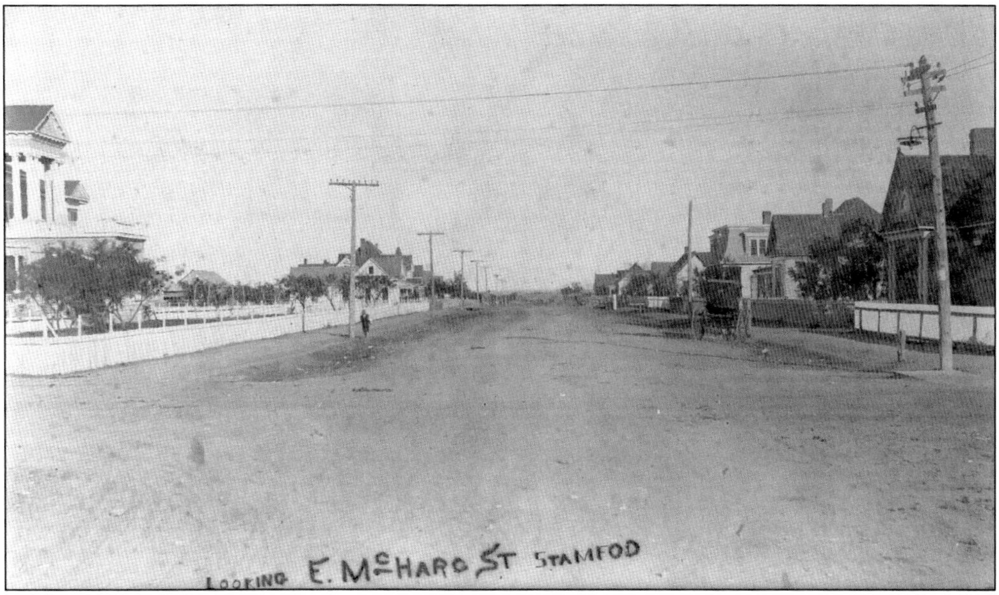

The first electric light plant was installed in 1900 and provided power to homes like these, on McHarg Street east of the Stamford Inn (far left). Lucien Larch, who opened his grocery store in 1901, lived on McHarg Street. A waterworks system was begun in 1899, and a water tower and mains were constructed the following year. Streets gained more definition but remained packed dirt.

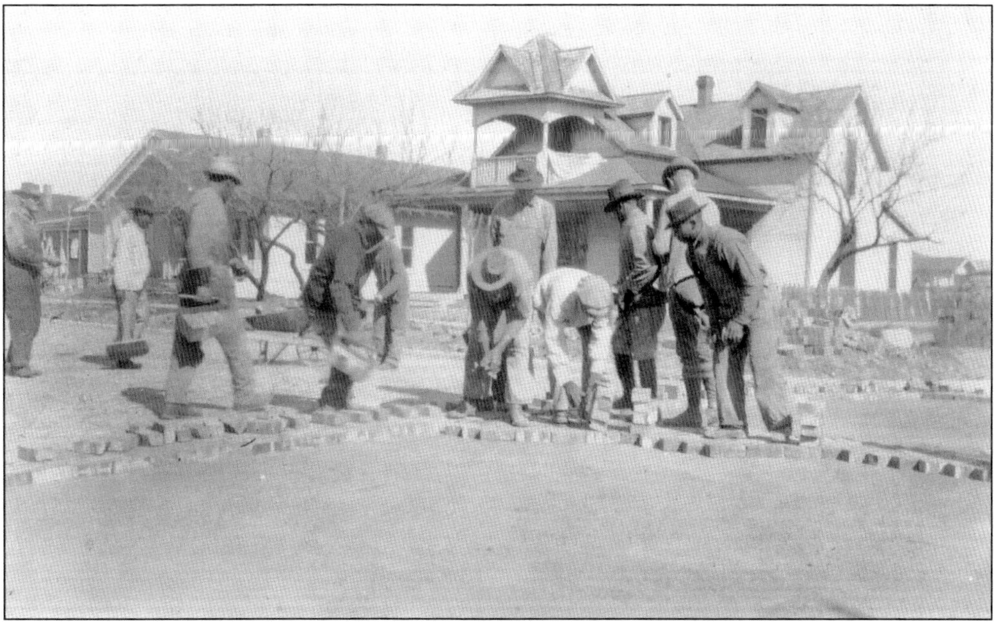

Streets surrounding the square were paved with bricks, and brick pavement slowly extended into residential areas. This photograph of a Stamford brick crew is from the 1920s, but the brick-by-brick process remained the same. By 1910, Stamford billed itself as "the paved city of Texas," with 16 blocks of vitrified brick pavement and 20 miles of concrete sidewalks. However, a 1911 letter from one resident commented, "There was more mud than brick streets." (Quoted in the 75th Anniversary Edition of the *Stamford American*, November 13, 1975.)

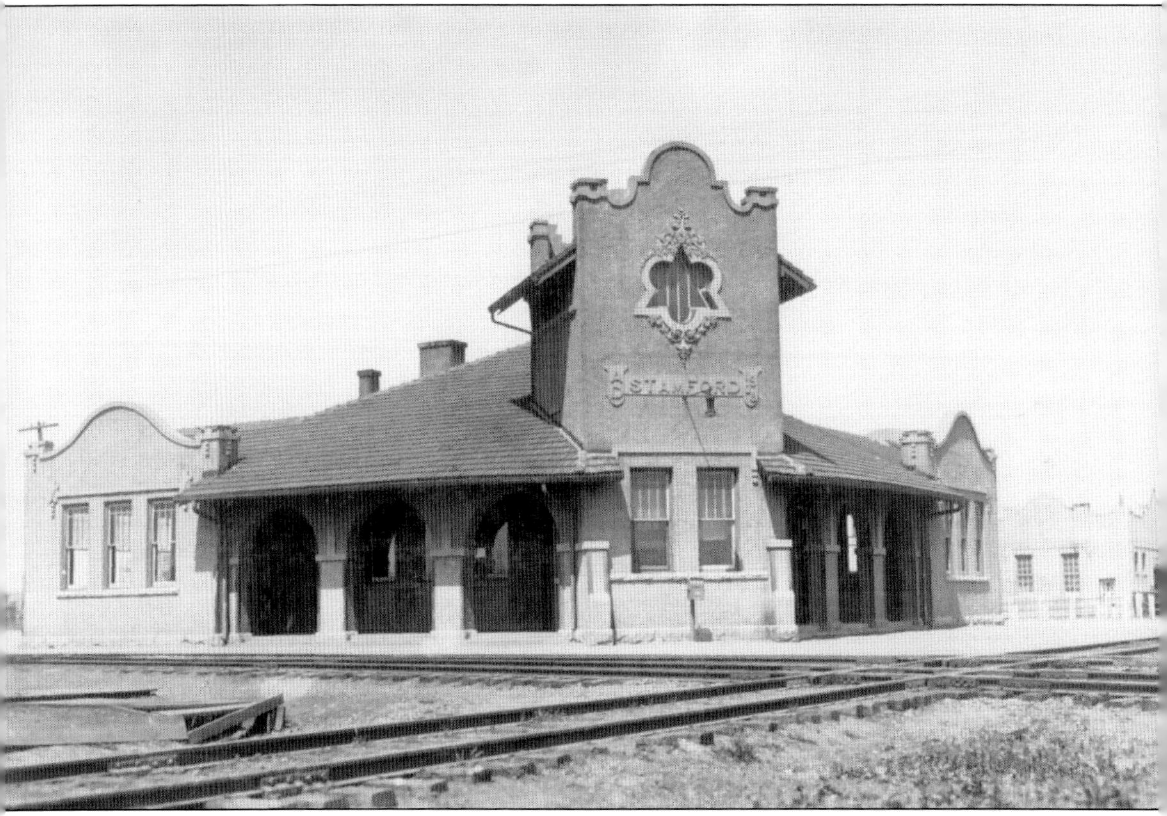

Railroad growth helped solidify Stamford's position as the gateway to central West Texas. The Texas Central expanded 42 miles west to Rotan in 1907. The Wichita Valley Railway connected Wichita Falls to Abilene and the Texas & Pacific Railroad. Several Stamford businessmen, including R.L. Penick, chartered the Stamford & Northwestern Railroad in 1909 with plans to build to Plainview, Texas. By the following year, the line reached Spur, 82 miles northwest, with bonuses of more than $223,000, the largest given in Texas for this amount of railroad. The Kansas City, Mexico & Orient Railway, a speculative venture planned to reach all the way from Kansas City to Topolobampo, Mexico, intersected the Stamford & Northwestern at Sagerton, 10 miles down the line. The Stamford Union Station depot, seen here in 1923, was built at a cost of $15,000 and welcomed passenger trains with Pullman coaches. Freight trains brought a wealth of goods for farmers, ranchers, and citizens of new towns that sprang up along the tracks like Tuxedo and Hamlin.

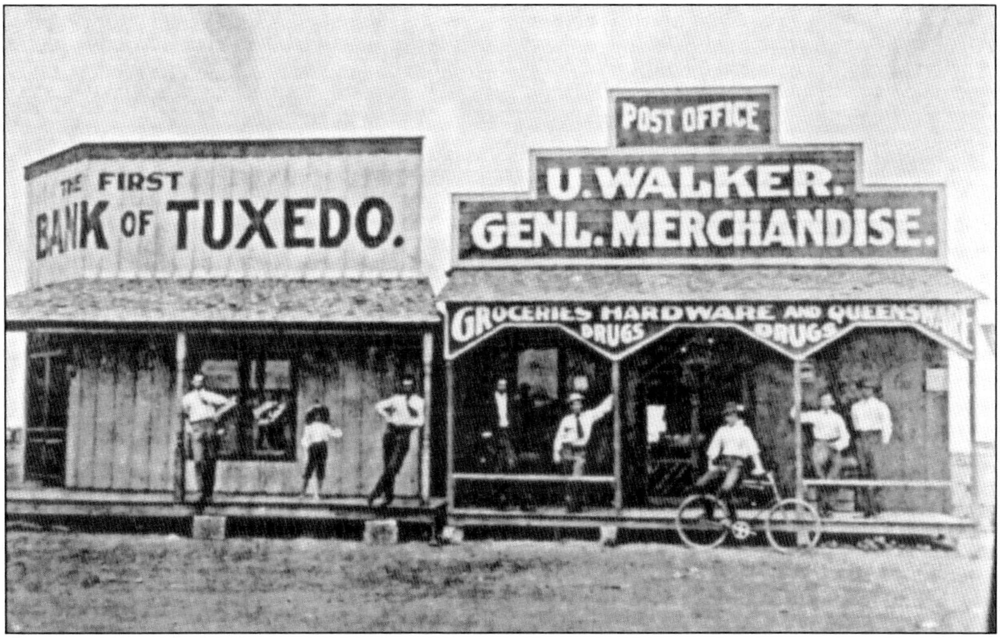

Tuxedo began in 1905 as the small community of Bonita, 10 miles west of Stamford. When the railroad arrived, the postal service required a different name. With 17 businesses by 1911, Tuxedo had dreams of challenging Stamford's success, but a massive fire the following year destroyed most of the community, and the town never regained its momentum. (Courtesy of Dwaine Stephens family, Tuxedo Reunion files.)

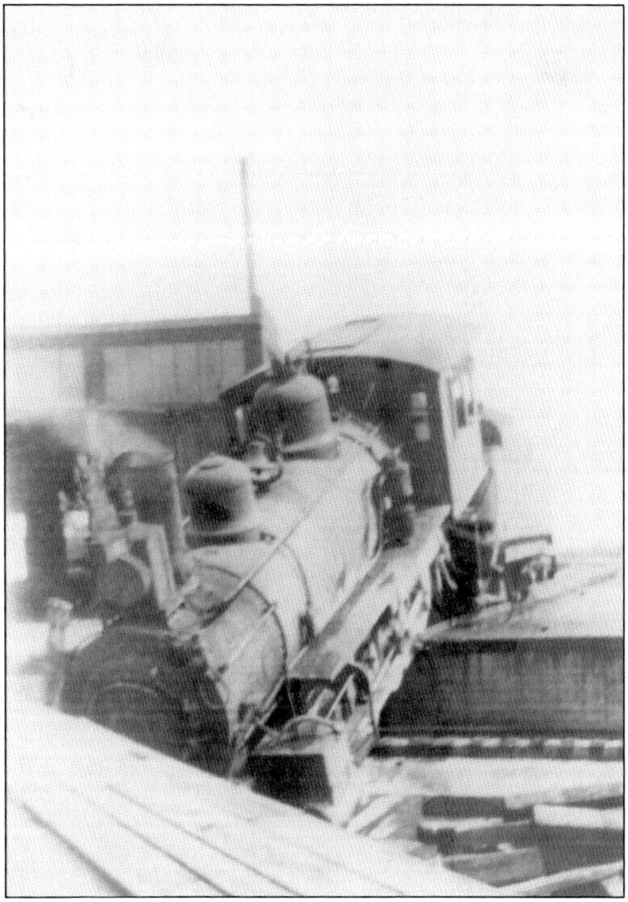

Everything did not always run smoothly, as seen in this undated photograph of an engine that ran off the turntable and into the pit at the roundhouse in Stamford. In these years, the roundhouse and machine shop employed more than 100 men to handle the rail traffic.

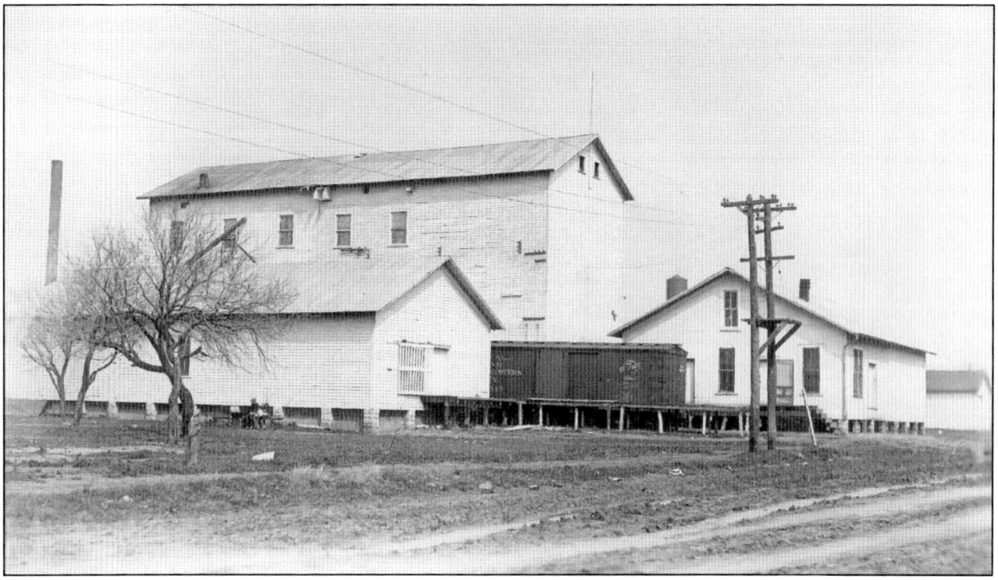

The railroad connections allowed Stamford to become a small manufacturing center. The Stamford Flour Mill and Elevator, established in 1900, was the city's largest industry. The Stamford Cotton Oil Company began in 1904 and was managed for a time by P.P. Berthelot. The iron foundry began operations in 1906. This structure may be part of the flour mill, seen in the early 1920s.

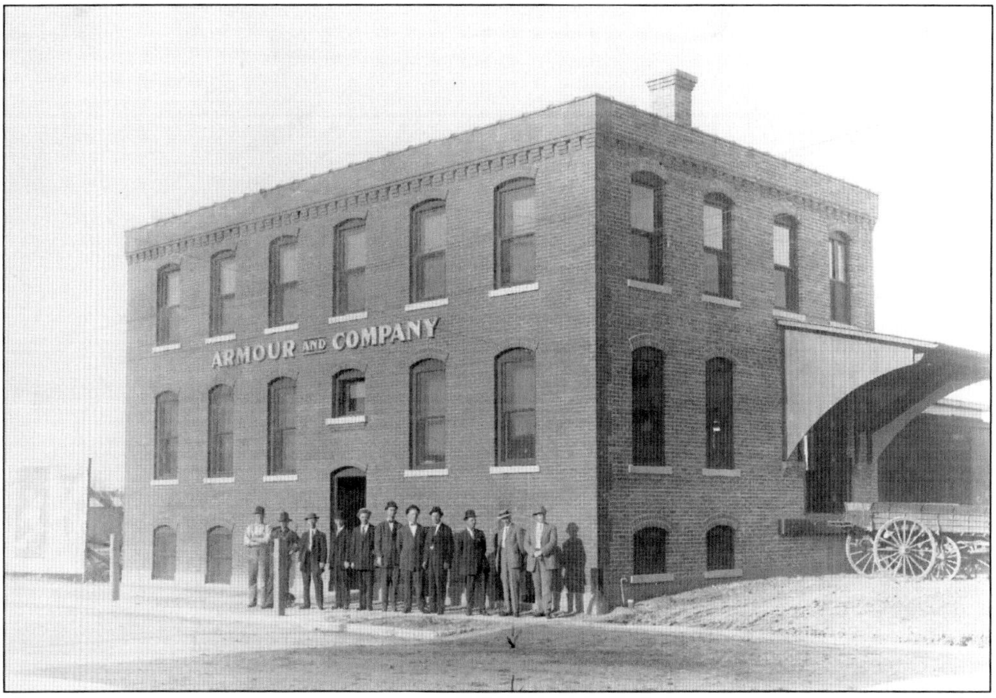

Several wholesalers made Stamford their West Texas headquarters, including grocers, produce houses, and even a piano manufacturer. Armour and Company, the Chicago meatpacking firm, opened a branch office in Stamford in 1909, and the volume of its business led the company to construct a $30,000 building. The only person identified in this photograph is H.P. Mowdy, second from the right.

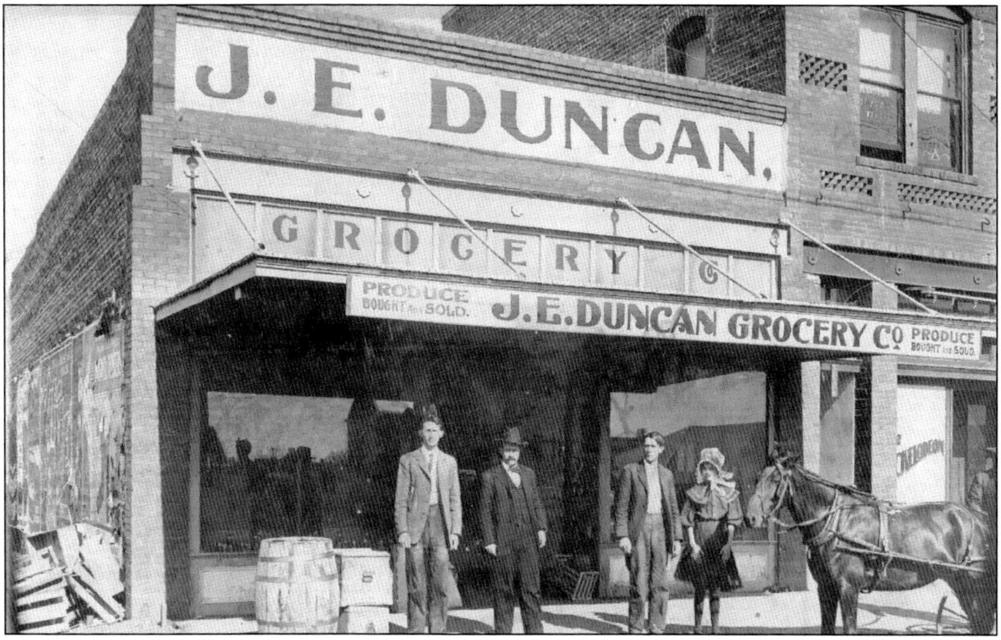

Retail businesses like J.E. Duncan Grocery Co. provided goods for the rapidly growing population. By 1909, Stamford had 75 retail establishments, including dry goods stores, drugstores, jewelers, and a steam laundry. Horses and wagons remained the primary transportation, but a nickelodeon provided movies next door to Duncan's. The grocer's wall was covered with posters advertising circuses, traveling vaudeville troupes, and Chautauqua tent shows. Every soda fountain had Dr. Pepper for 5¢ a glass.

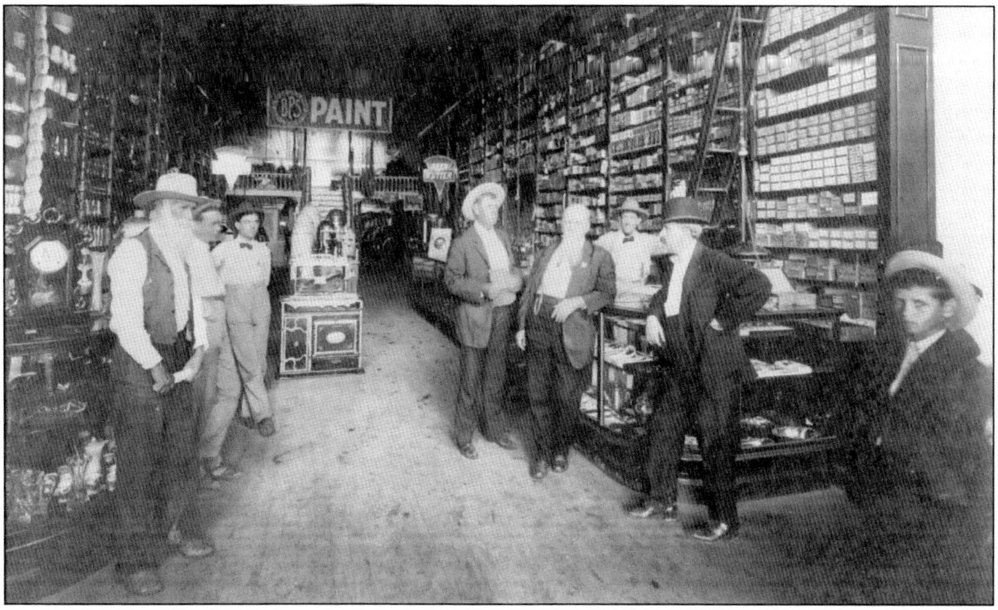

This undated photograph shows White's Hardware Store filled with a wide variety of goods, from clocks and dishes on the left to cutlery and boxes of marbles on the far right. A Detroit stove is in the center, and several buggies are in the back. Proprietor James A. White is second from the right, Ben Cullum stands at the ladder, and the others are unidentified.

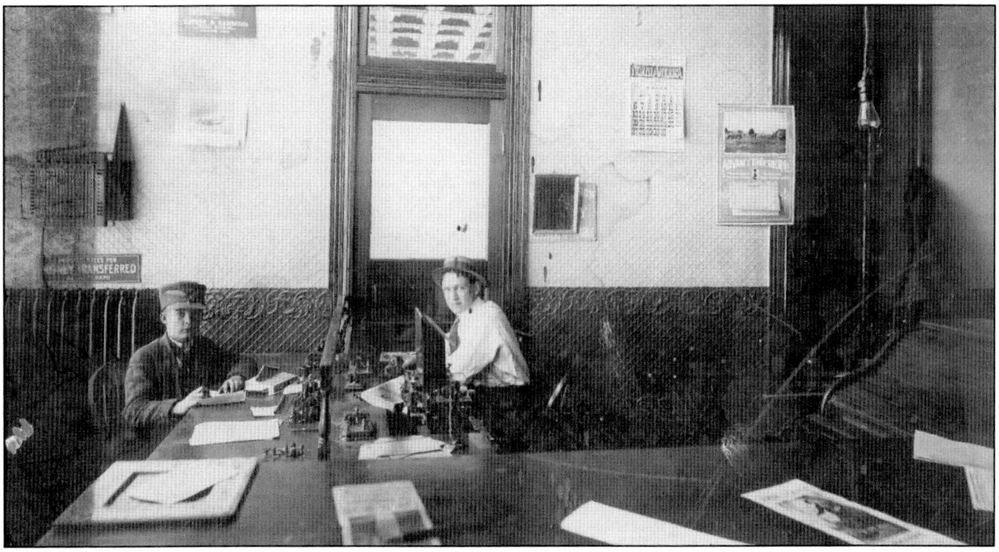

Residents also had access to multiple communication sources. The *Stamford News* was established in 1900. Methodist minister Samuel Gay served as the editor for several years. The newsstand in the Yates Drug Store carried the *Dallas News* by 1904. The two young telegraph operators in this 1910 photograph are identified as D. Gay and W.U. Smith.

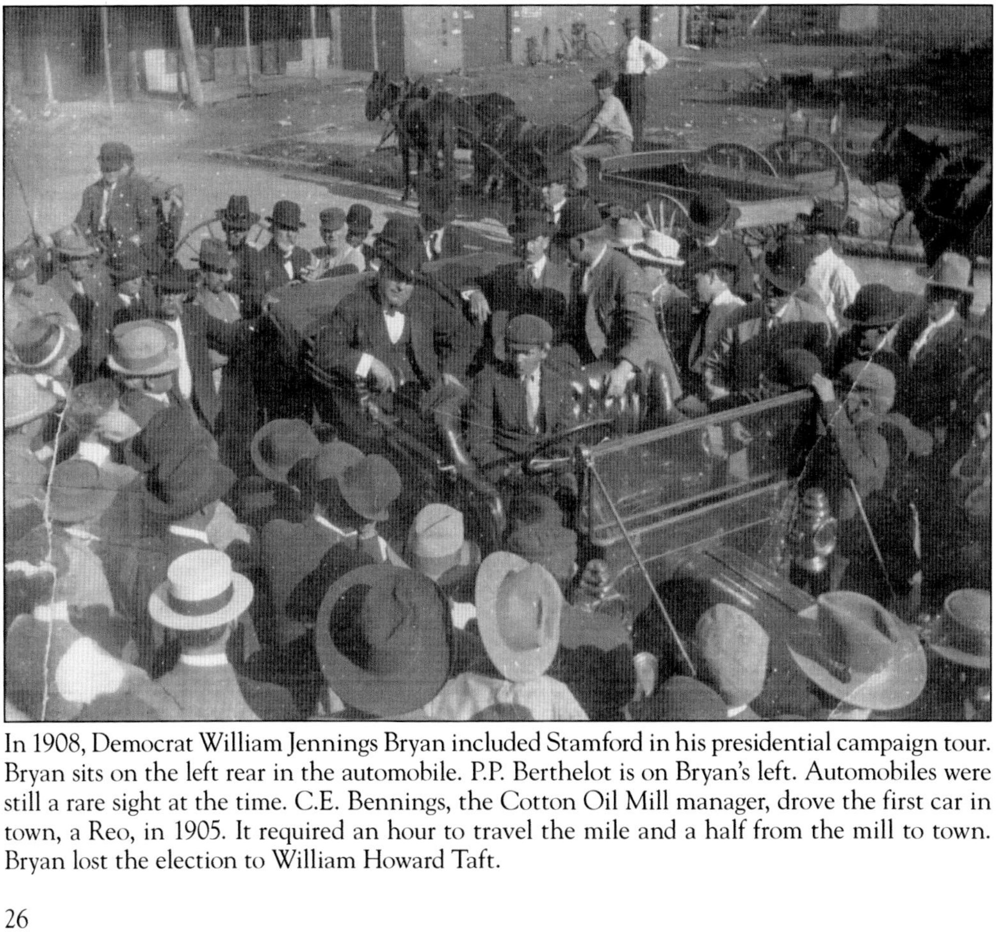

In 1908, Democrat William Jennings Bryan included Stamford in his presidential campaign tour. Bryan sits on the left rear in the automobile. P.P. Berthelot is on Bryan's left. Automobiles were still a rare sight at the time. C.E. Bennings, the Cotton Oil Mill manager, drove the first car in town, a Reo, in 1905. It required an hour to travel the mile and a half from the mill to town. Bryan lost the election to William Howard Taft.

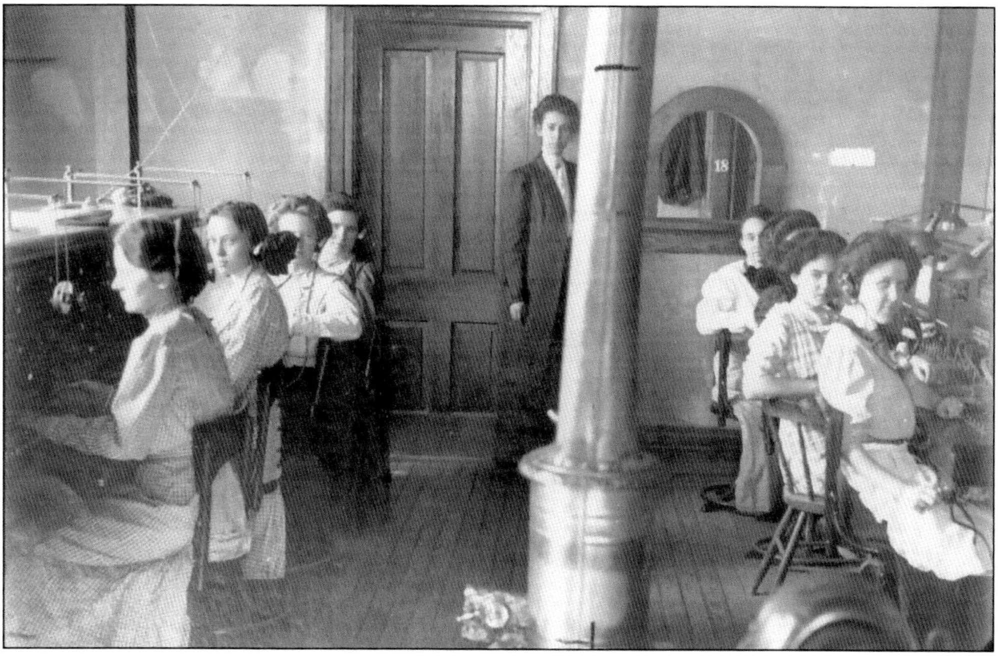

Stamford led much of West Texas in receiving phone service. In 1910, when Salome Keen started at the Stamford Southwestern Bell Telephone office, 400 residents had telephones, and the staff consisted of two people. By the time of this undated photograph, the service had clearly grown, requiring more equipment and operators.

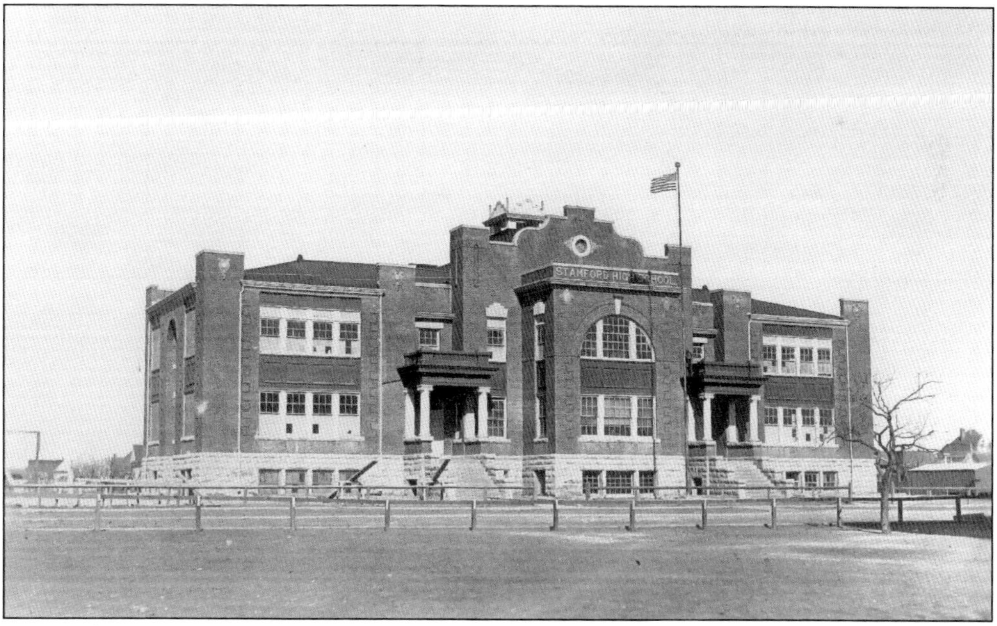

Stamford's early educational, religious, and cultural life was not neglected. The two cabooses that served as school buildings in the fall of 1900 were soon replaced with a frame building. Despite receiving no diploma, Stamford's first graduate, Lillie Ashburn, gained admittance to Baylor University. By 1904, the four-teacher staff issued diplomas to several of the 200 students. This redbrick building was begun in 1906 and dedicated in 1908.

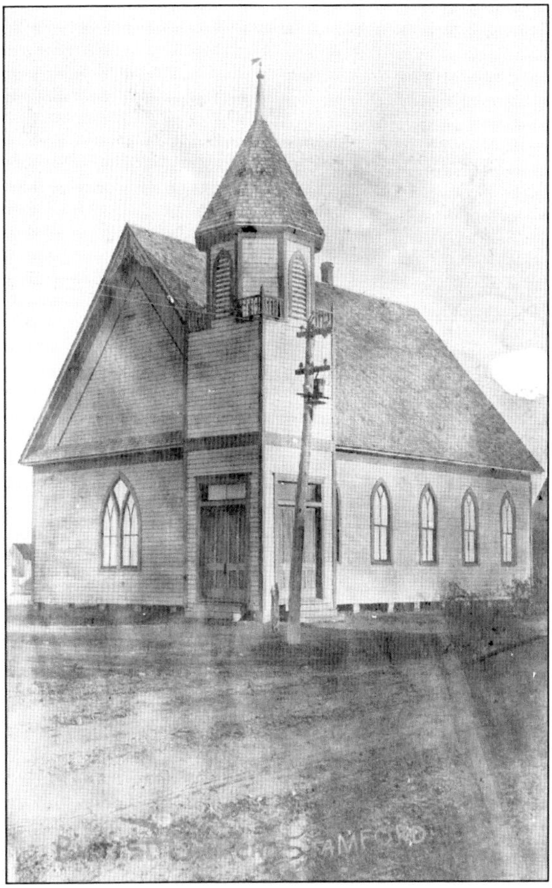

Church formation preceded Stamford's birth. Central Presbyterian was first, organized in September 1899 in an arbor on the W.J. Galbreath Farm. Within a year, the congregation erected the first church building in town, earning the reed organ promised by Henry McHarg for this accomplishment. First Baptist was formed by 27 adults and four children under a mesquite tree in a vacant lot, but they soon built the wood-frame structure seen here.

In 1905, Baptist pastor F.S. Groner challenged the congregation to construct a new brick church building. The cornerstone was laid in 1908, and the new facility on North Swenson Street, seen here, was dedicated the following year. By 1911, the church had more than 600 members and an annual budget of $5,000.

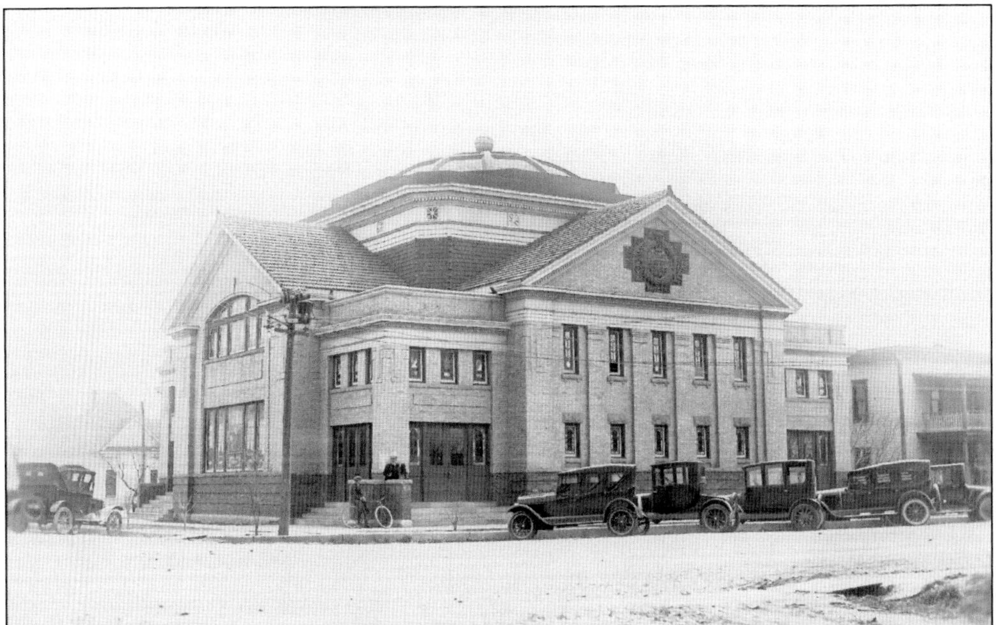

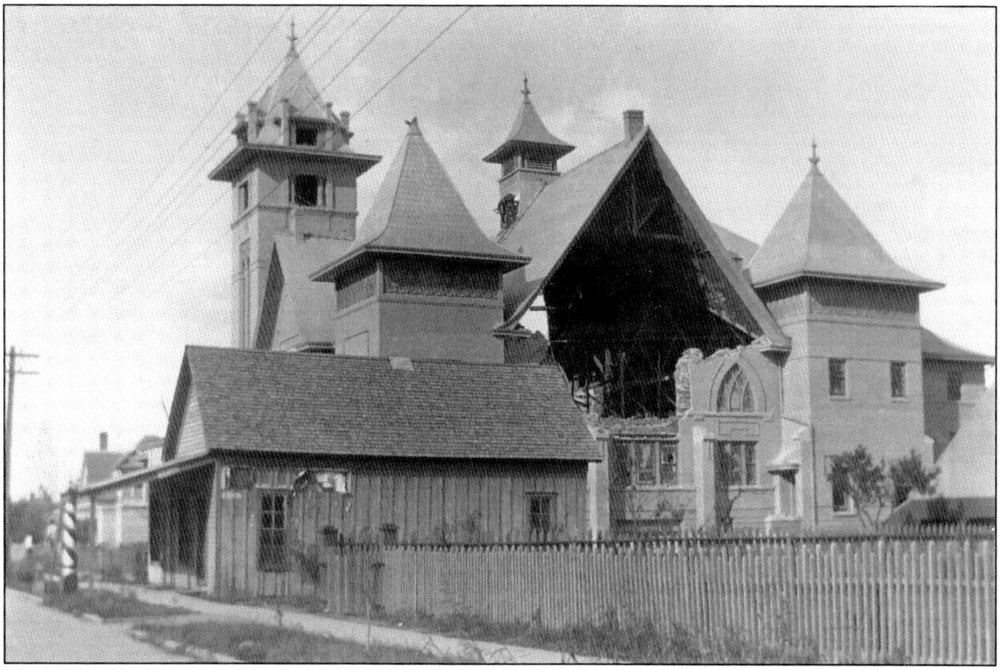

In September 1900, Rev. Samuel Gay, the editor of the *Stamford News*, led an organizational meeting of Methodists in Sledge Hall, located in Dr. John Sledge's office building on the south side of the square. Rev. Ike Hightower became the first pastor of the Stamford circuit, and the congregation built a small frame church on North Swenson Street. In January 1909, plans began for a larger church in a new location on East Hamilton Street, and the cornerstone for St. John's Methodist Episcopal Church, South, was laid in 1910. Construction began rapidly but slowed as funds declined. A storm also seriously damaged the church, demolishing a completed portion of the middle section of the building (see the photograph above). Rev. C.B. Meador became the pastor in the fall of 1911 and led the congregation into the new "highest church building between Fort Worth and El Paso" the following February.

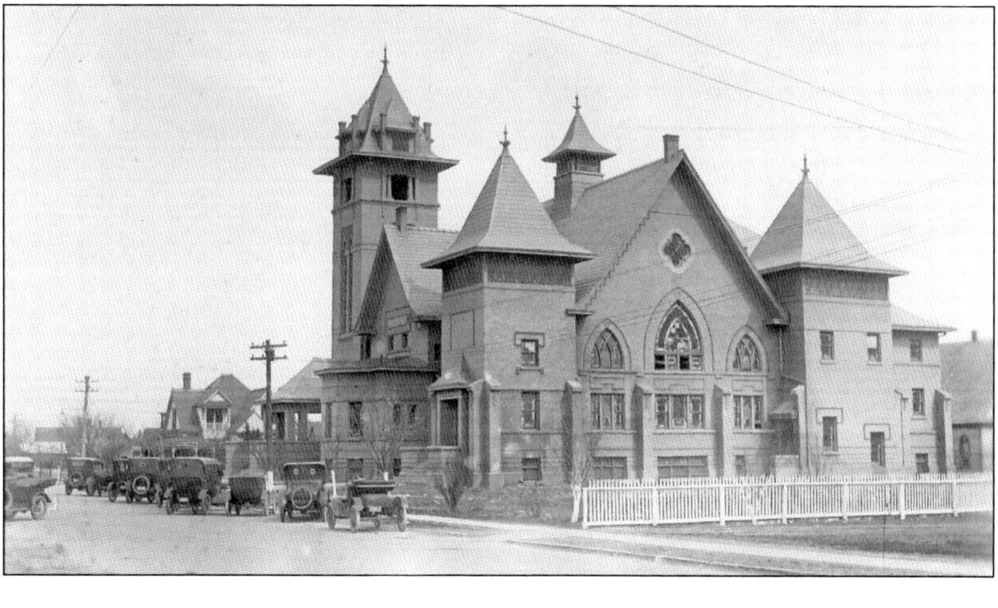

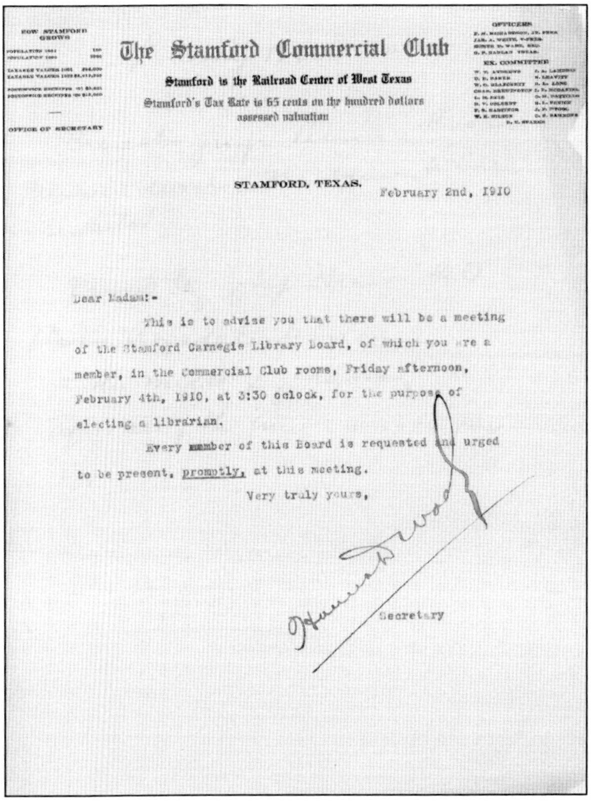

The Stamford Commercial Club

Stamford is the Railroad Center of West Texas

Stamford's Tax Rate is 65 cents on the hundred dollars assessed valuation

HOW STAMFORD GROWS

OFFICE OF SECRETARY

OFFICERS

EX. COMMITTEE

STAMFORD, TEXAS. February 2nd, 1910

Dear Madam:-

This is to advise you that there will be a meeting of the Stamford Carnegie Library Board, of which you are a member, in the Commercial Club rooms, Friday afternoon, February 4th, 1910, at 3:30 oclock, for the purpose of electing a librarian.

Every member of this Board is requested and urged to be present, promptly, at this meeting.

Very truly yours,

Secretary

Mrs. Willard Lee became the first president of the Stamford Twentieth Century Club. In 1907, the group reorganized as the Pierian Club—named after the spring in Macedonia, fabled as a source of artistic inspiration—and undertook the major project of securing funding from philanthropist Andrew Carnegie for a library. A fascinating correspondence file in the library, including this call for a meeting to select a librarian, traces the story of the club's success.

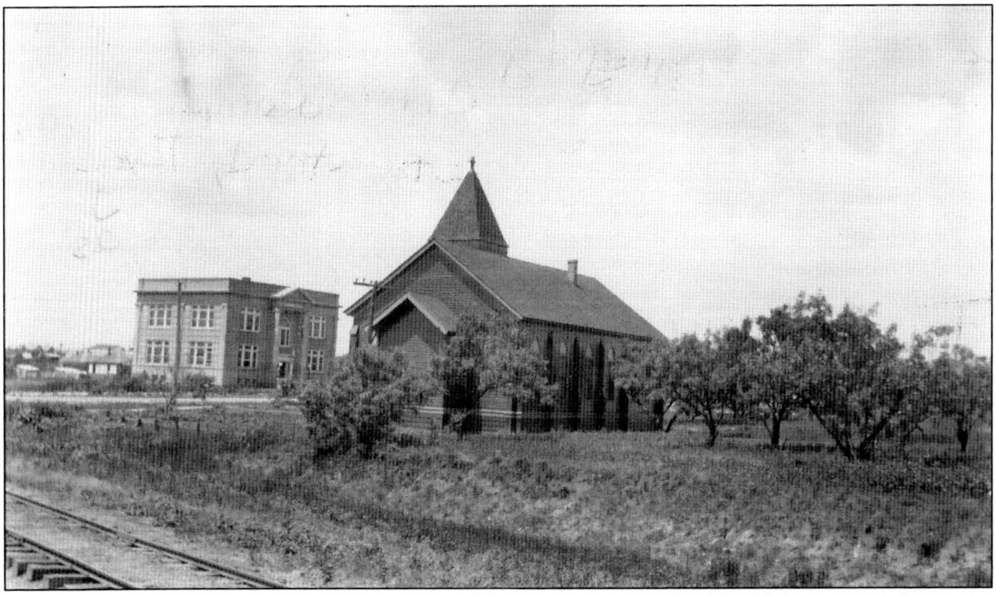

Stamford became the smallest town in the United States to be selected for one of the 1,600 Carnegie libraries. The three-story brick building trimmed in white stone (left background) was on East McHarg Avenue, near the Wichita Valley Railway tracks. The library opened in late 1910 with Sadie Ragsdale as the first librarian. (Courtesy of Southwest Collection/Special Collections Library, Texas Tech University, Lubbock, Texas, SWCPC, 132.)

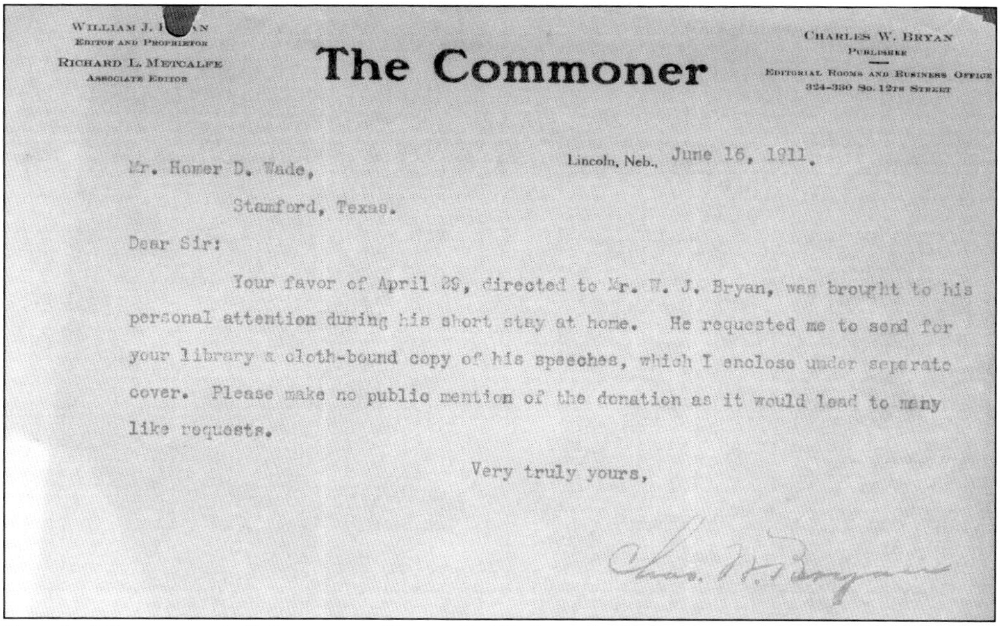

William J. B[illegible]an
Editor and Proprietor
Richard L. Metcalfe
Associate Editor

The Commoner

Charles W. Bryan
Publisher
Editorial Rooms and Business Office
324-330 So. 12th Street

Lincoln, Neb., June 16, 1911.

Mr. Homer D. Wade,

Stamford, Texas.

Dear Sir:

Your favor of April 29, directed to Mr. W. J. Bryan, was brought to his personal attention during his short stay at home. He requested me to send for your library a cloth-bound copy of his speeches, which I enclose under separate cover. Please make no public mention of the donation as it would lead to many like requests.

Very truly yours,

Chas. W. Bryan

Stamford Commercial Club secretary Homer D. Wade, emboldened by the successful acquisition of a Carnegie library, wrote to William Jennings Bryan requesting a book donation. Wade had served as Bryan's chauffeur during his 1908 visit. Bryan, popularly known as "The Great Commoner," provided a book of his speeches, but his publisher, Charles Bryan, requested that the gift not be publicized "as it would lead to many like requests."

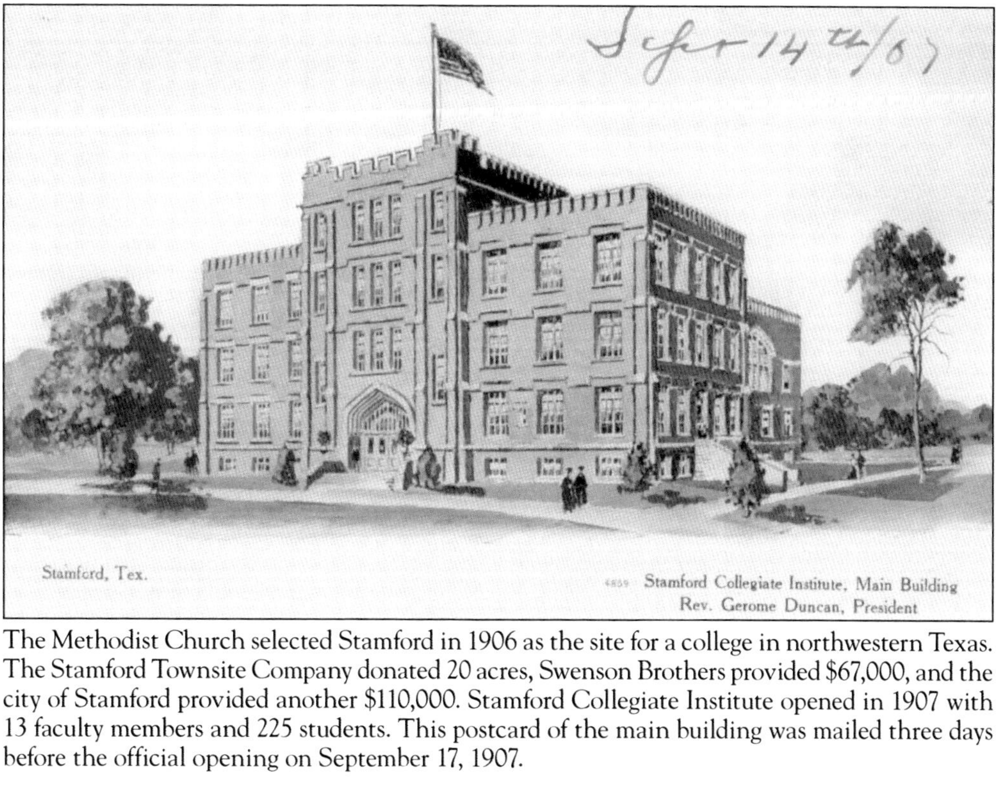

The Methodist Church selected Stamford in 1906 as the site for a college in northwestern Texas. The Stamford Townsite Company donated 20 acres, Swenson Brothers provided $67,000, and the city of Stamford provided another $110,000. Stamford Collegiate Institute opened in 1907 with 13 faculty members and 225 students. This postcard of the main building was mailed three days before the official opening on September 17, 1907.

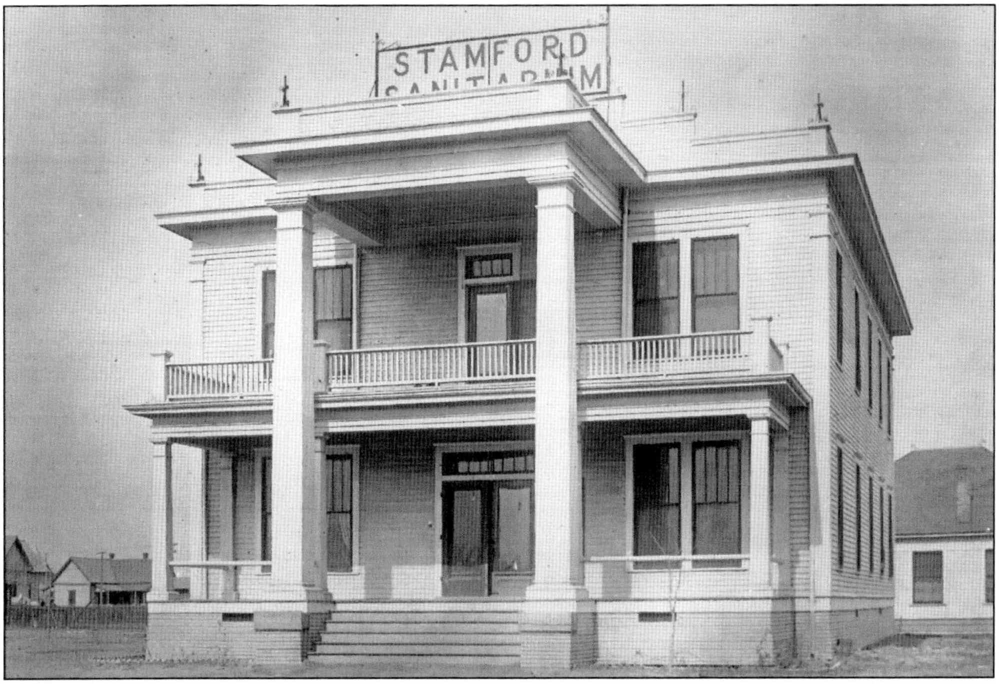

Though Stamford had several doctors from its founding, the city lacked a hospital facility. In 1910, Dr. Sam Webb of Albany and Dr. M.E. Lott of Navasota, surgeons for the Texas Central Railroad, built the 12-bed Stamford Sanitarium, with a 10-room annex for railroad patients, the first one between Fort Worth and El Paso. A professional nurses' training school was also organized in 1910.

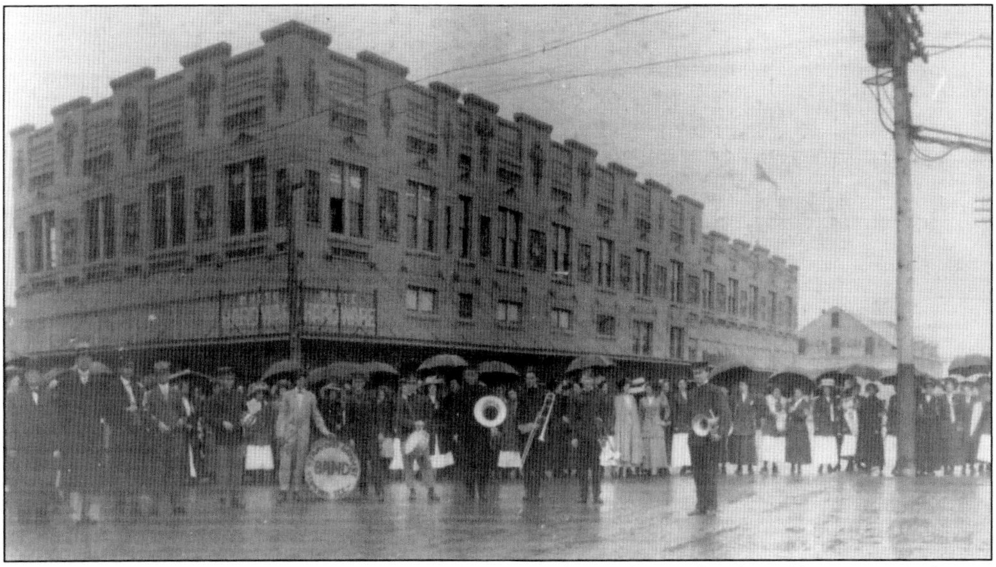

Joe Ward organized a town band in 1909, and 17-year-old Harley Sadler found he enjoyed playing trombone more than working in his father's general store. Drawn to entertainment, Sadler ran away with the Parker Brothers Carnival for several months. Returning home, he formed a small vaudeville troupe, launching a lifelong career as a traveling performer. Sadler may be the trombone player next to the tuba in this 1911 photograph.

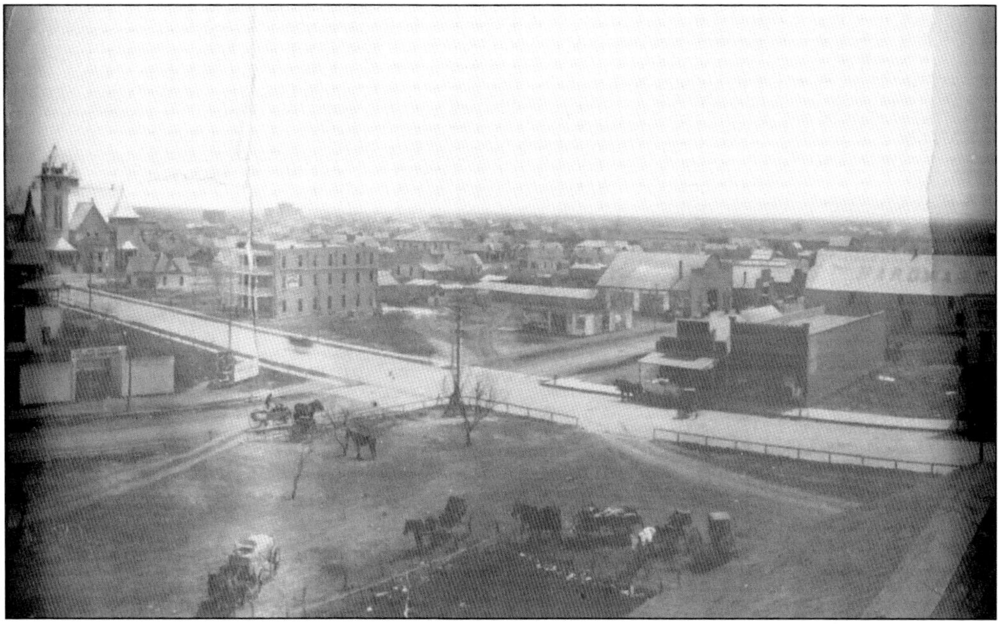

In 1985, Olin Lancaster, an 82-year-old resident, donated a remarkable panoramic photograph taken of Stamford in 1911 to the Cowboy Country Museum. Three sides of the square are captured in a view from atop the town hall. In this first segment along Hamilton Street, St. John's Methodist Church is on the left, the Stamford Collegiate Institute building is in the background, and the Stamford Livery is on South Wetherbee Street.

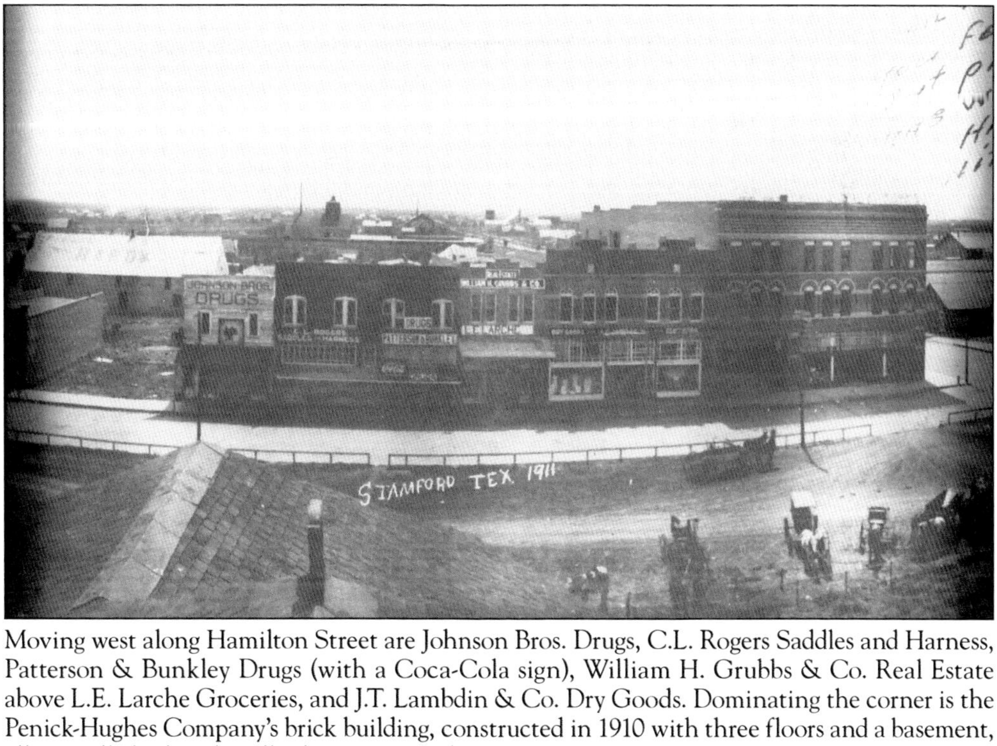

Moving west along Hamilton Street are Johnson Bros. Drugs, C.L. Rogers Saddles and Harness, Patterson & Bunkley Drugs (with a Coca-Cola sign), William H. Grubbs & Co. Real Estate above L.E. Larche Groceries, and J.T. Lambdin & Co. Dry Goods. Dominating the corner is the Penick-Hughes Company's brick building, constructed in 1910 with three floors and a basement, all specially built to handle the company's hardware business.

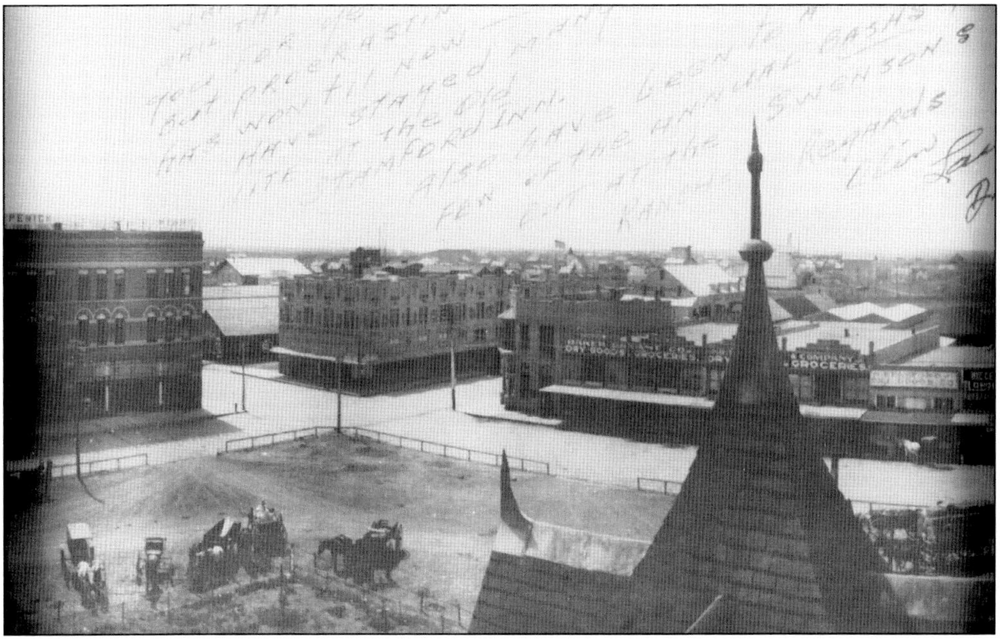

Lancaster inscribed the photograph thusly: "I've wanted to mail this to you for years but procrastination has won till now—Have stayed many a nite at the Old Stamford Inn. Also have been to a few of the annual bash's out at the Swenson Ranch." White Hardware is seen here across the street from Penick-Hughes. Along Swenson Street are the pioneer businesses Baker-Bryant Dry Goods and D.O. McRimmon Dry Goods.

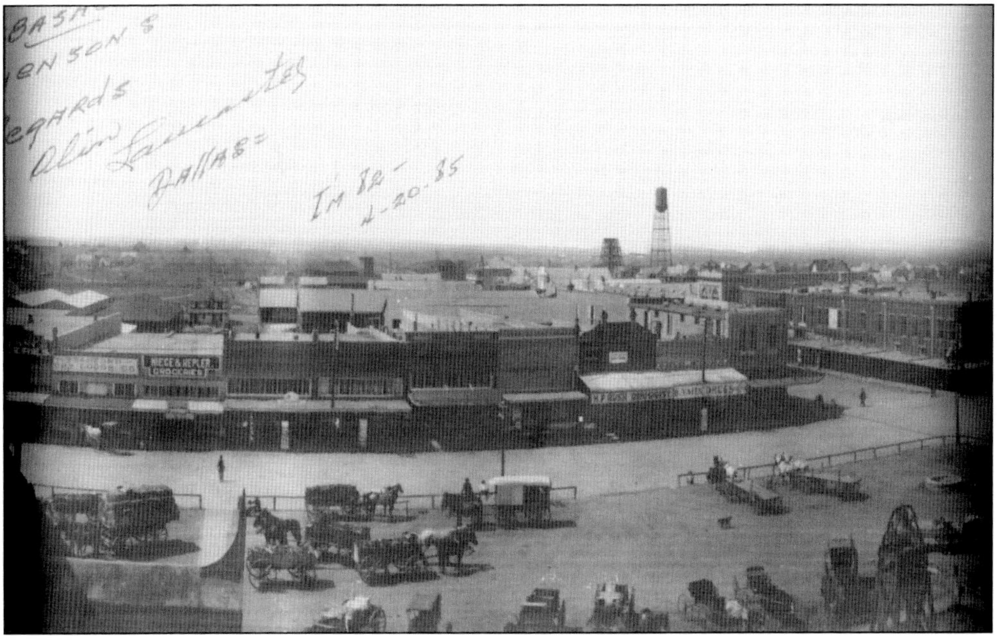

Continuing north along Swenson Street are the Stamford Dry Goods Co., Niece and Helper Groceries, several unidentified businesses (one with a barber pole), H.P. Rush Druggist, B. Yates Drugs, and Citizen's National Bank on the corner. There is not a single automobile in the photograph—only horses, buggies, and wagons.

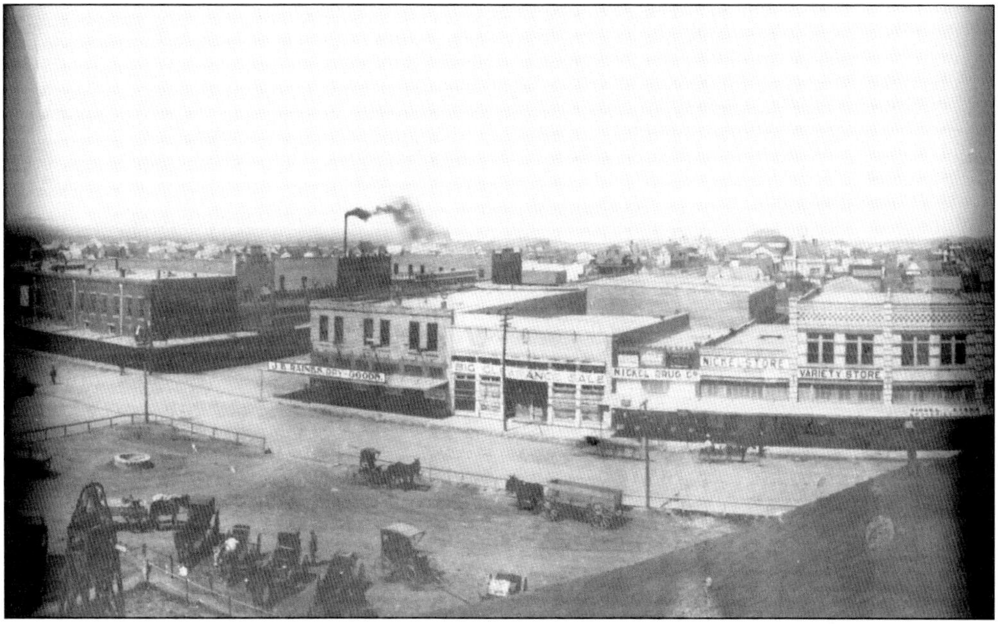

The First State Bank occupied a corner at Swenson and McHarg Streets. J.B. Raines Dry Goods has the first space on East McHarg. Next door is the abandoned Mistrot Bros. store, still sporting a "Big Clearance Sale" sign. Nickel Drug Co. also advertised Coca-Cola. First Baptist Church is behind the Nickel store. The Variety Store and Riddell and Evans Groceries share a building with decorative brick trim.

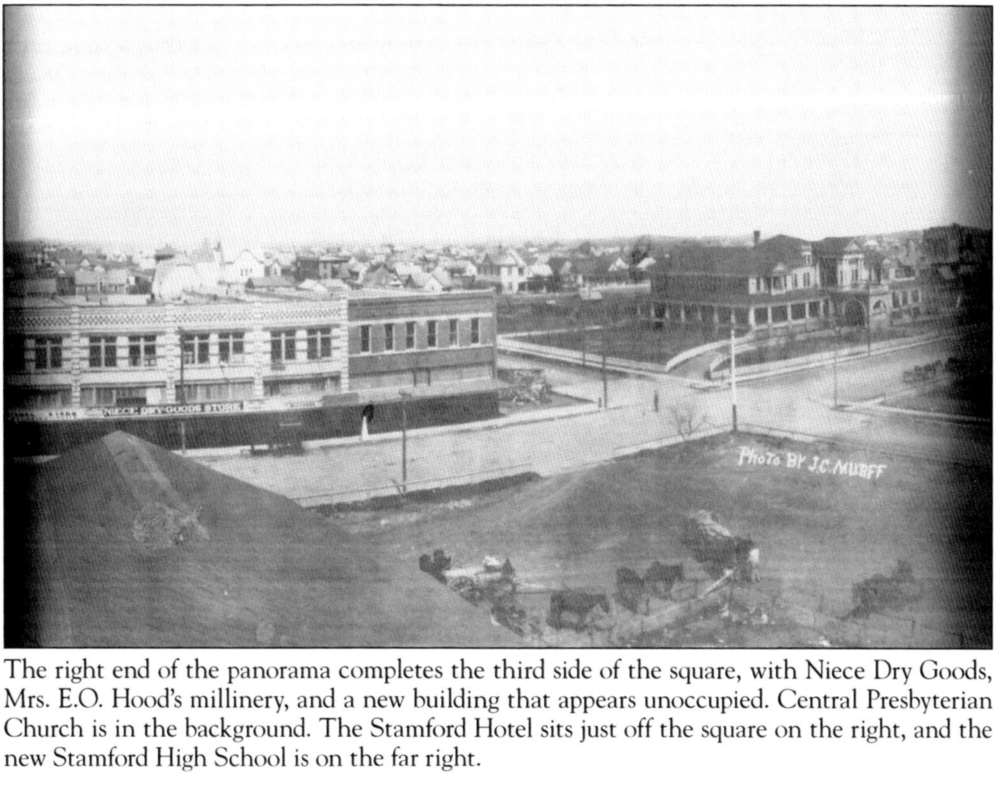

The right end of the panorama completes the third side of the square, with Niece Dry Goods, Mrs. E.O. Hood's millinery, and a new building that appears unoccupied. Central Presbyterian Church is in the background. The Stamford Hotel sits just off the square on the right, and the new Stamford High School is on the far right.

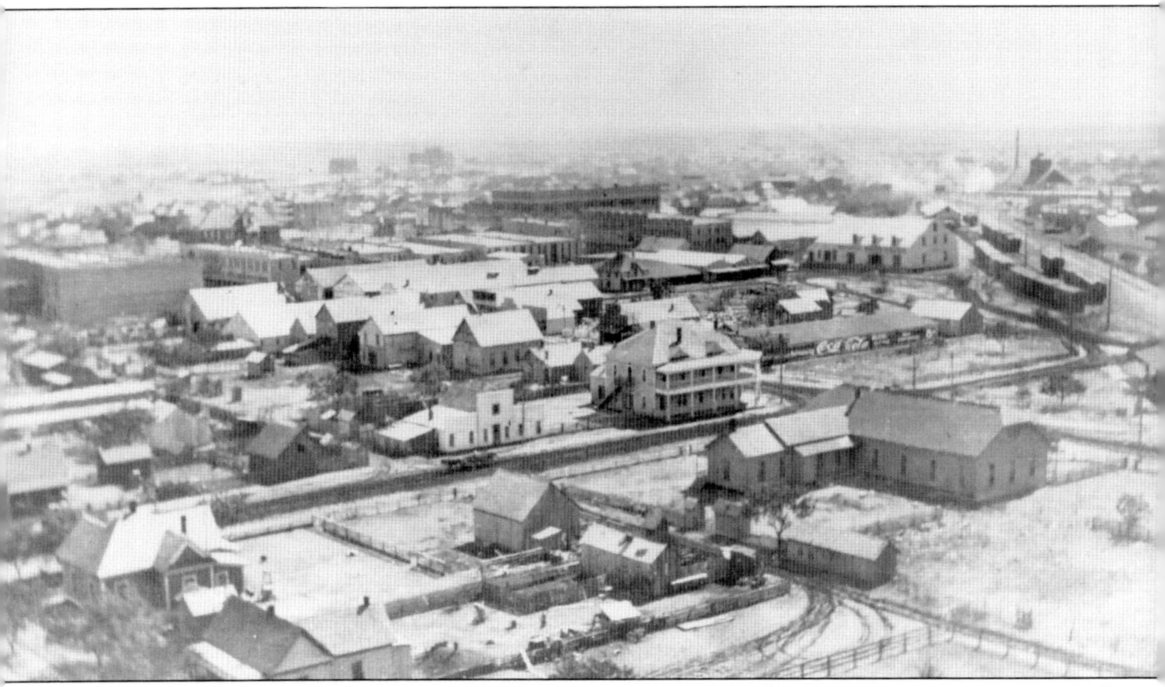

This 1910 view looking southeast from the city water tower shows a prosperous young city of 3,902 people where there had been only empty prairie a decade before. Rail lines run along the right of the photograph, and warehouses dominate much of the foreground. The huge Penick-Hughes Building anchors the town square near the photograph's center. The town hall is almost lost in the jumble of buildings on the left. The following year, the Texas Knights of Pythias held their annual convention in Abilene. Mayor Charles Brewington and Homer Wade led a special delegation to hijack the convention for a day. Seven rail coaches of Pythians rode the Wichita Valley Railway to Stamford for a reception and banquet at the Stamford Inn. Wade, the secretary of the Commerce Club, wrote an article for the *Abilene Daily Reporter* in which he bragged that Stamford "is destined to become not only a jobbing center, but a railroad center, a manufacturing center, an educational center and in truth and in fact the metropolis of West Texas."

Two

BEFORE STAMFORD

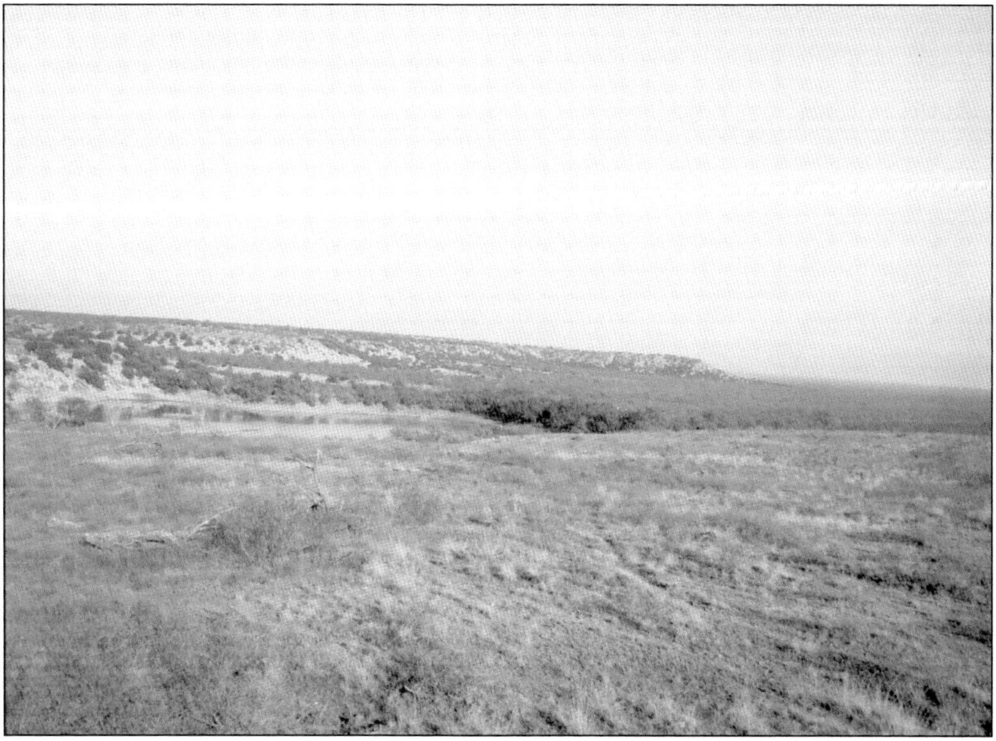

For centuries, only buffalo and Indians traversed West Texas. Jacob Howard, a black soldier in the 11th Infantry stationed at Fort Griffin, Texas, in the early 1870s, described the country around Flat Top Mountain (seen here) thusly: "For over 200-miles in any direction there was not a railroad or a village let alone a town or city, only mail stations here and there on the trails between forts."

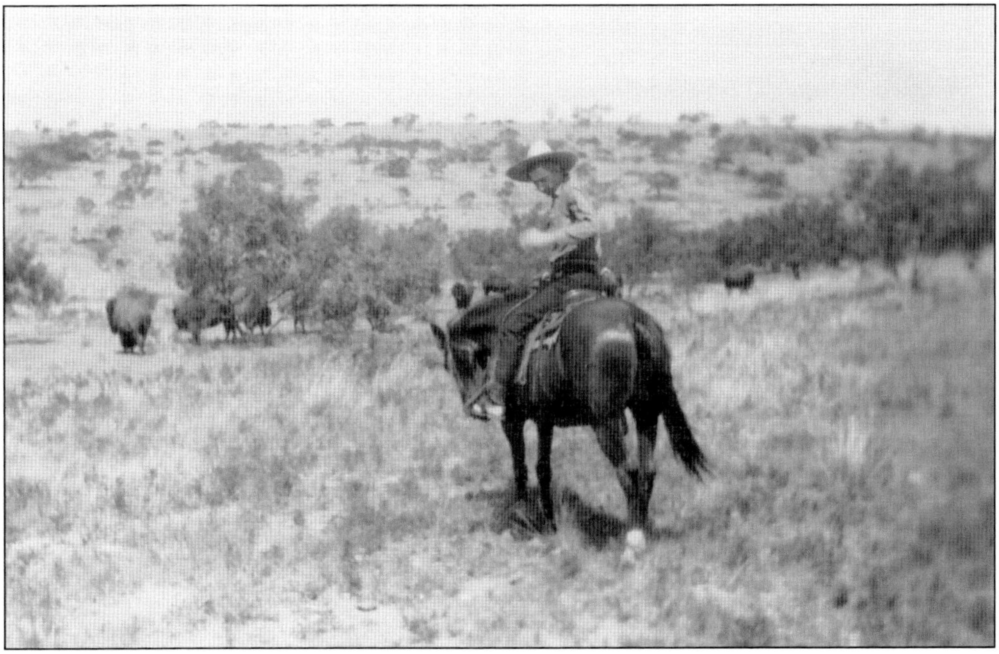

The rolling plains were excellent grasslands, with the Clear Fork of the Brazos wandering across them, rich in game. An 1872 surveying party estimated that there were 50,000 buffalo here. The group spent a tense time huddled in a ring of wagons while a huge stampede thundered around them. By 1879, hundreds of cattle had been driven into the region, and the buffalo became only a nuisance, ignored here by an unidentified cowboy.

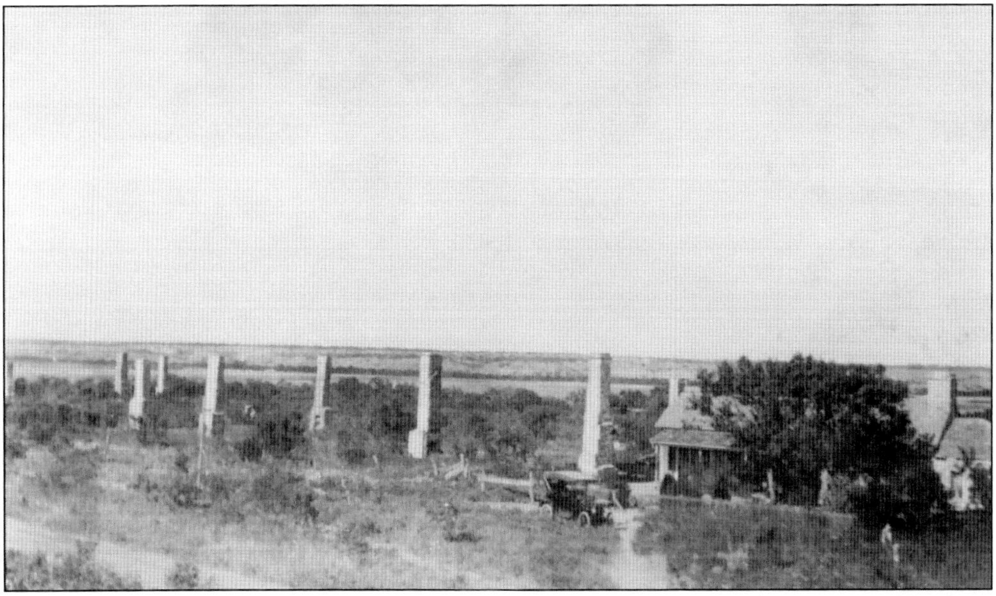

By the early 1900s, all that remained of Fort Phantom Hill were scattered stone ruins like these barracks chimneys. Established in 1853, the fort became the first settlement in Jones County. A lack of adequate fresh water and vegetables led to its abandonment in 1854. Fire destroyed the log walls and thatched roofs. In 1858, it became Station 54 on the Southern Overland Mail–Butterfield stagecoach line.

In the summer of 1866, Charles Goodnight, Oliver Loving, and 18 cowboys drove 2,000 head of cattle from Texas to New Mexico, establishing the trail named for them. Years later, Goodnight helped historian J. Evetts Haley retrace their route on this map, which began at Fort Belknap and followed the old stage lines past Fort Phantom Hill on its way west. (Courtesy of the Nita Stewart Haley Memorial Library, Midland, Texas.)

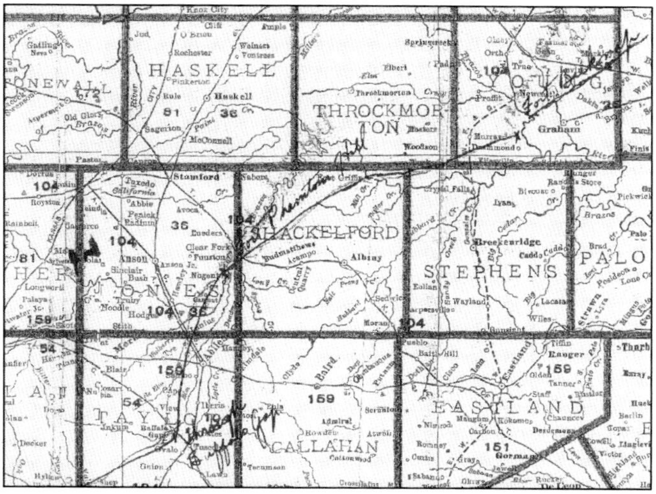

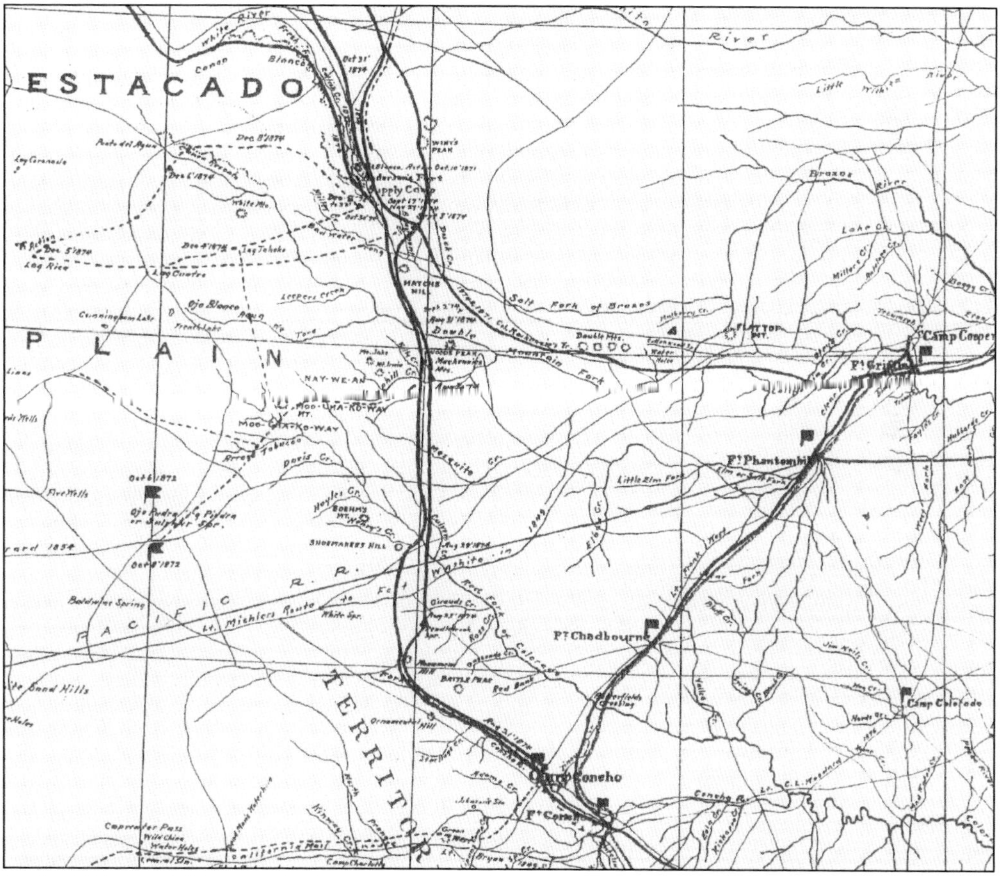

In the 1870s, Col. Ranald Mackenzie led several military expeditions against nomadic Indians on the Southern Great Plains. This 1927 map of his campaigns includes the route blazed west from Fort Griffin by several hundred troopers and supply wagons in 1871 and 1874. The trail south of Flat Top Mountain and the Double Mountains was used over the next 20 years by settlers moving west and buffalo hunters carrying hides east to Fort Griffin. (Courtesy of the Nita Stewart Haley Memorial Library, Midland, Texas.)

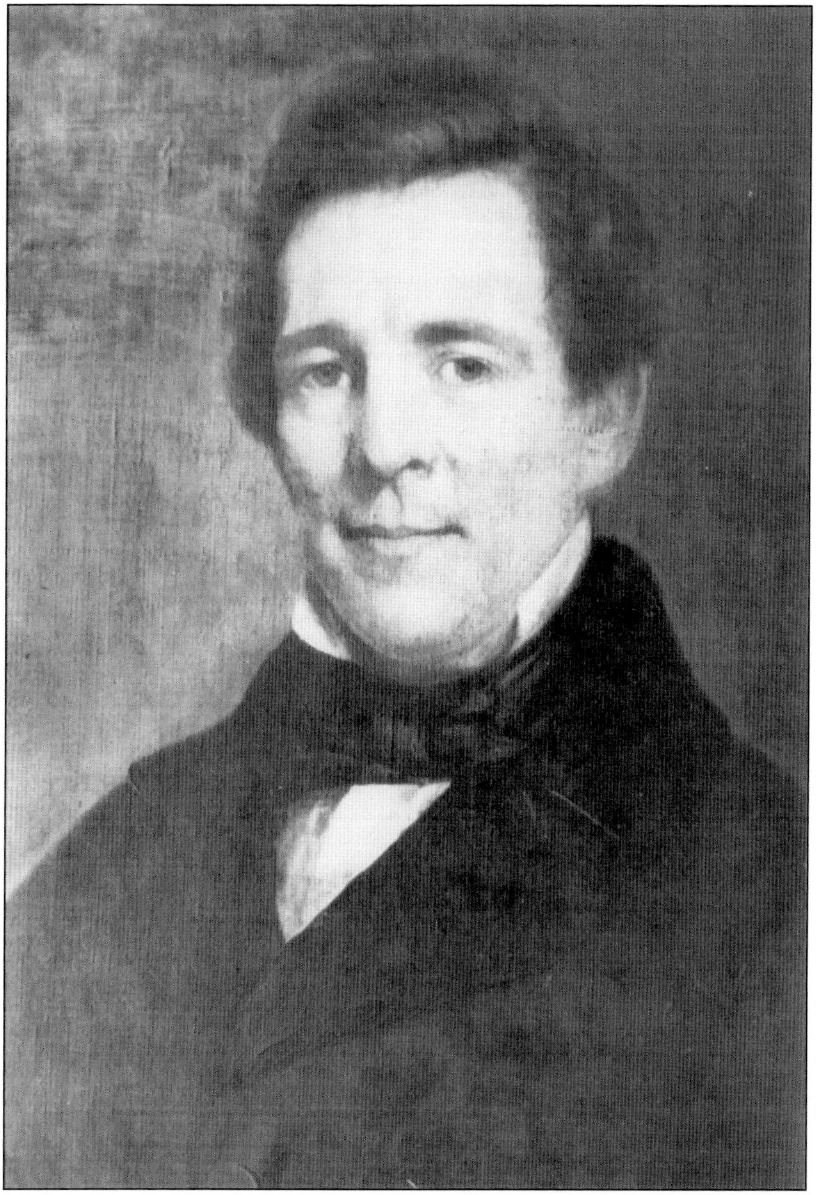

Swante Magnus "S.M." Swenson is reported to be the first Swedish immigrant to Texas, arriving in 1838 by way of New York. He partnered in the mercantile business, peddling goods by wagon to area plantations. Moving to Austin, he successfully launched another mercantile enterprise. He then invested in railroad land grants, acquiring 100,000 acres in northwestern Texas, still Indian country, which made him perhaps the largest landowner in Texas at the time. Swenson also helped other Swedes immigrate to Texas. A friend of Stephen F. Austin, he contracted to furnish the new governor's mansion in 1854. His opposition to Texas secession in 1861 eventually forced him to flee to Mexico. After the Civil War ended, Swenson settled first in New Orleans and later in New York, where he created the banking house of S.M. Swenson and Sons. In 1882, Swenson returned to Texas to inspect his West Texas lands for development. Swenson leased his vast domain to his sons, Erick and Swen, who operated them as the Swenson Brothers Cattle Company, with their brand an extended M sandwiched between two reversed S's.

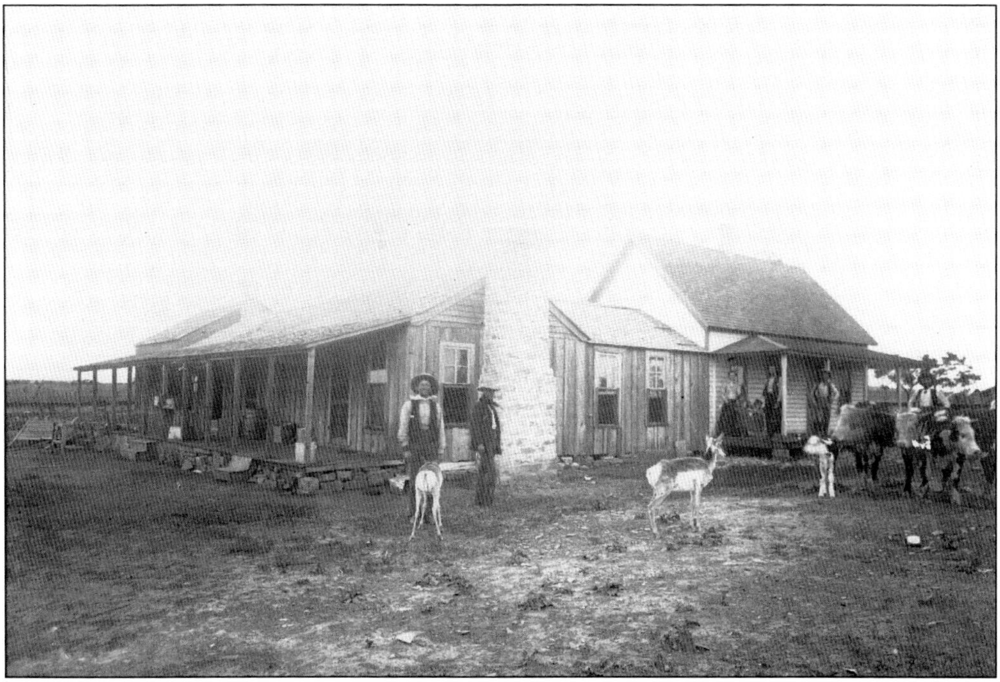

S.M. Swenson established three ranches in West Texas. The Flat Top was named for the prominent mesa it encompassed. The Throckmorton, seen here, was the largest and was originally named the Eleonora for Swenson's daughter. The 50,000-acre Ericksdahl Ranch became some of the area's first fenced land. The first stock brought to the ranches included more than 1,000 Durham Hereford shorthorns. The initial horse herd included Spanish and Arabian stock.

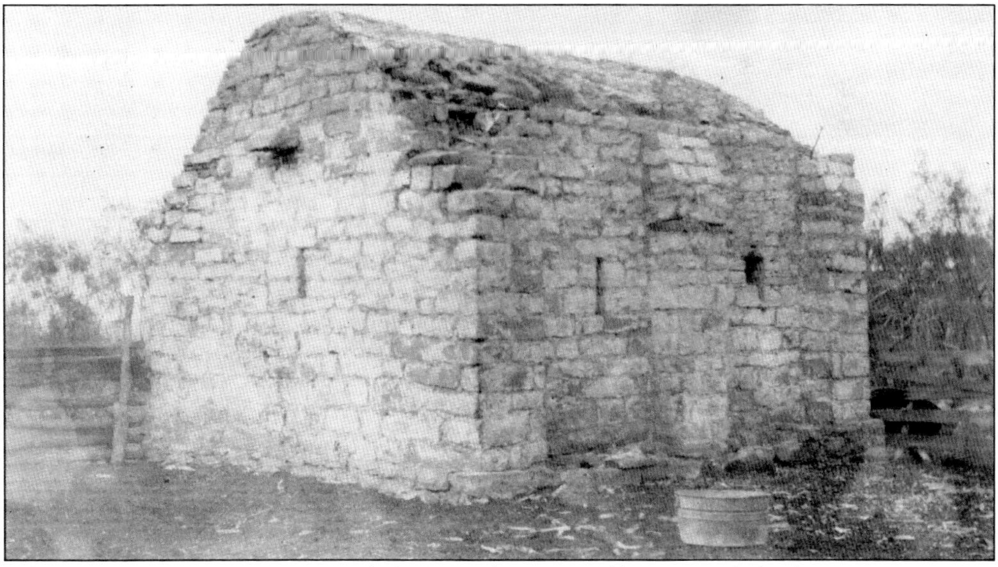

After 1875, a town grew up around the Fort Phantom Hill ruins, and the first commissioners' court of Jones County met there. Fort buildings, like the old powder magazine seen here, were utilized for storage or as sources of building stone. However, the new town was short-lived. In 1879, Jones City (later renamed Anson) became the county seat. By the 1890s, Phantom Hill was again largely abandoned.

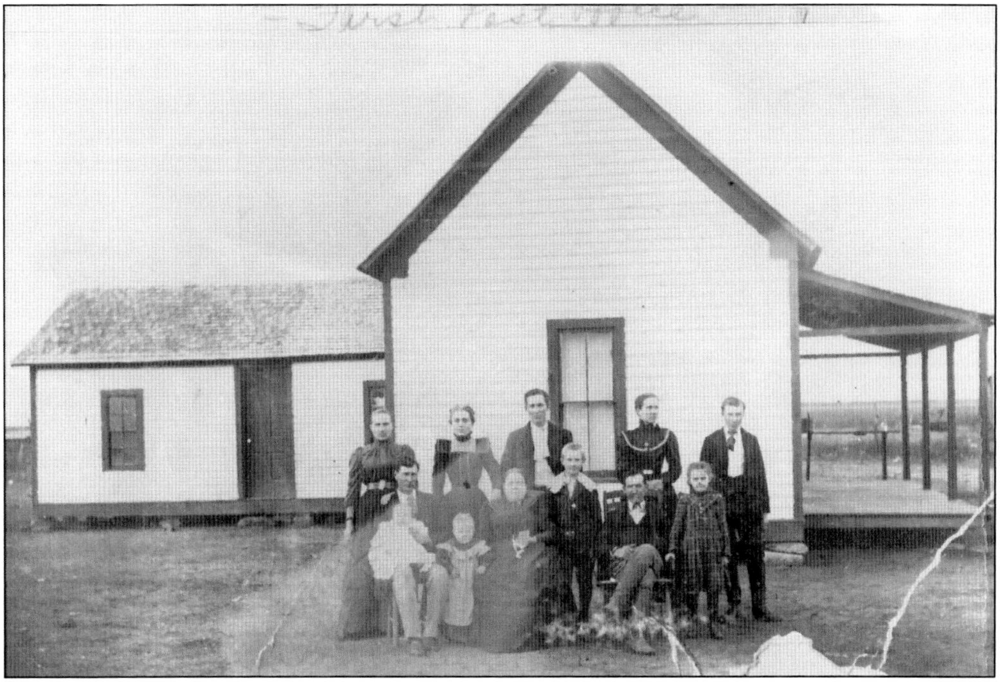

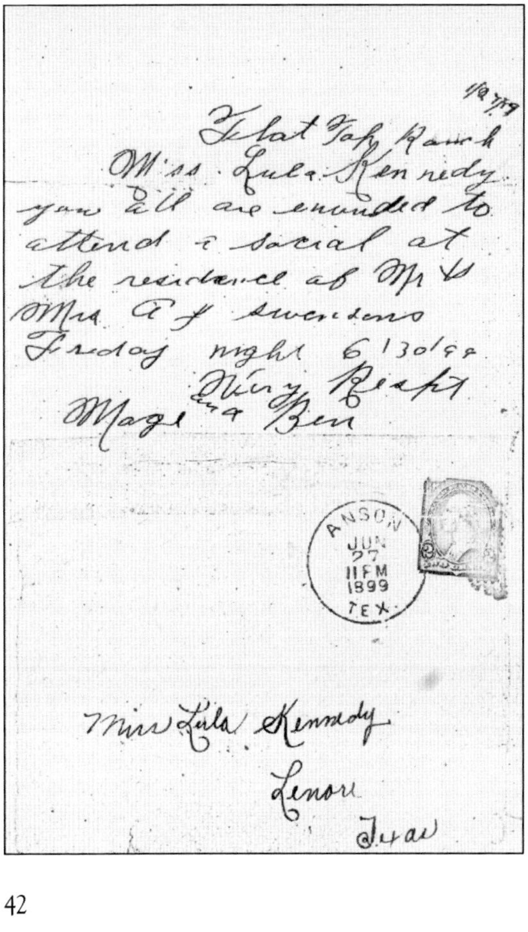
Flat Top Ranch
Miss Lula Kennedy
you all are invited to
attend a social at
the residence of Mr &
Mrs A J Swensons
Friday night 6/30/99
Very Respt
Maggie & Ben

ANSON JUN 27 11 PM 1899 TEX

Miss Lula Kennedy
Lenore
Texas

In 1881, the *Fort Griffin Echo* mused, "Is West Texas a farming country?" Despite the hardships of weather and long, difficult hauls to get crops to market, "nesters" built brush fences and began growing cotton, corn, wheat, and oats. J.J. Kennedy bought his farm in 1896 for $2 an acre. Kennedy, seen here with his family, also operated the Lenore post office.

This note inviting Lula Kennedy to a social at the Flat Top Ranch disproved any enmity between farmers and cattlemen. The greatest threat to both was drought, and the scattered farms and ranches made isolation a real hardship. Pioneer J.O. Moore recalled his wife's loneliness, saying, "The howl of the coyote and the buzz of the rattlesnake's warning were about the only company Amanda had." Stamford would change all that.

Three

LAND AND CATTLE

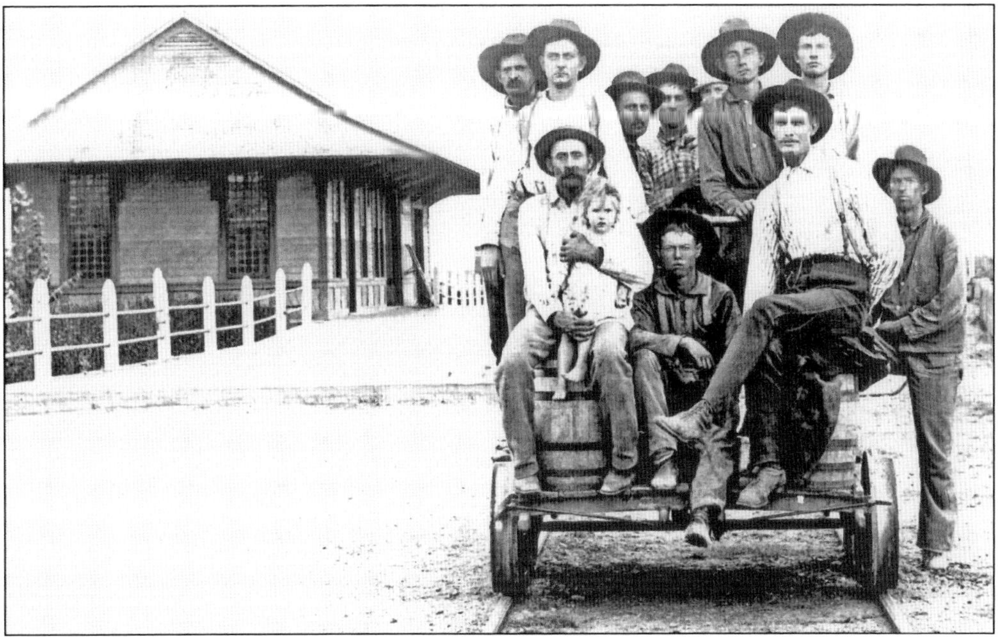

This group on a handcart at Stamford's railroad depot is not identified, but the young child implies that they are more than transient railroad workers. More likely, they represent the thousands who flowed through the new community seeking a chance to profit from the rich agricultural lands. The land's potential brought them all, from the Swenson land barons to immigrants hoping to obtain a few acres of rich soil.

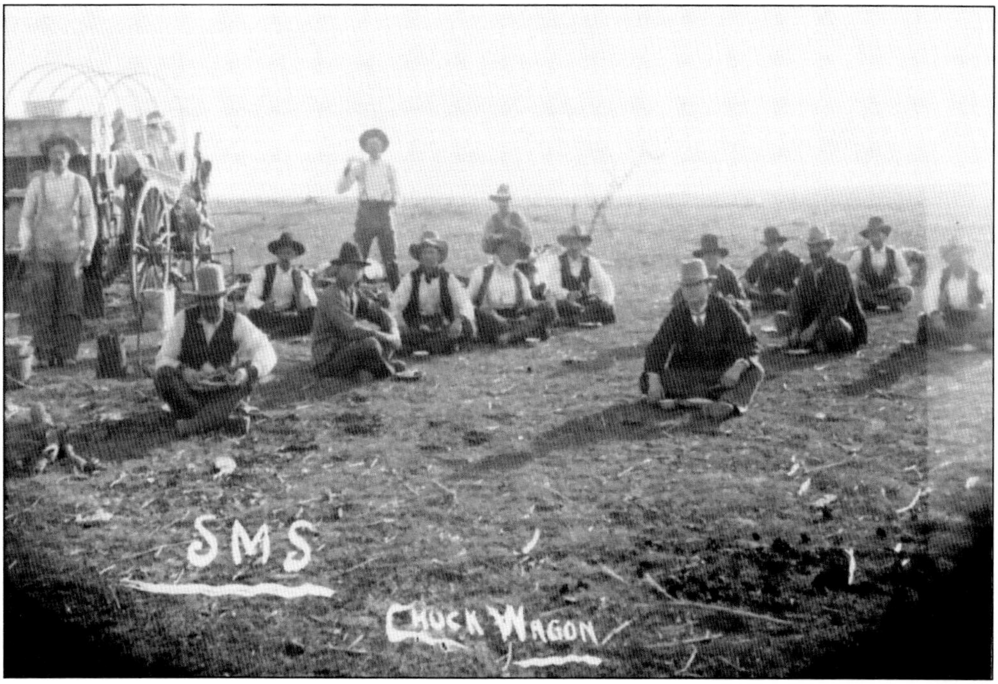

The expeditions ending the Indian threat and the elimination of the buffalo herds opened West Texas for cattle ranching. Large enterprises like Swenson Brothers brought cattle to the region. Herds were maintained on the range by small groups of hired cowboys, young men who were comfortable eating from a chuck wagon (left) and sleeping on the ground.

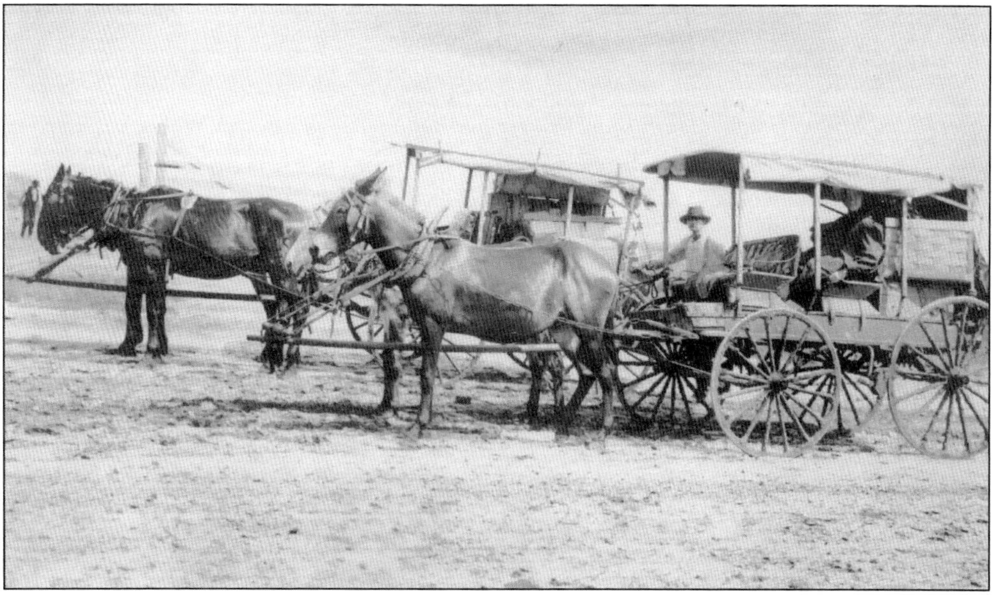

The cattleman could walk his herd to distant markets with free grass to eat along the way. Farm produce was dead weight, as expenses limited how far it could be profitably carried. Yet hardy pioneer farmers like this unidentified couple did venture west in whatever conveyance they could afford to try surviving with subsistence farming and grain crops for a few head of stock. (Courtesy of Swenson Land and Cattle Company.)

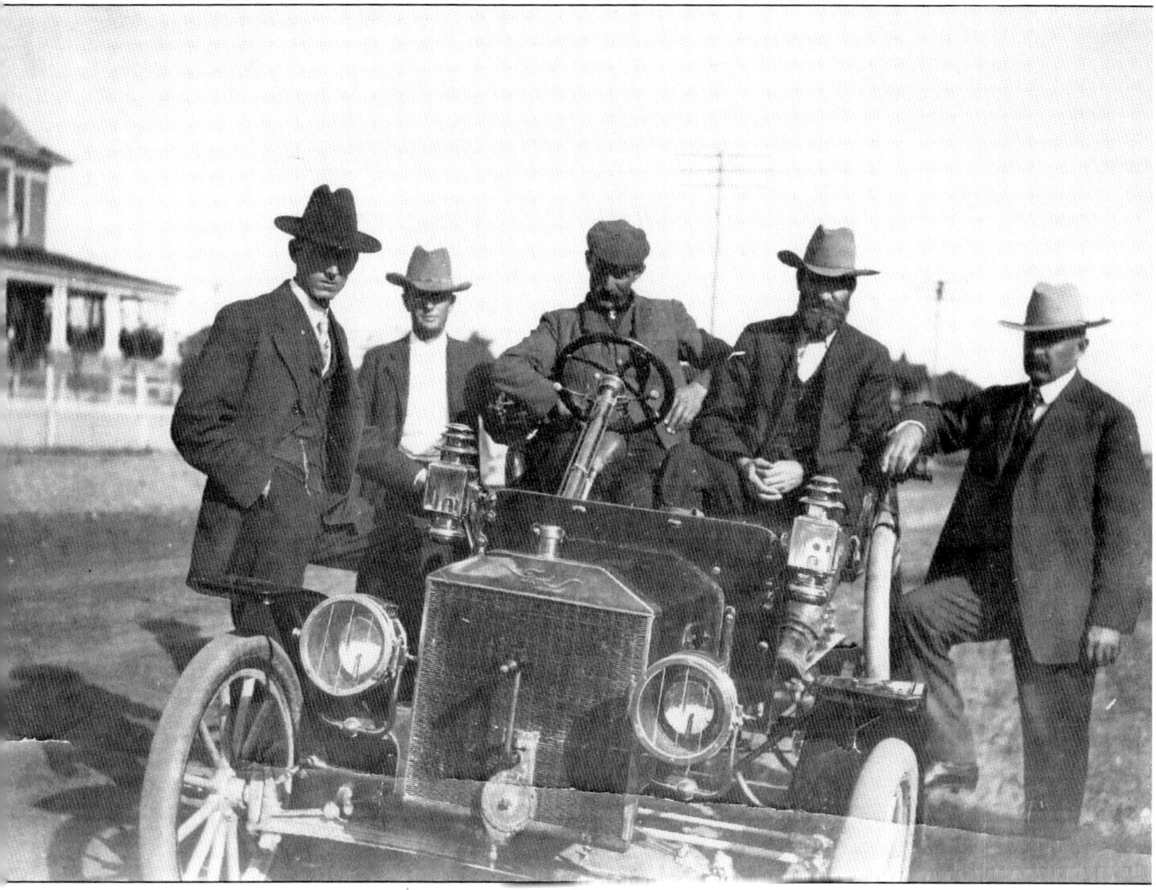

Erick and Swen Swenson remained New Yorkers but made annual trips to the Texas ranches. The man who supervised the development of the Swenson interests into a cattle empire was Andrew John Swenson (seated in the car on the right). On a return visit to Sweden, S.M. Swenson persuaded his nephew Andrew to immigrate to America in 1882 at the age of 18. The next year, Andrew and his friend Joe Ericson traveled from Louisiana to Jones County in a mule-drawn wagon to work for the Swenson ranches. In 1897, A.J., as he was most commonly known, became superintendent of the SMS ranches, working with ranch manager Frank Hastings, who had supervised the breeding and sale of Hereford cattle at the Armour operation in Kansas City before being hired by the Swensons in 1902. In 1906, Swenson Brothers purchased 100 registered Hereford heifers. Bred to Hereford bulls, they created the foundation stock for the SMS herd. When Hastings died in 1922, A.J. Swenson became the manager of the Swenson ranching interests. (Courtesy of Swenson Land and Cattle Company.)

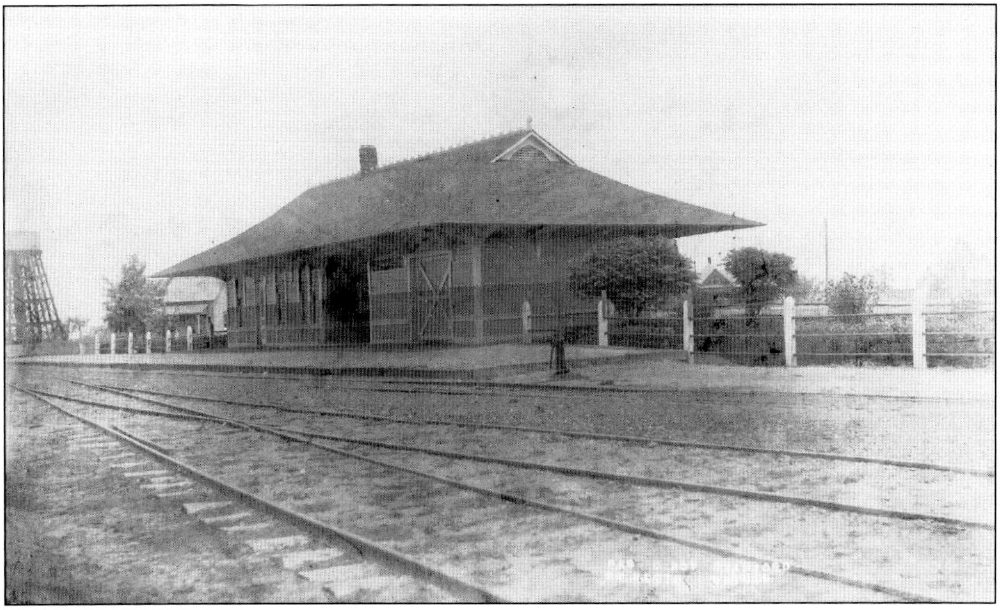

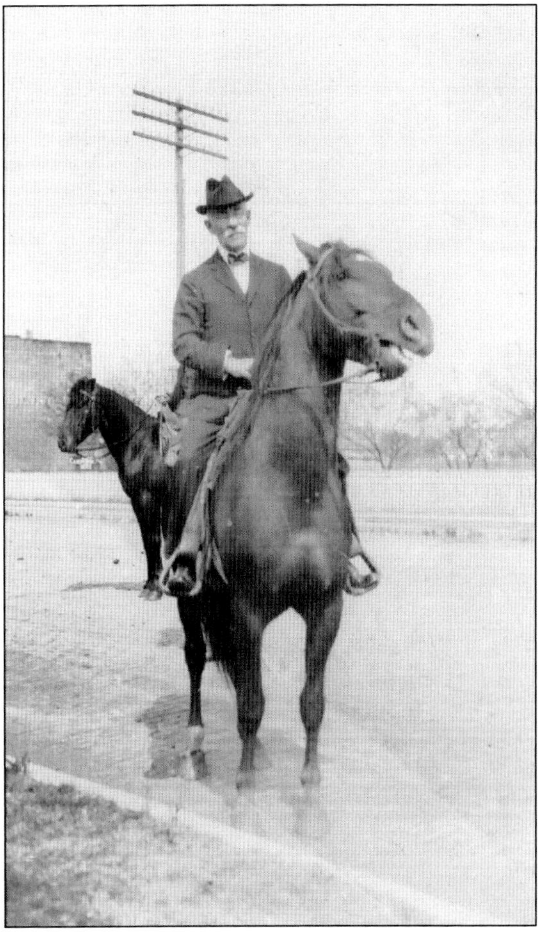

The Stamford depot, though deserted in this photograph, frequently bustled with new arrivals. In 1904, the depot had 104 immigrant boxcars filled with opportunity-seeking settlers. The following year, the depot reported $50,000 in freight business, including five fully loaded immigrant cars. The population of Jones County more than tripled between 1900 and 1910, reaching 24,299.

The Swenson brothers determined some of their lands were better suited to farming and began selling off 40,000 acres. Erick Swenson, seen here in Stamford, took an active role encouraging South Texas Swedes to relocate to the Ericksdahl—translated as "Erick's valley"—Ranch along California Creek. Between 1904 and 1906, a total of 300 settlers from Georgetown bought land for $10 to $16 per acre. (Courtesy of Swenson Land and Cattle Company.)

With the Ericksdahl community barely underway in 1905, Rev. L.J. Sanquist and Dr. J.S. Stamline came from the Austin area to establish a Lutheran church, meeting in local homes. At the second service, A.J. Swenson served a chuck wagon dinner to all those present. In January 1906, the congregation of Bethel Lutheran Church was organized with 19 charter members. The building is seen here around 1915. (Courtesy of sweame.org.)

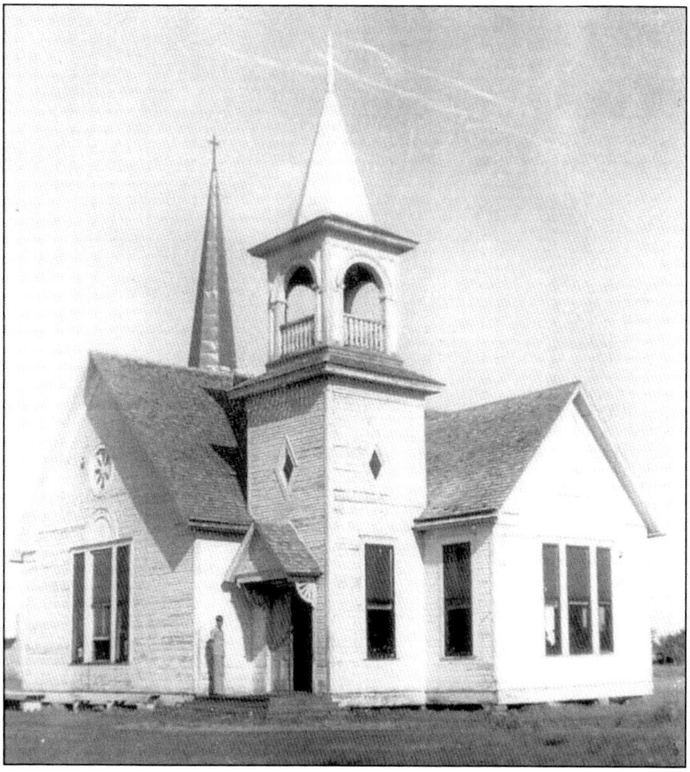

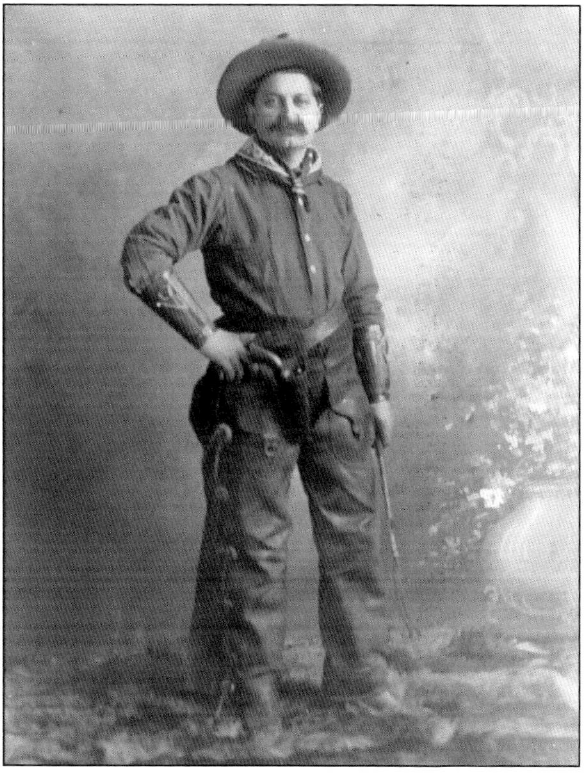

The Stamford area was cosmopolitan from its beginnings. Urban and rural Texans came to the new community, and Swedish immigrants farmed or worked as SMS ranch cowboys. R.L. Penick was originally from Missouri, while P.P. Berthelot was a French Canadian. Charlie Lackademia, seen here in cowboy gear in 1915, was a merchant of Greek ancestry who ran a candy shop and soda fountain in Stamford.

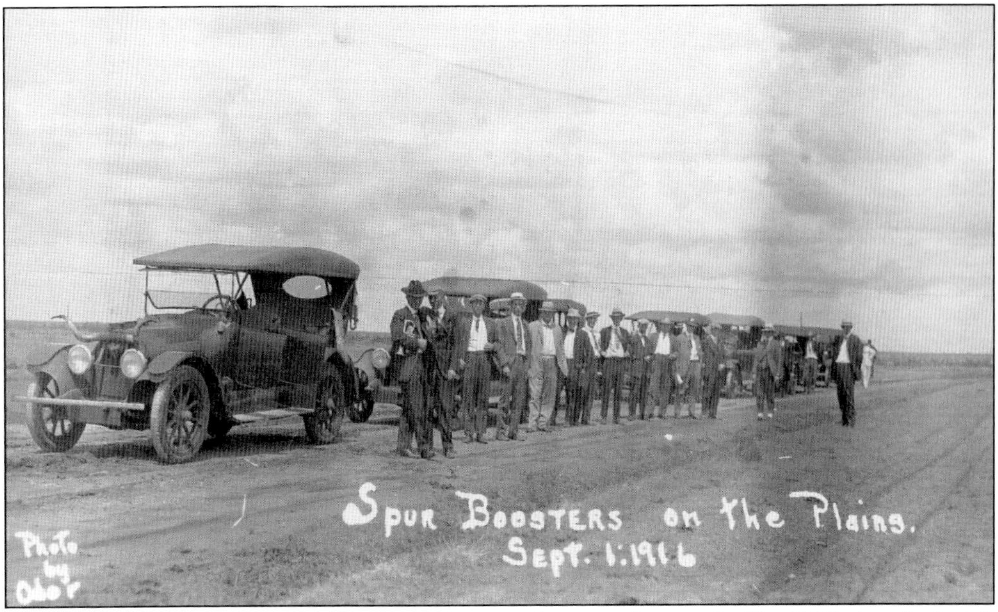

The transition from open range to a ranch economy became the standard by 1900. As it had with Ericksdahl lands, Swenson Brothers undertook a second colonization project to convert range land to corn and wheat lands. In 1908, Erick Swenson oversaw the purchase of the Spur Ranch for $1.4 million. Land sales included booster expeditions such as this one. (Courtesy of Swenson Land and Cattle Company.)

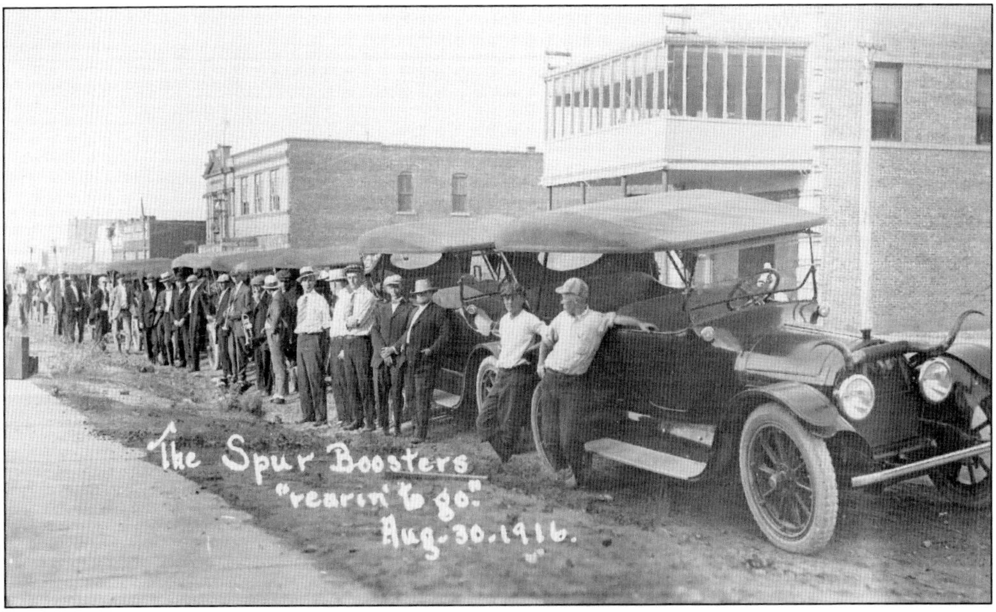

The Espuela Cattle Company, with approximately 439,000 acres in Dickens, Kent, Crosby, and Garza Counties, began in 1883. A London-based group of Scotsmen acquired the ranch in 1885 and later sold it to the Swenson interests. To facilitate land sales, the Swensons helped finance the Stamford & Northwestern Railroad 82 miles northwest from Stamford to the new city of Spur, from which automobile expeditions were launched. (Courtesy of Swenson Land and Cattle Company.)

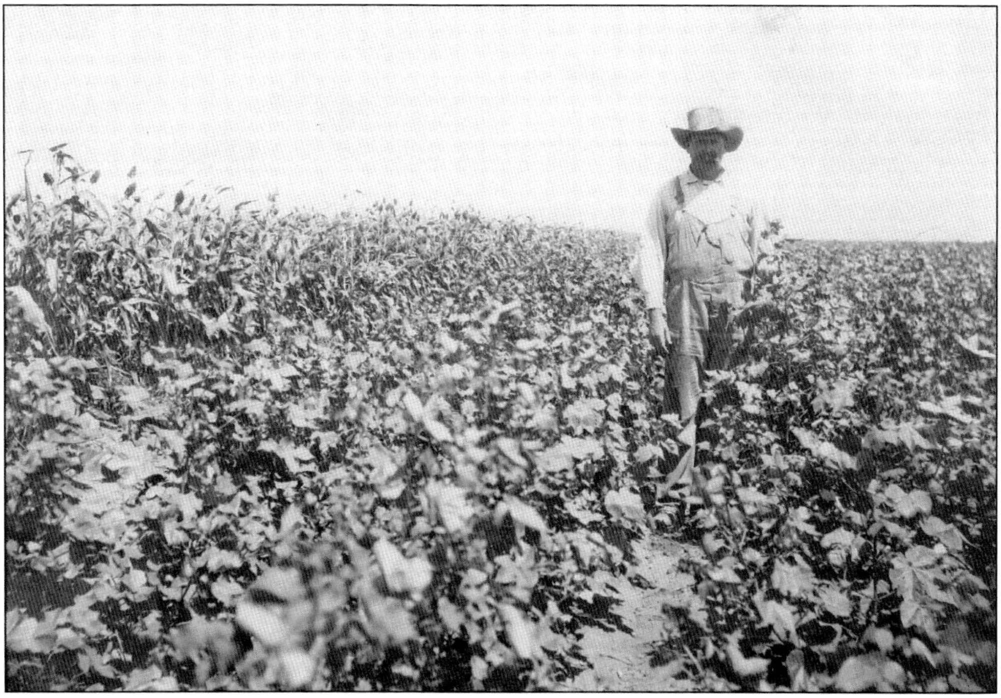

Like Stamford, Spur was a Swenson project. In its first 30 days in 1909, the town grew from a railroad terminal to a population of more than 700 with 50 businesses, a telephone system, and a public school. Selling lots as small as 160 acres at $15 per acre to farmers like C.D. Copeland, seen here, the Spur farmlands sold for approximately $3 million overall. (Courtesy of Swenson Land and Cattle Company.)

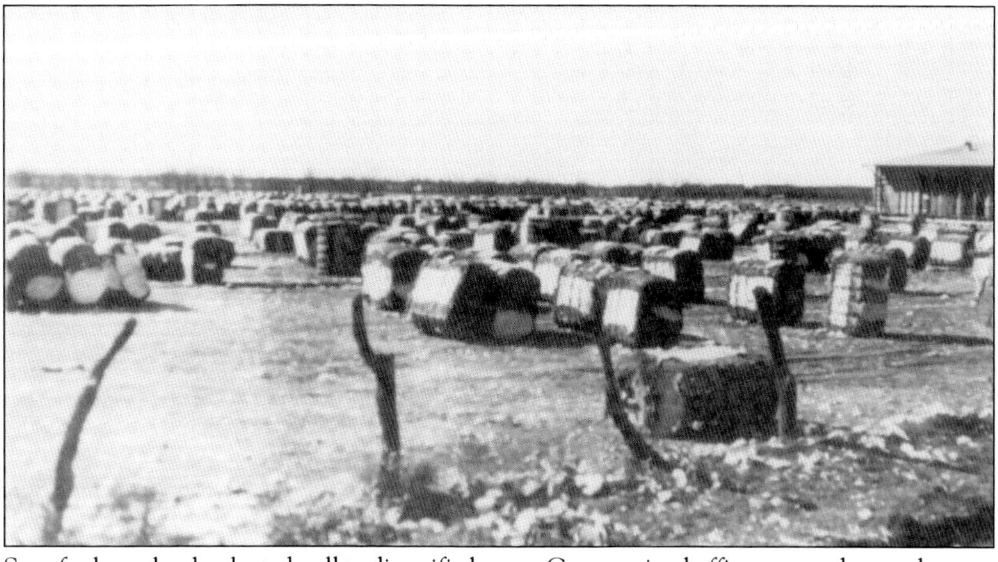

Stamford area lands adapted well to diversified crops. Corn, maize, kaffir corn, garden truck crops, and fruits all did well. Hogs joined cattle as profitable livestock. However, cotton became the principal cash crop. In 1905, a world-record 40,000 cotton bales shipped from the area. By 1909, Stamford had two cottons gins, each with a capacity of 100 bales a day. (Courtesy of Swenson Land and Cattle Company.)

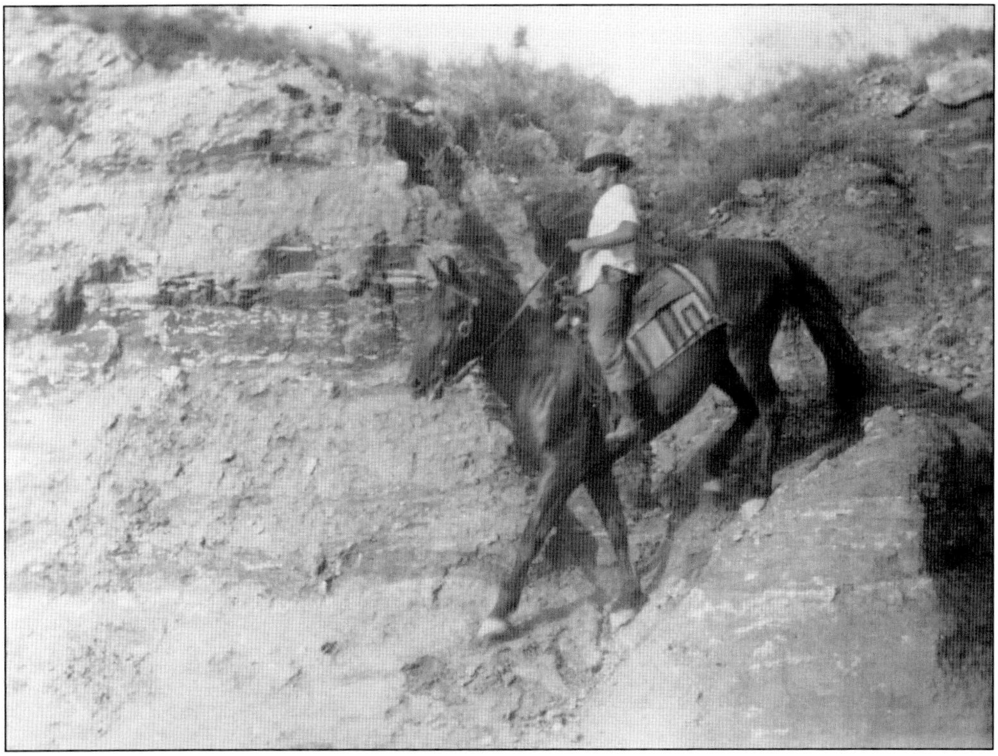

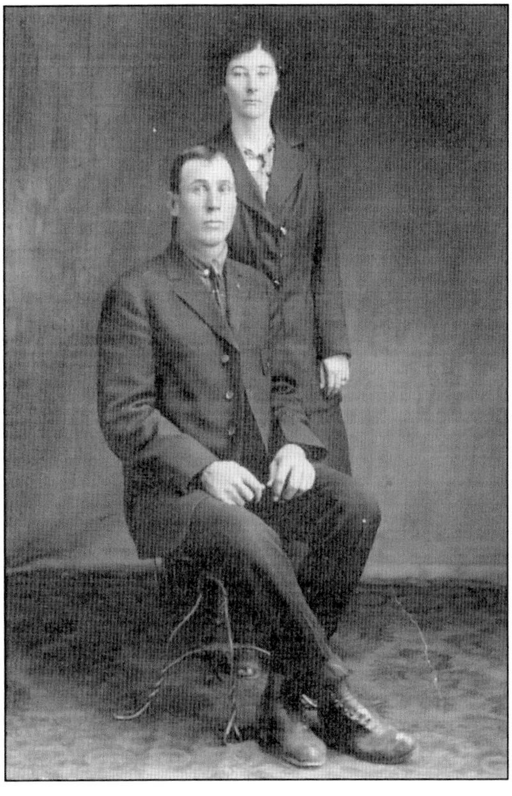

The Swensons also acquired young John Selmon, seen here riding down the Caprock Escarpment, with the Espuela Cattle Company. The 16-year-old Selmon rode 400 miles to West Texas in 1900. Fellow cowboys once persuaded the young man to ride the notorious bronco Towelface. After being pitched off, he remarked, "That's a scandalous bucking booger!" The laughing cowboys dubbed him "Scandalous John," and the nickname stuck for life. (Courtesy of Swenson Land and Cattle Company.)

John Selmon continued working on the Espuela Ranch (renamed Spur Ranch) and was a natural at all aspects of ranch work. In 1915, he married Emma Zinn, whose family ranched in Crosby County. The Spur lacked married housing, so the young couple, seen here, temporarily worked as ranch cooks. In 1919, Selmon became the foreman of the Flat Top Ranch, 12 miles northwest of Stamford. (Courtesy of Tony Selmon.)

The Swenson brothers exemplified the phenomenon of eastern capitalists financing western cattle businesses. Erick and Swen made their first ranch inspections in a buggy. By 1910, they traveled in a Pierce-Arrow touring car chauffeured by Swedish cowboy Carl Hedburg. In this undated photograph, Erick Swenson stands nearest the car. Cowboy Jake Raines has his back to the camera, and behind him is ranch superintendent A.J. Swenson.

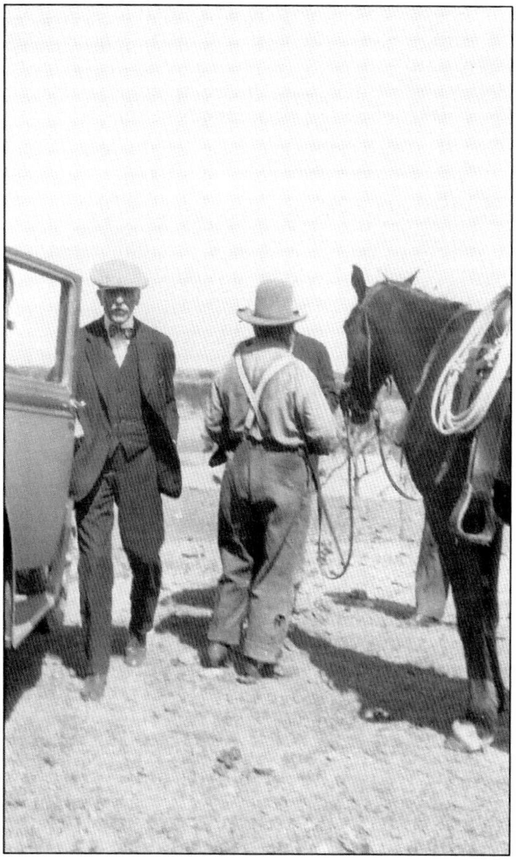

Many cowboys remained wage hands throughout their careers. Some aspired to eventually have land and cattle of their own. Others, however, held grander ambitions. Jake Raines, seen here on his horse Cheyenne, never married and banked his wages, which compounded at 10 percent. By the end of his 30 years of service to the SMS ranches, Raines was a millionaire.

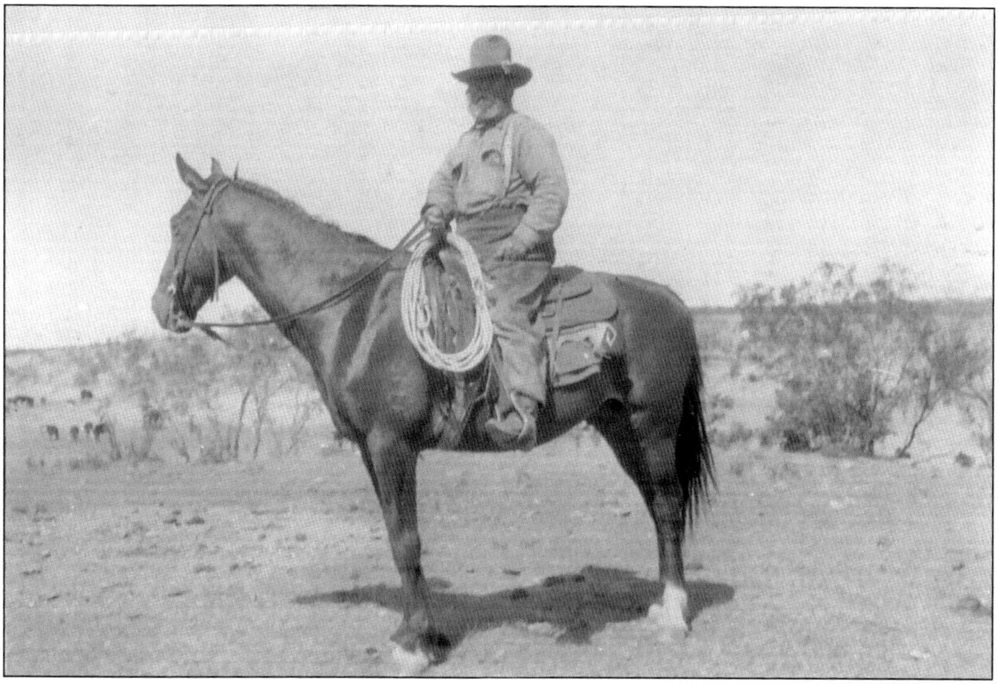

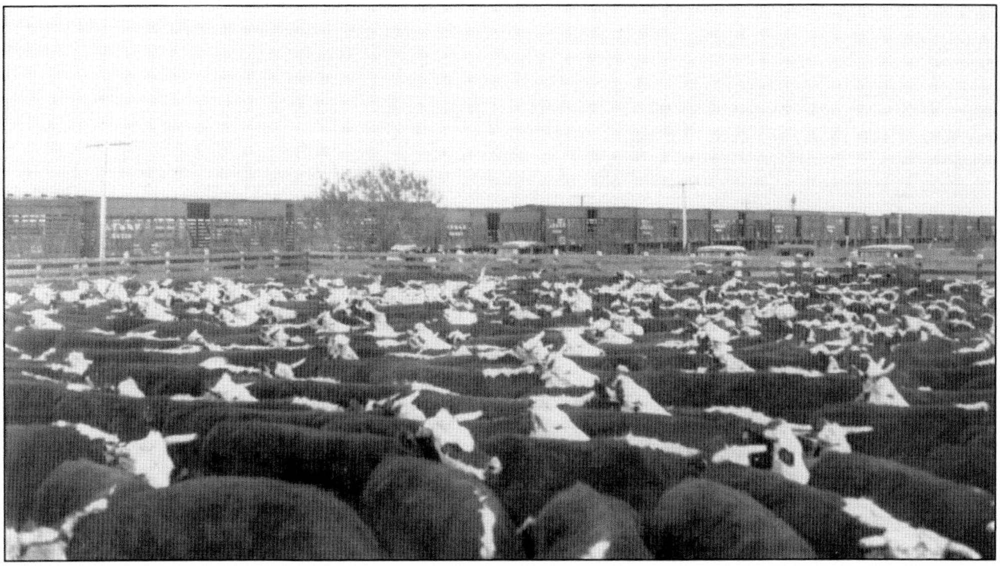

The Swenson brothers hired 42-year-old Frank Hastings to improve the SMS stock. Hastings applied his experience in the Hereford cattle business to produce two innovations. He pioneered the development of large-scale cattle feeding, constructing a 5,000-head facility in Stamford. Here, SMS Herefords await shipping around 1929. (Courtesy of Swenson Land and Cattle Company.)

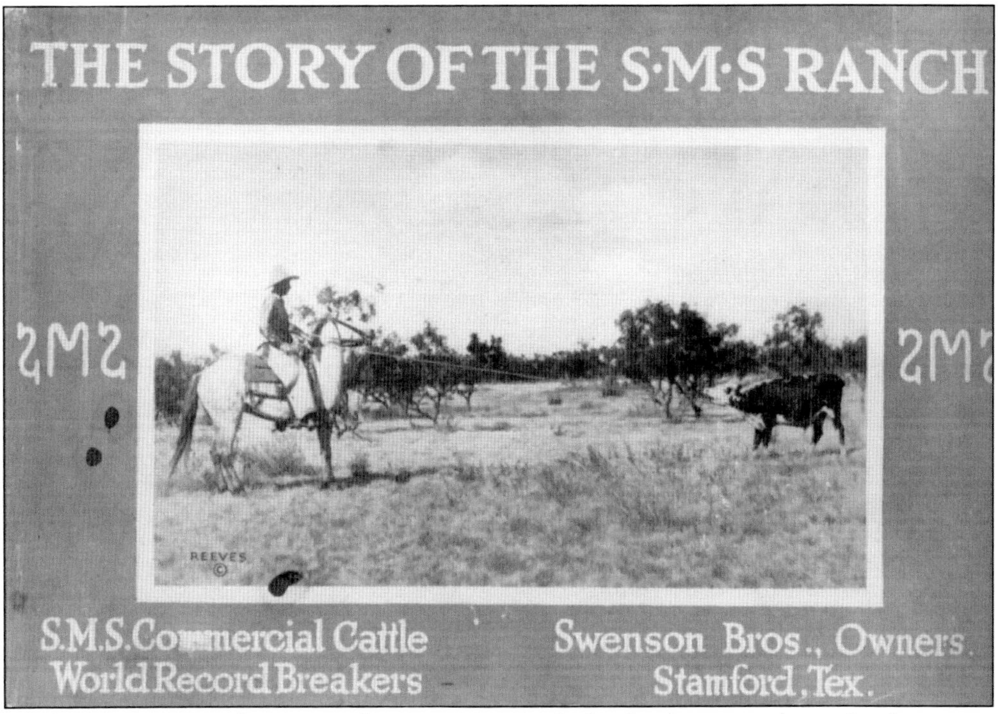

Frank Hastings created a new marketing strategy with the development of a mail-order system for selling SMS-registered cattle to operations in the Midwest. He produced annual booklets for prospective customers, with photographs and descriptions of the ranch and cattle. Hastings's personal integrity and that of the Swensons led purchasers, for the first time in history, to buy cattle sight unseen. This is the cover of the 1922 catalog.

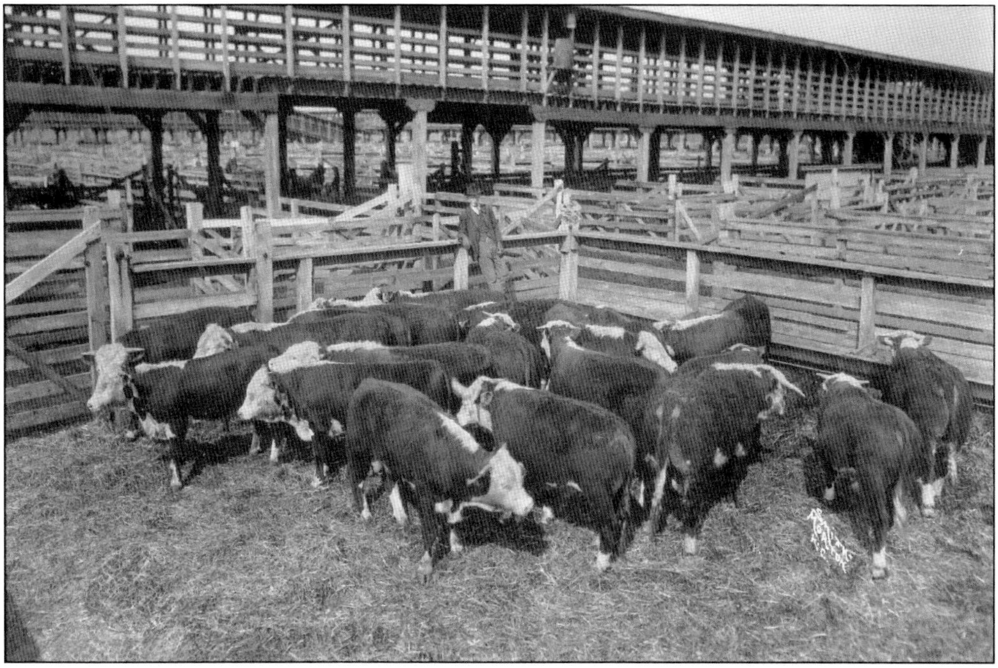

Registered Swenson cattle were promoted at national carload shows across the nation. In 1918, a carload of SMS cattle won Grand Champion of the Chicago International Stock Show, the first time commercial cattle won over purebred lots. The SMS brand became famous across the nation. This promotional photograph shows an unidentified man examining SMS cattle shipped to the Kansas City stockyards. (Courtesy of Swenson Land and Cattle Company.)

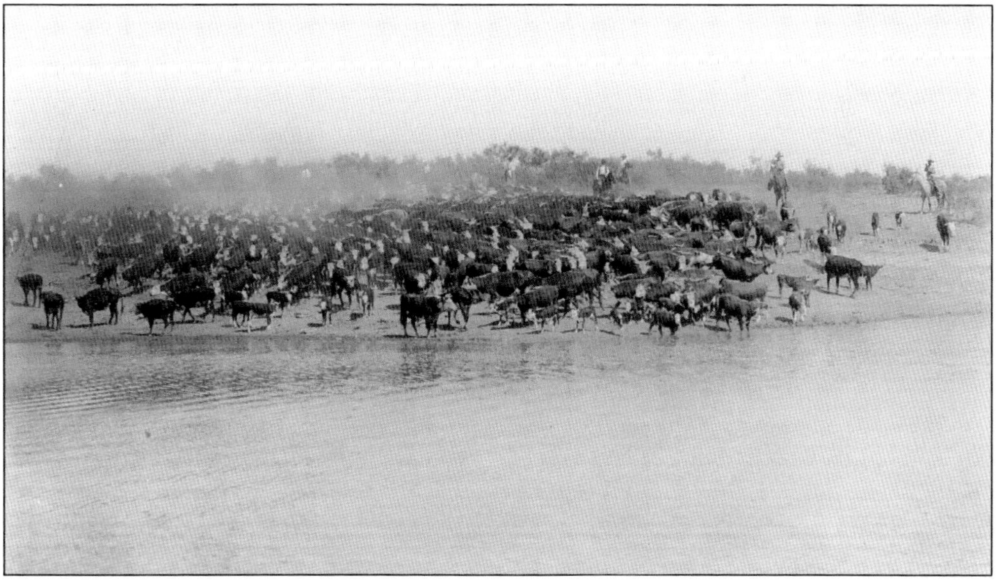

In cattle-drive images such as this one from the Flat Top Ranch, registered Hereford cattle replaced the half-wild longhorns. The initial issue of the monthly *Cattleman* magazine was printed in Stamford in 1914 for the Cattle Raisers Association of Texas. The association was founded in 1877, making it the oldest and largest organization of its kind in the United States. (Courtesy of Swenson Land and Cattle Company.)

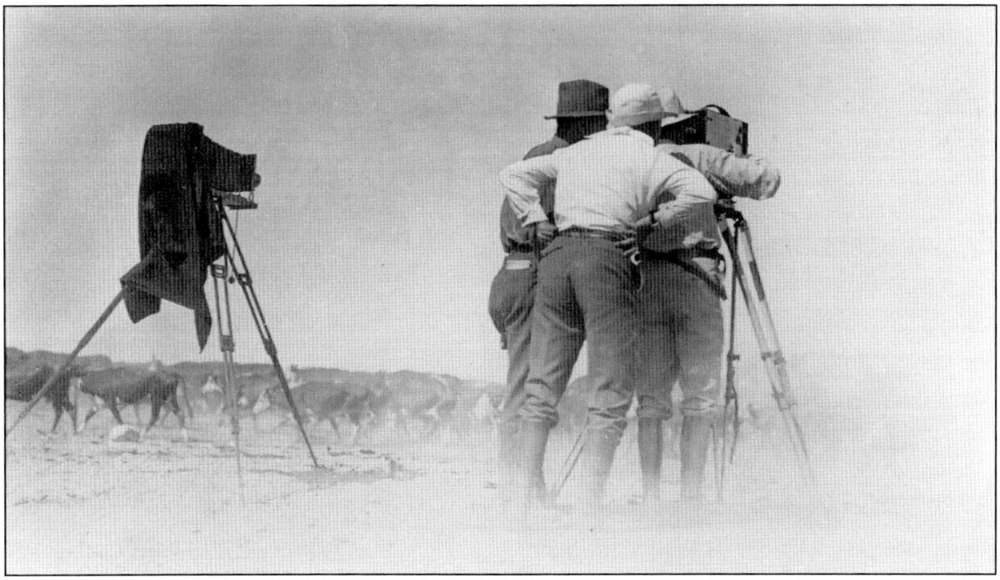

The SMS booklets included specifics on the stock, information about the ranches, and testimonials from satisfied customers. In addition, each booklet contained numerous photographs of cattle and ranch scenes. To obtain high-quality pictures, Swenson Brothers contracted with professional photographers to create the images for each booklet. This rare photograph captures three unidentified photographers and gives some insight into the difficulties they faced. (Courtesy of Swenson Land and Cattle Company.)

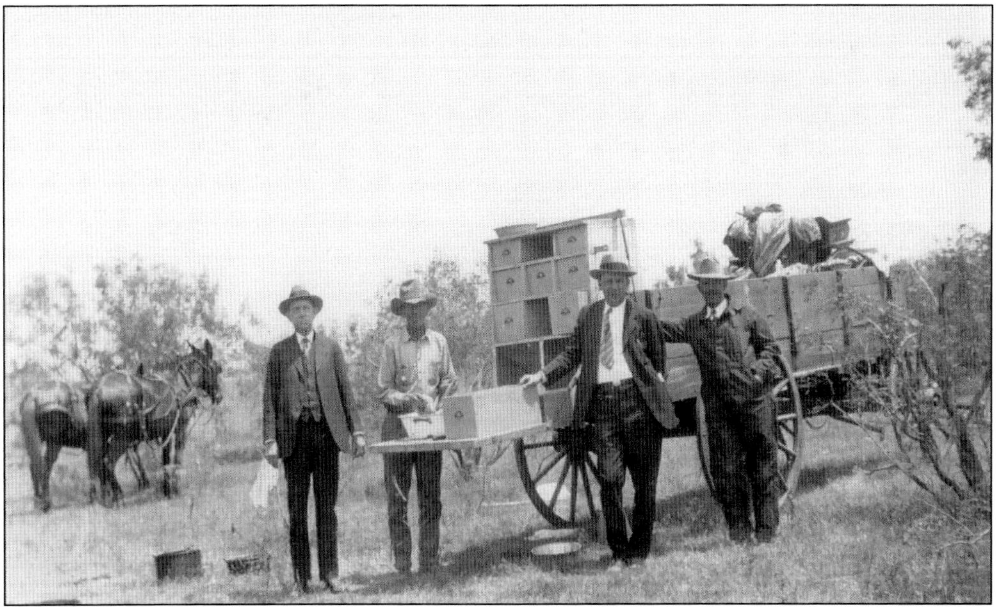

From the beginning, the SMS ranches were a 20th-century enterprise, with collaboration between New York financiers, railroad entrepreneurs, and Swedish immigrants. Early photographs contain contradictory images, like this one of unidentified businessmen in suits dining at a chuck wagon. Horses, wagons, railroads, and automobile transportation intermingled. Yet much ranch work still resembled what was done in the previous century, and nostalgia for the earlier days on the range remained a powerful force.

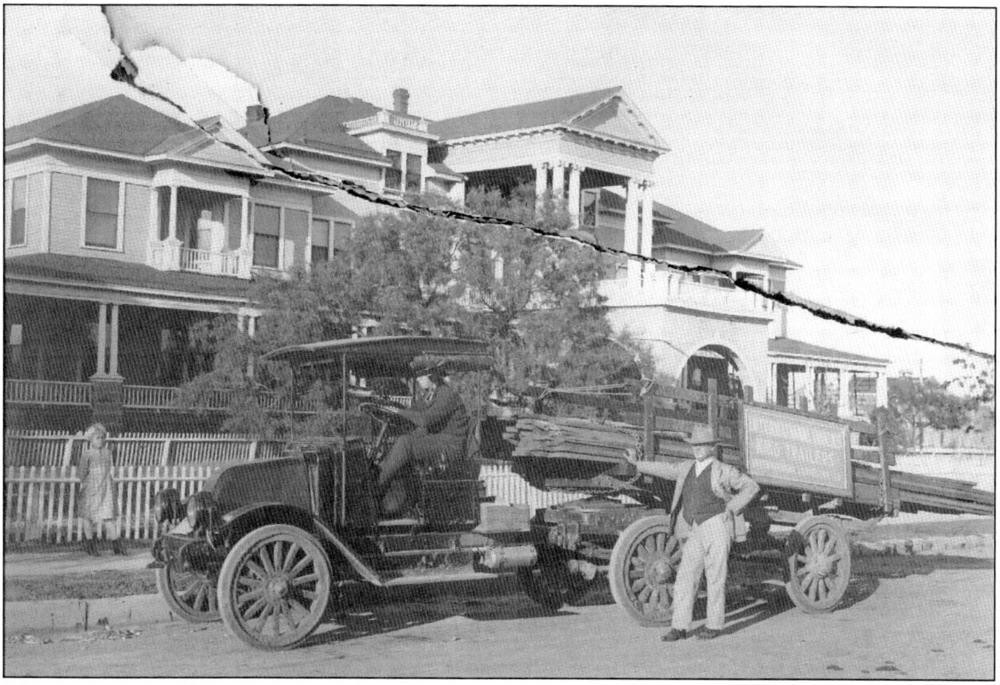

This International Harvester truck and King Trailer was the first truck owned by the Swenson Brothers enterprise. It was purchased in 1917 for use on the Spur Ranch. The unidentified men pose with the new vehicle in front of the Stamford Inn. The growing mechanization of ranch work was not a feature promoted by the first SMS booklets. (Courtesy of Swenson Land and Cattle Company.)

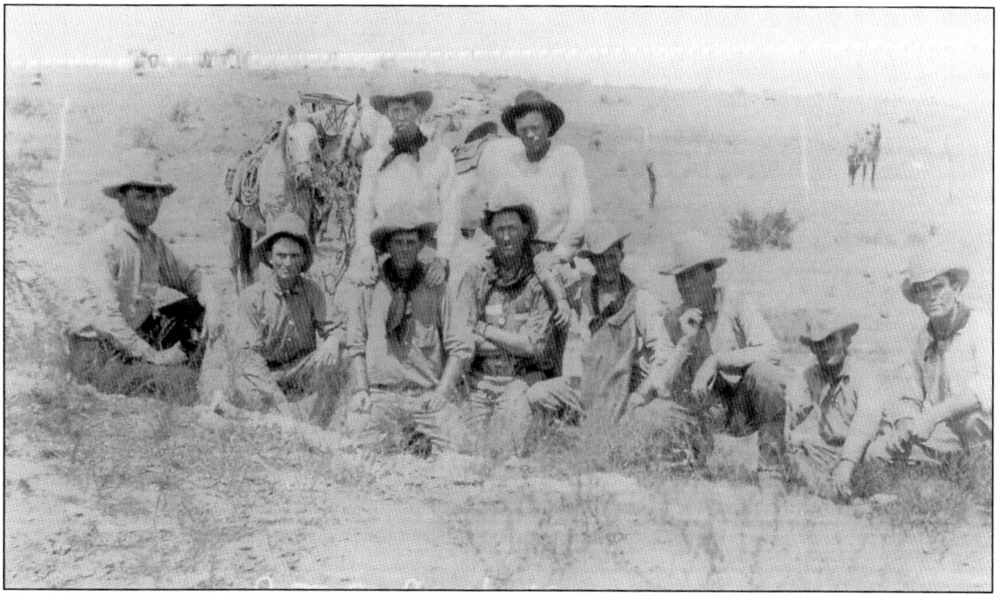

This photograph is captioned "SMS Cowboys" but has no names or dates. In the West, work, honor, and dignity often resided in the phrase "ride for the brand." The brand, a legal symbol of ownership, also became a mark of loyalty. The photographers hired by the SMS ranches captured this spirit as they recorded the roundup work for the annual booklets.

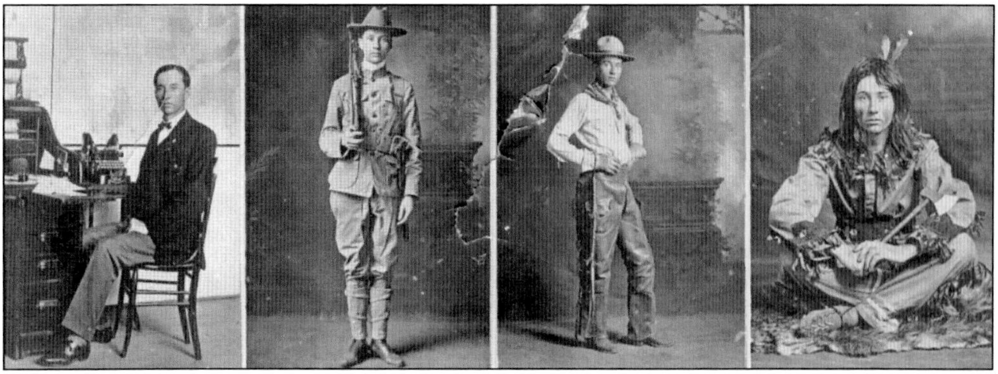

Stamford photographer Ray Rector produced a rich collection of SMS ranch images. Rector was an infant when his family moved from Hamilton County, Texas, to a West Texas farm southwest of Stamford in 1873. He worked as a cowboy on the XIT Ranch in the Texas Panhandle before moving back to Stamford, where he acquired a photographic studio in 1902. The young man produced this composite of self-portraits in different outfits.

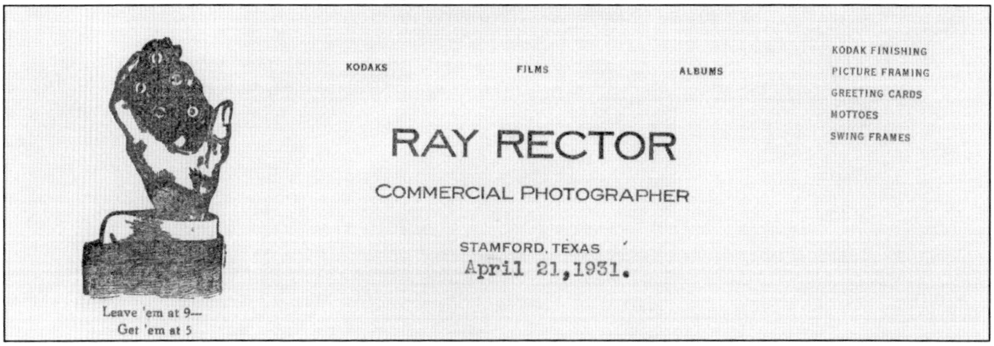

KODAKS FILMS ALBUMS

KODAK FINISHING
PICTURE FRAMING
GREETING CARDS
MOTTOES
SWING FRAMES

RAY RECTOR

COMMERCIAL PHOTOGRAPHER

STAMFORD, TEXAS

April 21,1931.

Leave 'em at 9—
Get 'em at 5

Rector operated a studio on the square for portraits. He also made popular photographs recording life in the young city of Stamford, from street scenes to circus parades, church socials, and special events. His stationery promised fast film development, claiming, "Leave 'em at 9—Get 'em at 5."

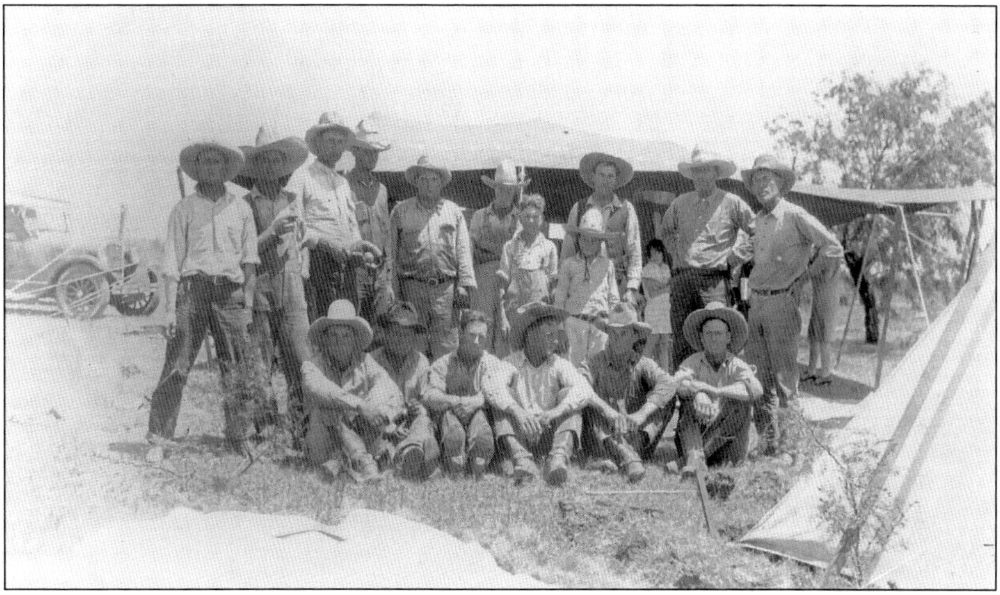

Ray Rector found recording life at area ranches in the early 1920s his favorite work. In this Rector photograph, Flat Top cowboys pose in front of the chuck wagon, with an automobile seen faintly in the left background. Foreman John Selmon stands at the back, seventh from left in a black vest. One young cowhand, Cleo Shipman, standing third from left, holds a baseball and glove, perhaps ready for a bit of lunchtime recreation.

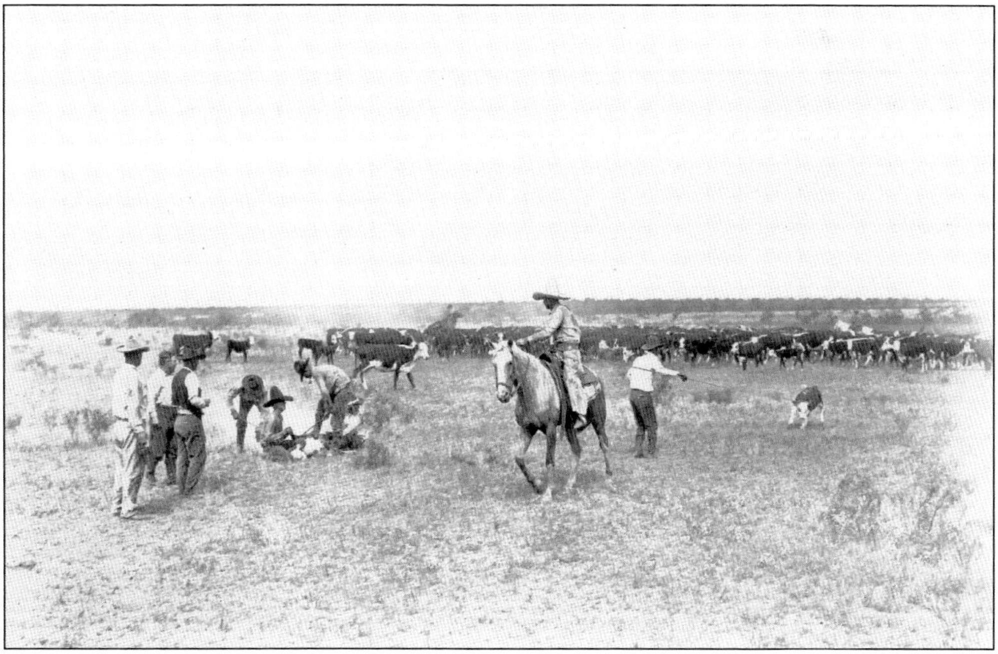

Frank Hastings filled the SMS promotional booklets with iconic ranch images taken by Rector and other photographers. Near the back of the booklet, he included the article "Some Glimpses Into Ranch Life." He apologized for the fragmentary nature of his comments but added, "What is put down is entirely true and real." This photograph provides a look at the roping and branding work during a roundup.

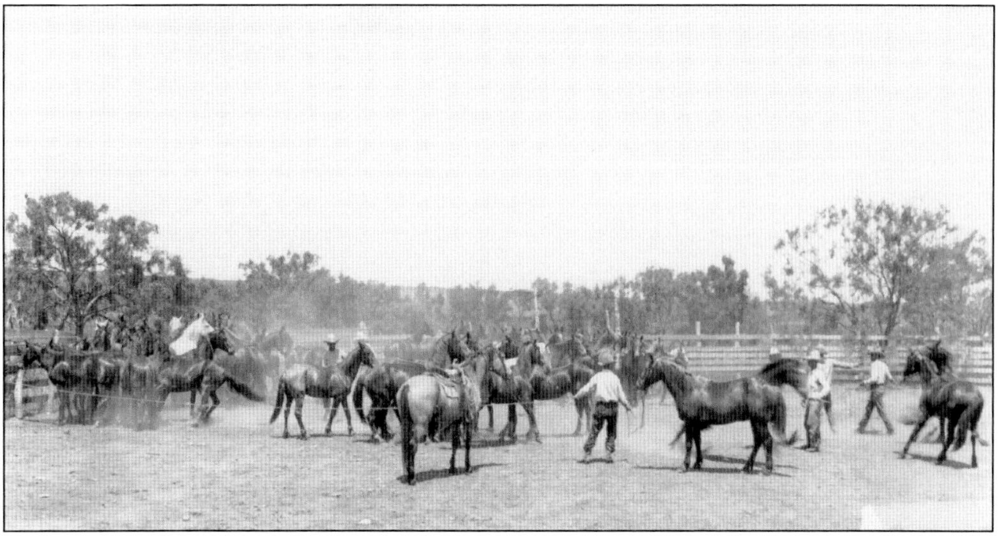

The Flat Top Ranch employed a few cowboys full-time. More hands were hired at branding time to help with the roundup. The saddle-horse herd, or remuda—Spanish for "change of horses"—was as important as the cowboys. The SMS ranches had 500 horses for "cow-work," with eight to 10 for each cowboy. All horses had distinctive names like Big Enough, Monkey Face, and Sail Away Brown.

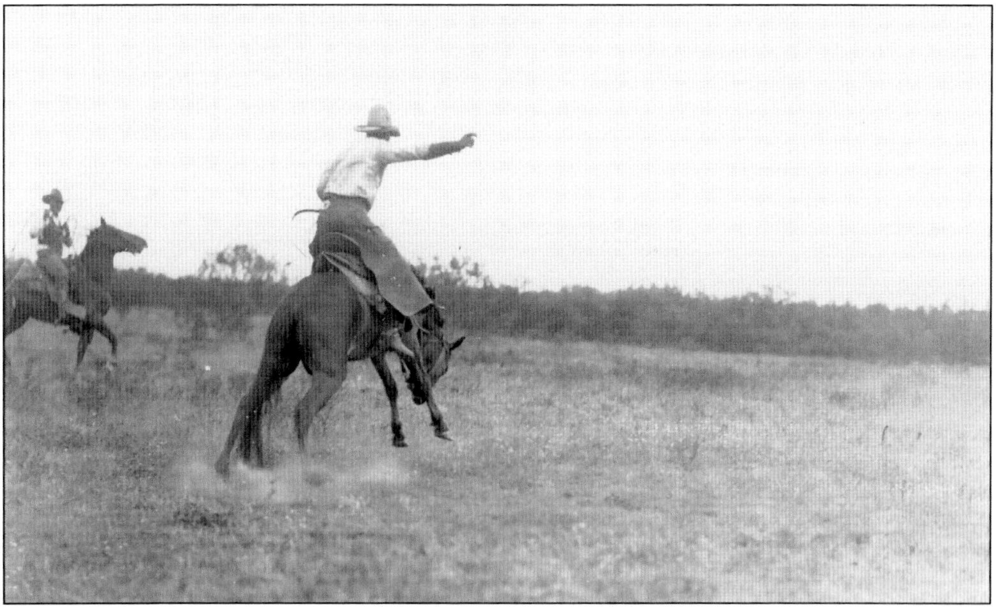

Ray Rector took this action shot of Cleo Shipman working as a "bronc buster" to break a new horse for riding. Roy Phillips rides alongside with a lasso. Shipman grew up in Hamlin, another town created by the Texas Central's extension westward from Stamford. As a Flat Top cowboy, Shipman broke new ponies to the saddle until a goring by a bull damaged his bronco-riding career.

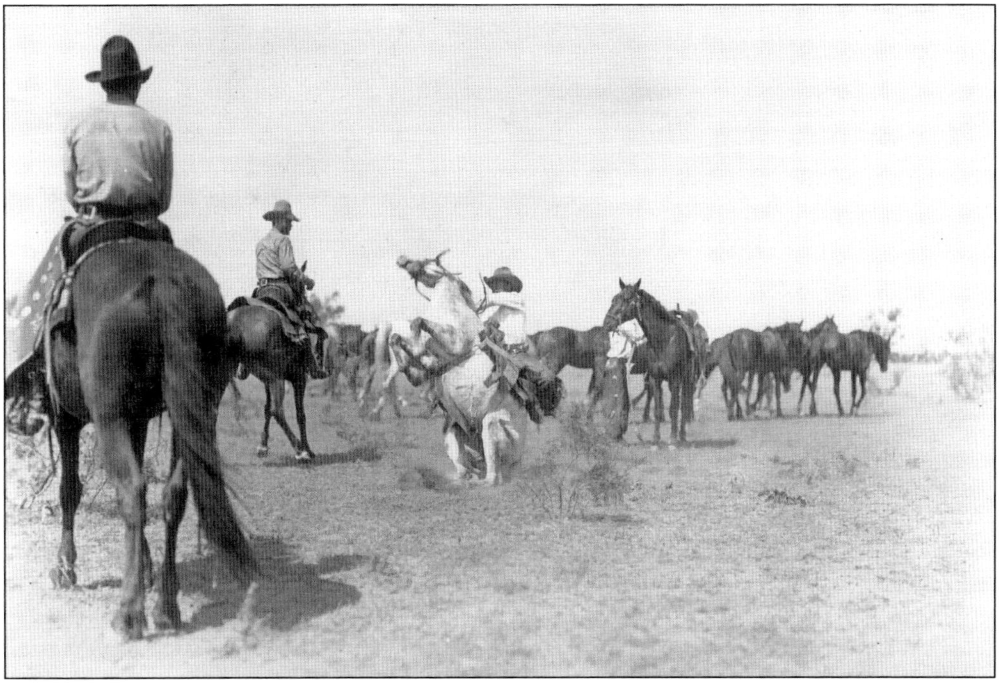

Taken years before the advent of high-speed cameras, this unusual photograph catches a dramatic moment in a ride gone dangerously wrong on the SMS ranch. The rearing horse falls backward as his rider struggles in the saddle with only a split second to avoid serious injury. For years, many old-time cowboys considered this the most remarkable horse photograph in existence.

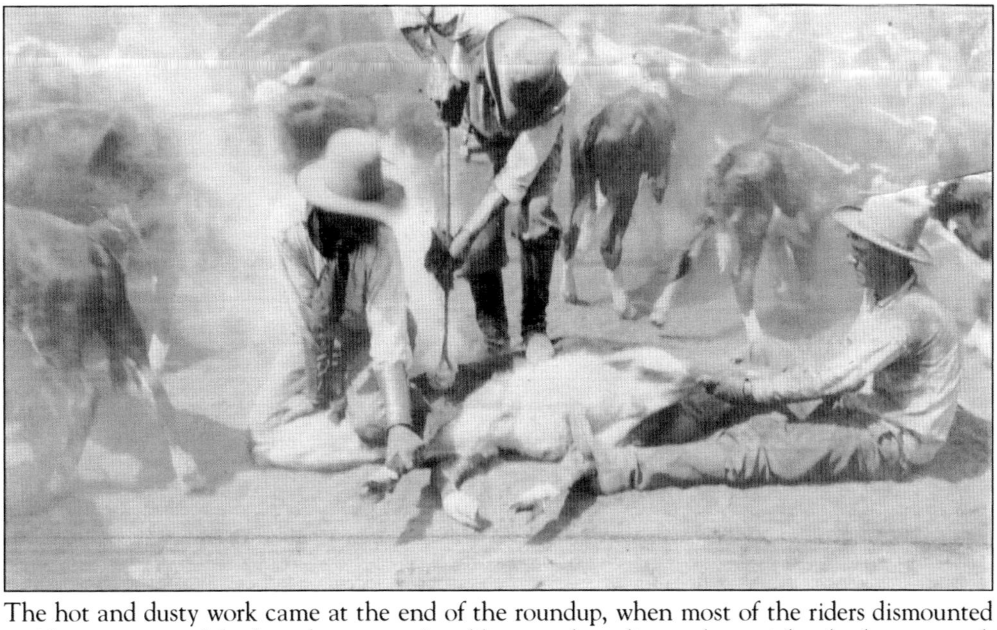

The hot and dusty work came at the end of the roundup, when most of the riders dismounted and became part of the branding team. In addition to branding, calves might also be castrated, vaccinated, and earmarked. An earmark is a cut or mark in the ear of livestock to indicate ownership. Ranches registered earmarks along with their brands. The calves recovered within 10 to 15 days.

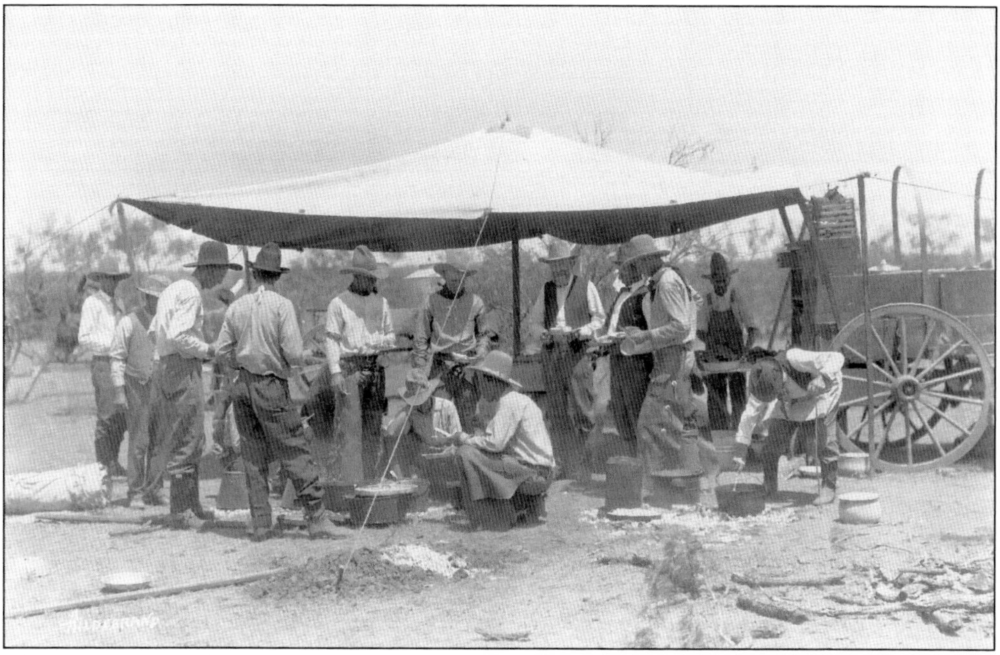

The roundup crew did not work with a time clock, instead following "sun hours." Wagon outfits were headquarters, and the chuck wagon carried food, bedding, and tents, with food prepared from the back of the wagon on open fires. The "hoodlum" wagon (in background) carried the water barrel, wood, and branding irons. Ranch superintendent A.J. Swenson (center) might have been "wagon boss," but around the chuck wagon, the cook had the final word.

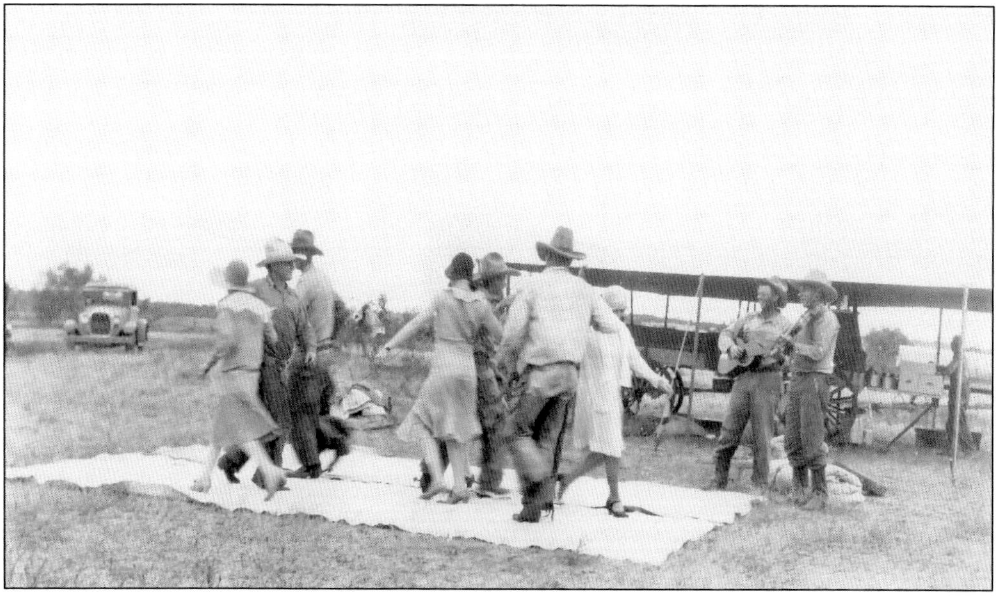

When the ladies visited, there was time to organize an impromptu dance. Here, on a wagon-sheet dance floor, avid square dancers Vira Owen (with cloche hat) and Mary Reeves (with large hat) guide the turns while John Selmon (right) joins the impromptu band. Folklorist professor John Avery Lomax, the pioneer collector of cowboy songs, visited the SMS Flat Top Ranch in 1916 to gather material for a lecture at Princeton University on cowboy dialect.

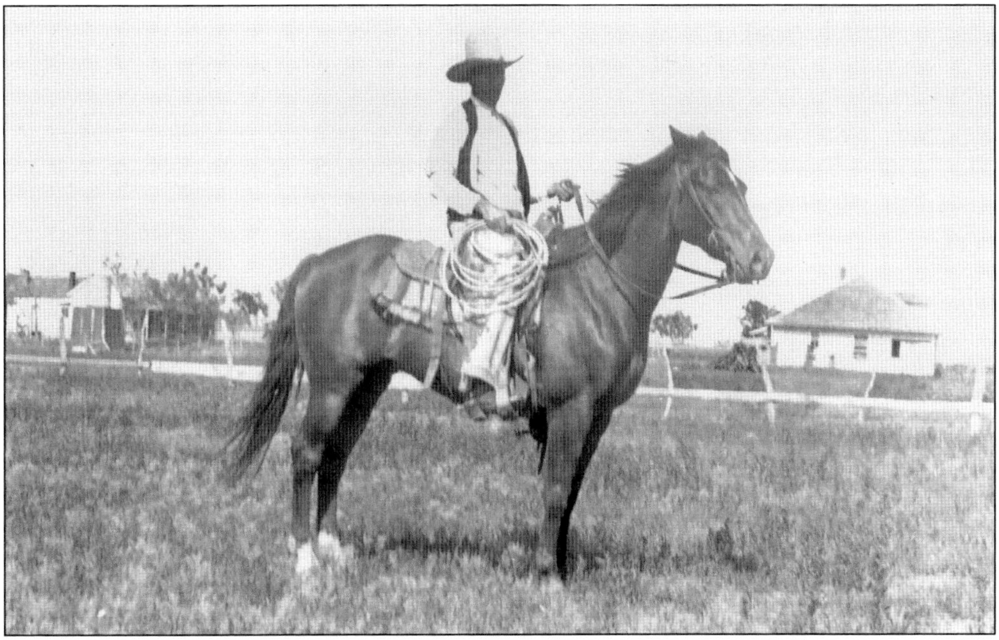

In 1934, Prof. John Lomax, assisted by his son Alan, made thousands of field recordings of folk musicians nationwide to expand the collection of the Archive of American Folk Song, founded in 1928. On December 6, 1935, Lomax recorded a collection of square-dance calls, fiddle tunes, and original songs at the Flat Top Ranch, including two square-dance calls in the Texas drawl of John Selmon. (Courtesy of the Cleo Shipman family.)

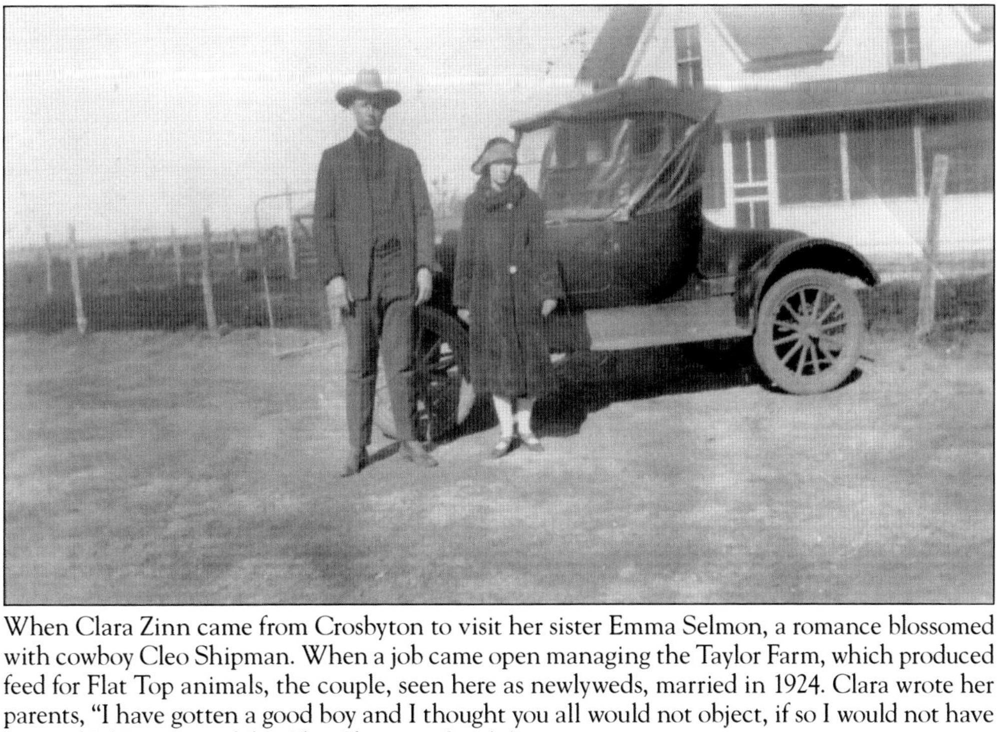

When Clara Zinn came from Crosbyton to visit her sister Emma Selmon, a romance blossomed with cowboy Cleo Shipman. When a job came open managing the Taylor Farm, which produced feed for Flat Top animals, the couple, seen here as newlyweds, married in 1924. Clara wrote her parents, "I have gotten a good boy and I thought you all would not object, if so I would not have married." (Courtesy of the Cleo Shipman family.)

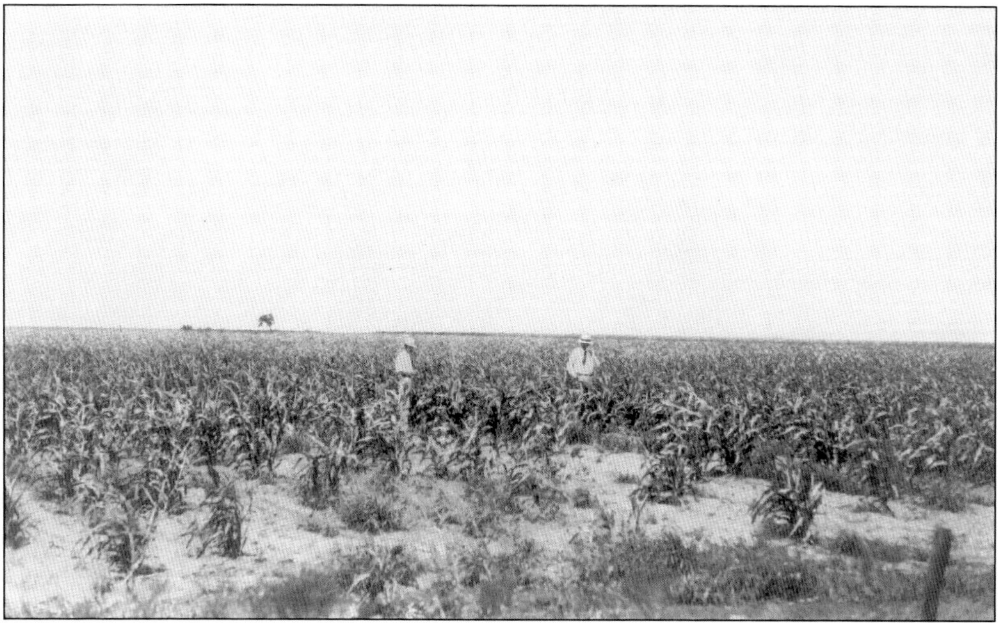

As the cowboy-turned-farmer Shipman demonstrated, farmers and ranchers frequently partnered rather than fought. Some farms provided livestock feed. The Taylor Farm, on Flat Top Mountain, grew oats for horses and grain that was bundled into cattle feed. Others produced wheat or corn, like this field near Stamford. Cotton became the principal cash crop.

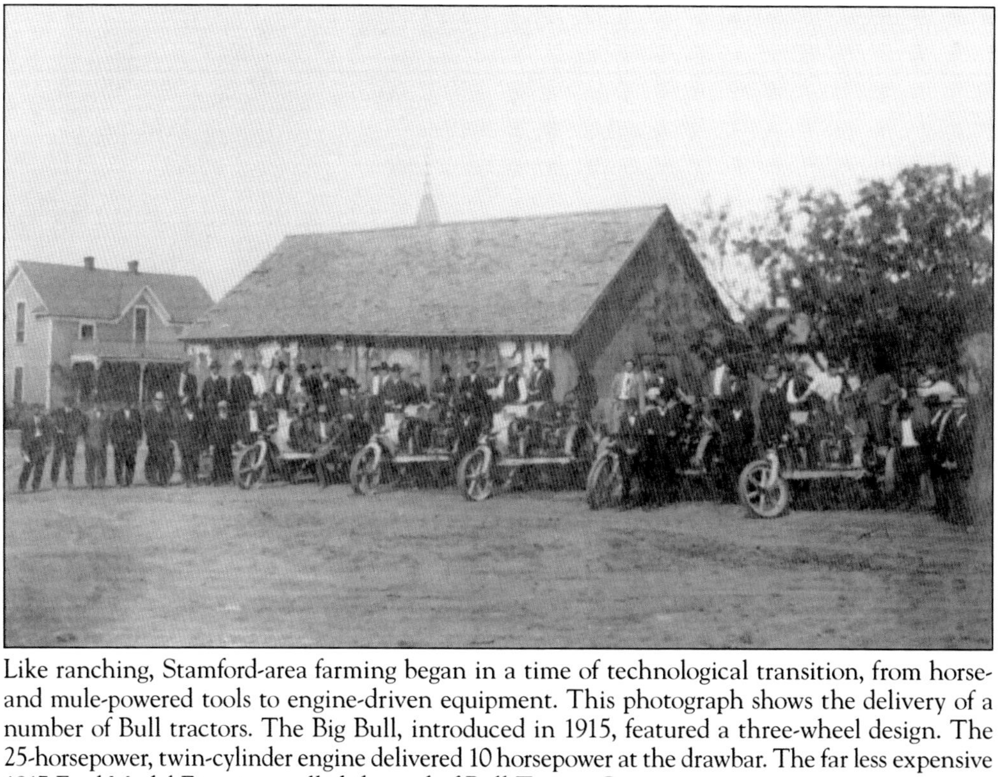

Like ranching, Stamford-area farming began in a time of technological transition, from horse- and mule-powered tools to engine-driven equipment. This photograph shows the delivery of a number of Bull tractors. The Big Bull, introduced in 1915, featured a three-wheel design. The 25-horsepower, twin-cylinder engine delivered 10 horsepower at the drawbar. The far less expensive 1917 Ford Model F tractor spelled the end of Bull Tractor Company.

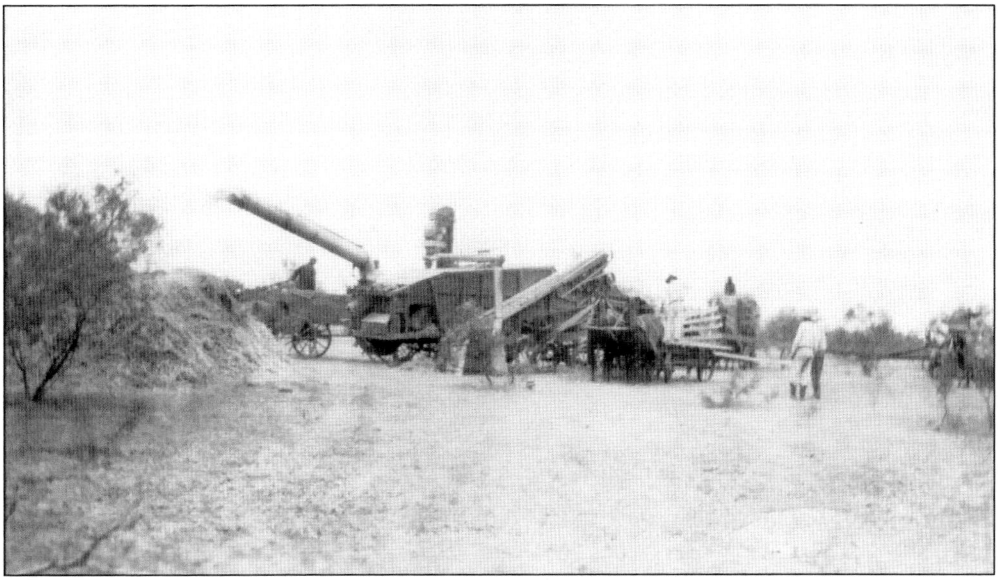

Also like ranching, changes in farm technology did not occur overnight. As this photograph of threshing demonstrates, horse-drawn wagons worked alongside the McCormick Deering threshing machine, and harvesting work remained labor-intensive. Smaller farmers pooled equipment and worked together to bring in one another's crops. Wagons remained the primary vehicle for carrying crops to markets and shipping points. (Courtesy of the Cleo Shipman family.)

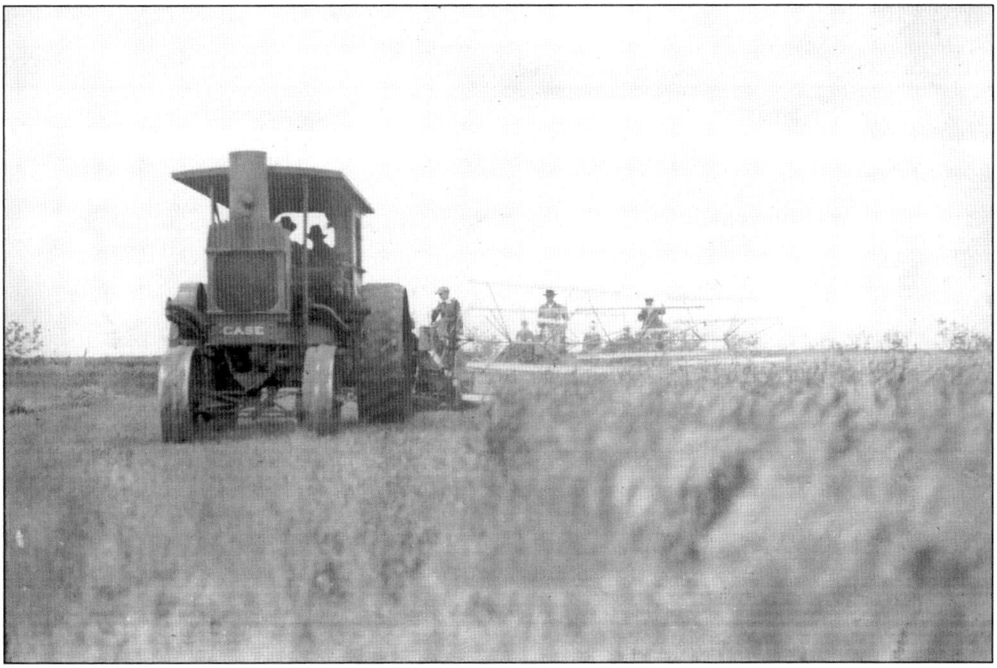

J.I. Case began manufacturing this tractor, the Case 20-40, in 1912. With some modifications, the 20-40 was produced until 1919. The original 40-horsepower engine was a two-cylinder and was powered by kerosene. The original sale price of a 1912 Case was $2,100. The engine-powered tractor and reaper-binder combination resulted in faster and more economical harvesting. Railroad extension north and west from Stamford allowed for cheaper delivery of large farm equipment.

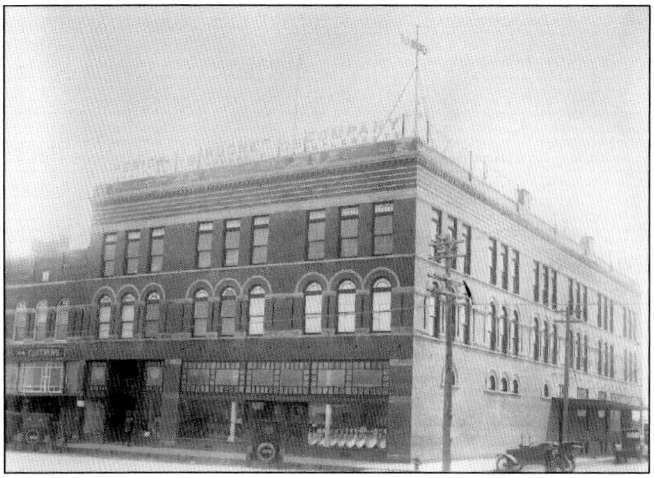

The Penick-Hughes Company of Stamford became a major retail and wholesale distributor in response to farming demand. The three-story building seen here included a switchboard to manage calls. Salesmen traveled to farms throughout West Texas. In a dramatic publicity event, the firm purchased an entire trainload of 40 cars of farm implements. Following the train's arrival, a banquet for 125 guests was held at the Stamford Inn.

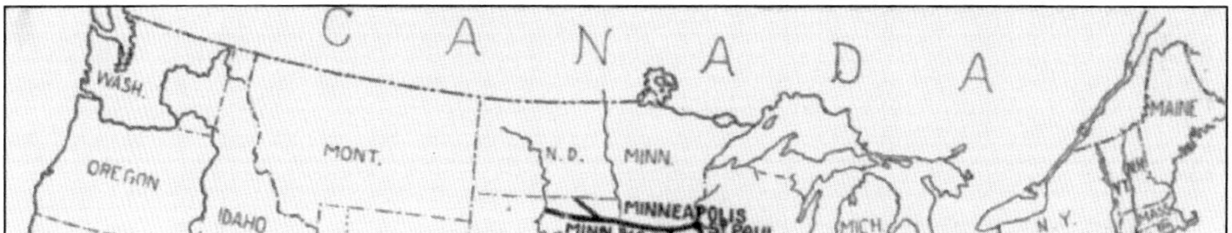

Another railroad stimulated agricultural growth in 1905 when the Kansas City, Mexico & Orient Railway line passed 14 miles west of Stamford, creating the community of Sagerton. The Orient, as envisioned in this 1909 map in the *American Review of Reviews*, would connect Kansas City with the Pacific Ocean. When the Stamford & Northwestern was laid in 1909, tiny Sagerton had two separate depots for a time.

By the early 1920s, the landscape was filled with cultivated land. Simple wood-frame houses were visible in all directions, representing dreams large and small. Away from the railroad, travel remained primitive, and local communities like Sagerton, Avoca, and Tuxedo formed small rural schools and churches. This 1918 winter scene of the road near Spur demonstrates how hazardous automobile travel was. (Courtesy of Swenson Land and Cattle Company.)

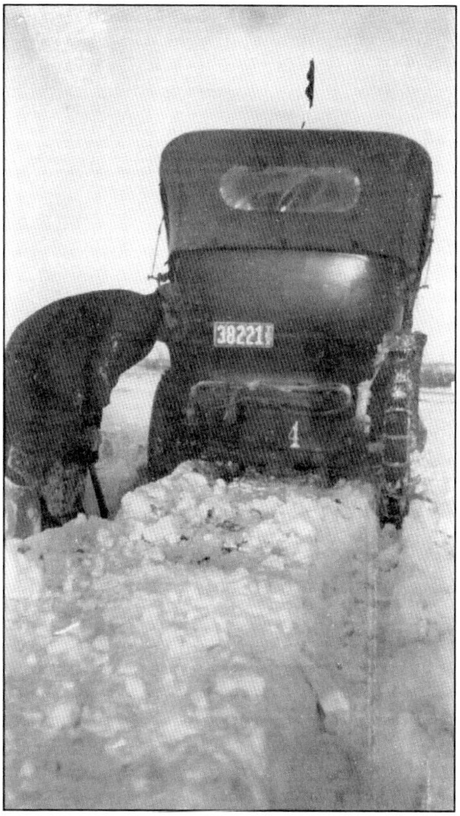

Family was important in agricultural life. Children joined the family work force at an early age, but formal education was also desired as soon as schools could be formed. Love and care were equally important. Rugged ranch foreman John Selmon found this Shetland pony for his son Tony and brought it home in the back of his Model T automobile for the young boy, who is seen here mounted with his woolly chaps. (Courtesy of the Cleo Shipman family.)

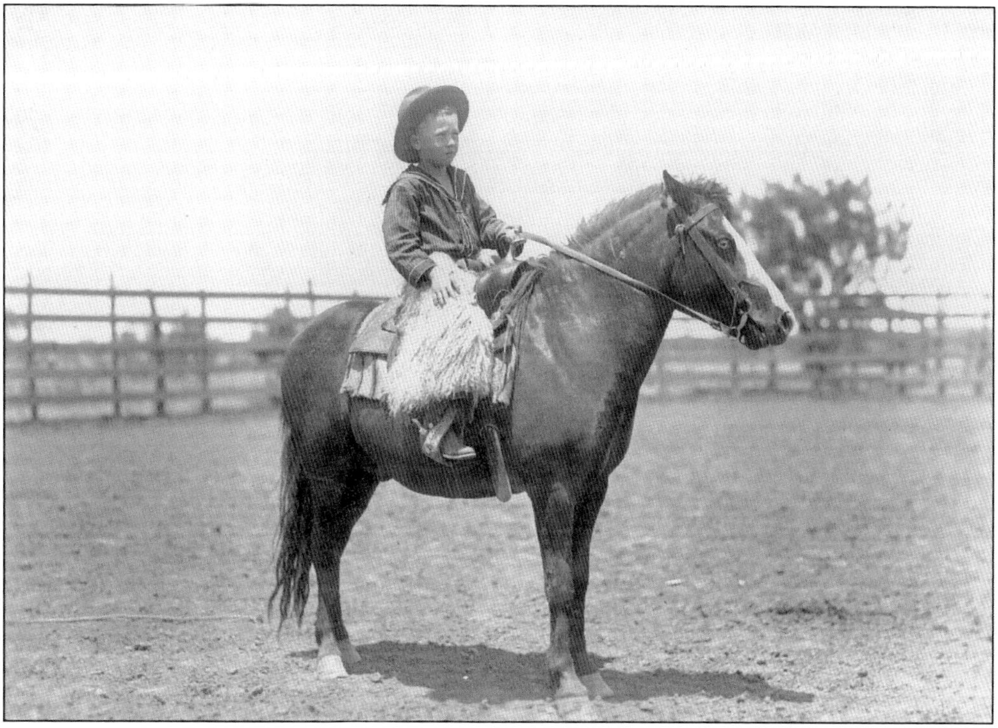

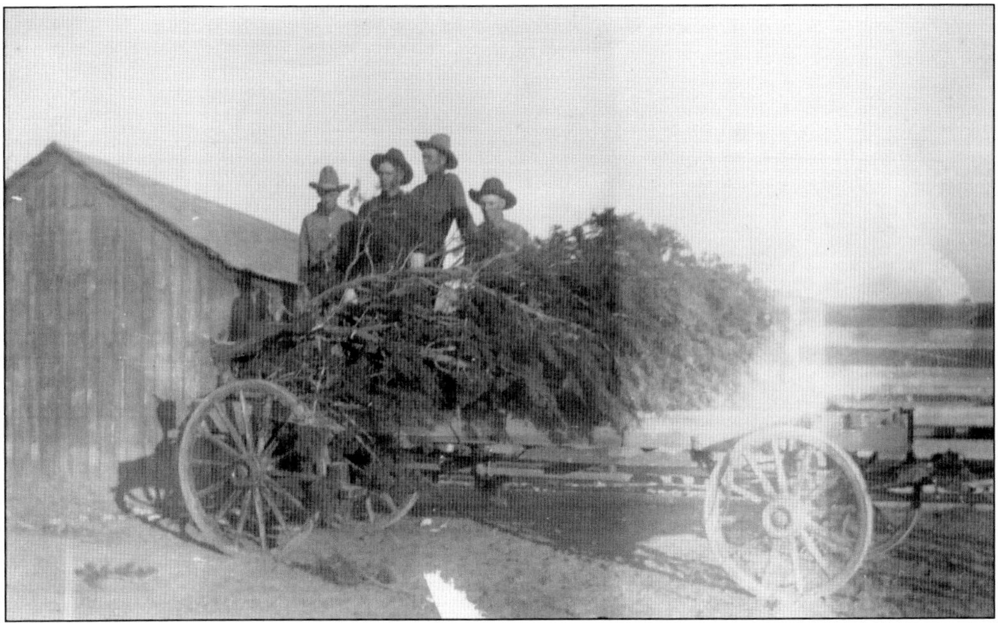

Despite the hard work and the lack of luxuries, farm and ranch communities found time to celebrate life. Geraldine Smith recalled Christmas gatherings at Tuxedo School, and similar events recurred across the prairies. Smith remembered, "We always had a cedar tree that was cut and brought from Flat Top Mountain," like the one seen here. She added, "It was a hilarious time for every one there and everyone was there." (Courtesy of the Cleo Shipman family.)

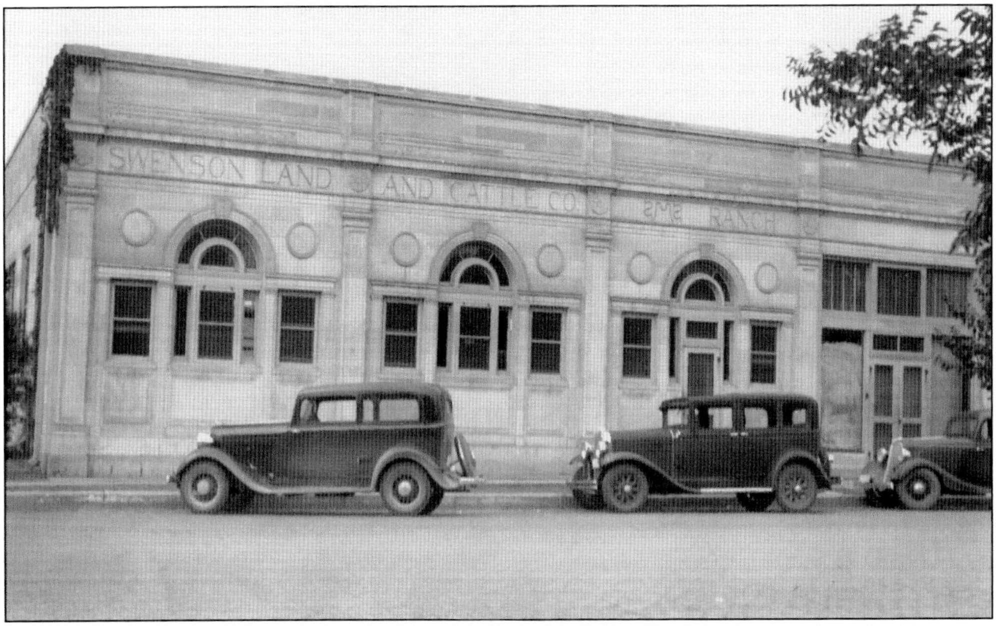

In 1926, the Swenson ranches, except for the Spur Ranch, were incorporated as the Swenson Land and Cattle Company, with headquarters in Stamford. This new office was constructed just off the main square, across the street from the Stamford Inn. The company name and famous SMS brand were incorporated into the building facade, a permanent reminder of the importance of land and cattle to Stamford's success. (Courtesy of Swenson Land and Cattle Company.)

Four

Good Times, Tough Times

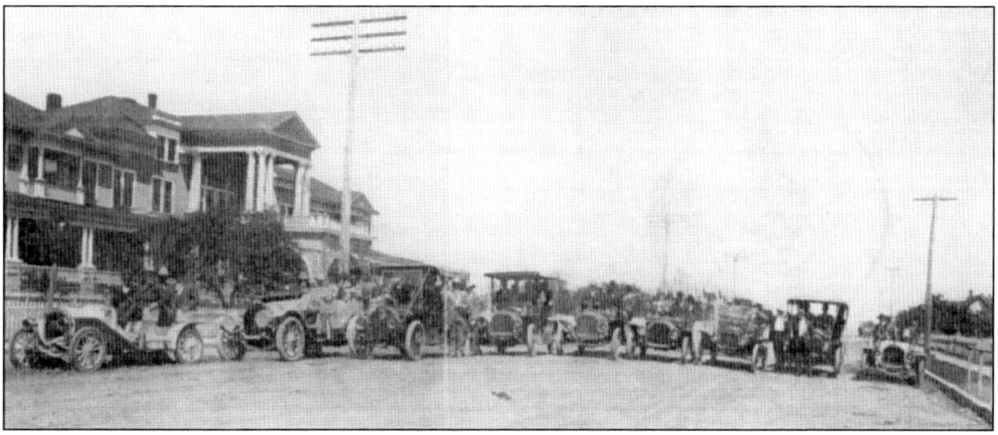

The 1910 First National Bank brochure entitled this shot of automobiles filling the street in front of the Stamford Inn "Entertaining visitors." By the 1910s, Stamford was a thriving community whose leaders had dreams of an even greater future. The reality over the next few decades would prove far rockier than they ever envisioned.

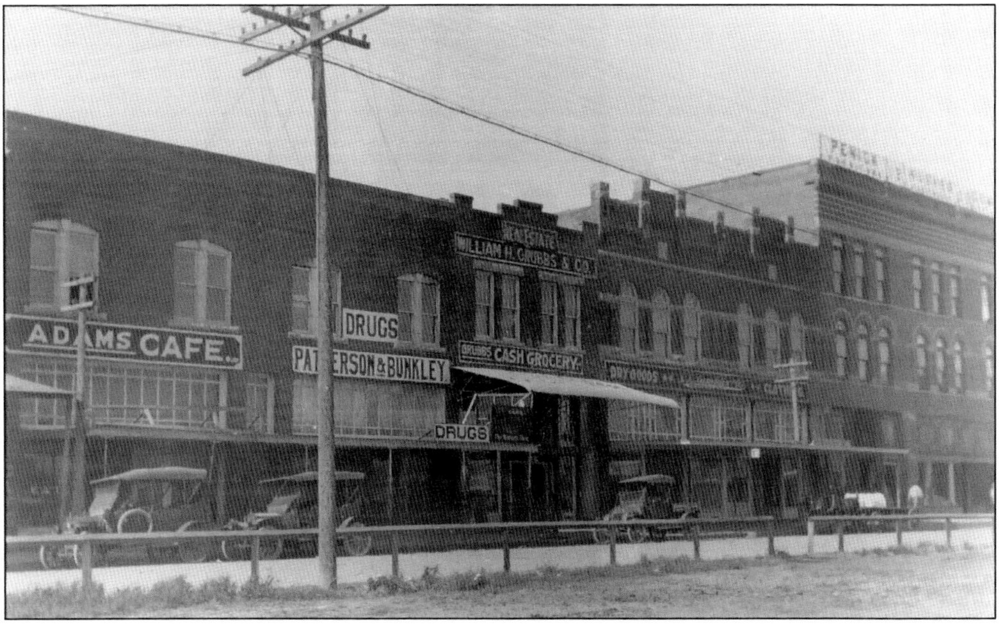

Automobiles, though less common than the bank brochure implied, were becoming a regular feature of Stamford life. By the time this photograph was taken, around 1915, the square offered parking for both automobiles and horse and buggies (right) and a rail for tying up horses. Businesses along Hamilton Street included the Adams Café, Patterson & Bunkley Drugs, William Grubbs Cash Grocery and Real Estate, J.A. Lambdin Dry Goods, and Penick-Hughes Hardware.

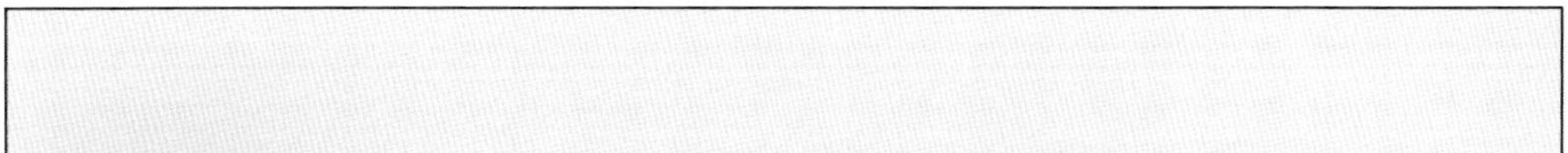

This 1914 photograph of the west side of the square looks north along Swenson Street and reveals the wide variety of transportation forms. Early automobiles share the street with buggies, bicycles, and horse- and mule-drawn vehicles. Several wagons, including one with a cover, sit on the right, inside the railing. By this date, Stamford featured three wholesale grocery houses, a large oil mill, and an ice plant.

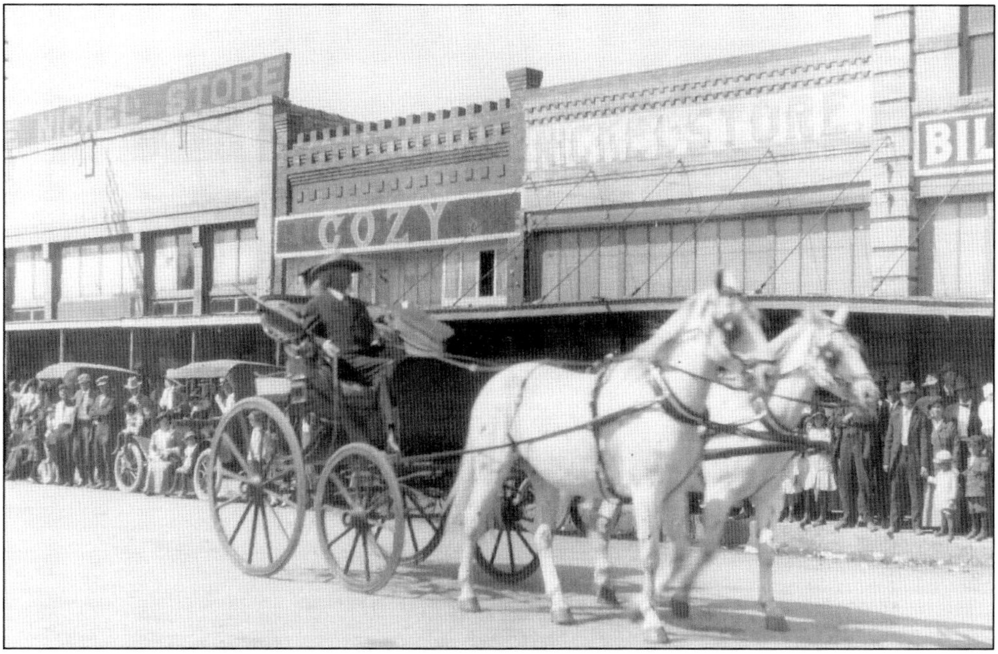

In 1915, a bit of the Old West came to Stamford when William "Buffalo Bill" Cody (seated in buggy) came to town. After years of successful touring with his Wild West Show, Cody went bankrupt in 1914. As a condition of paying off his debts, Cody agreed to perform with the Sells-Floto Circus, owned by Harry Tammen, the editor of the *Denver Post*. Cody died two years later.

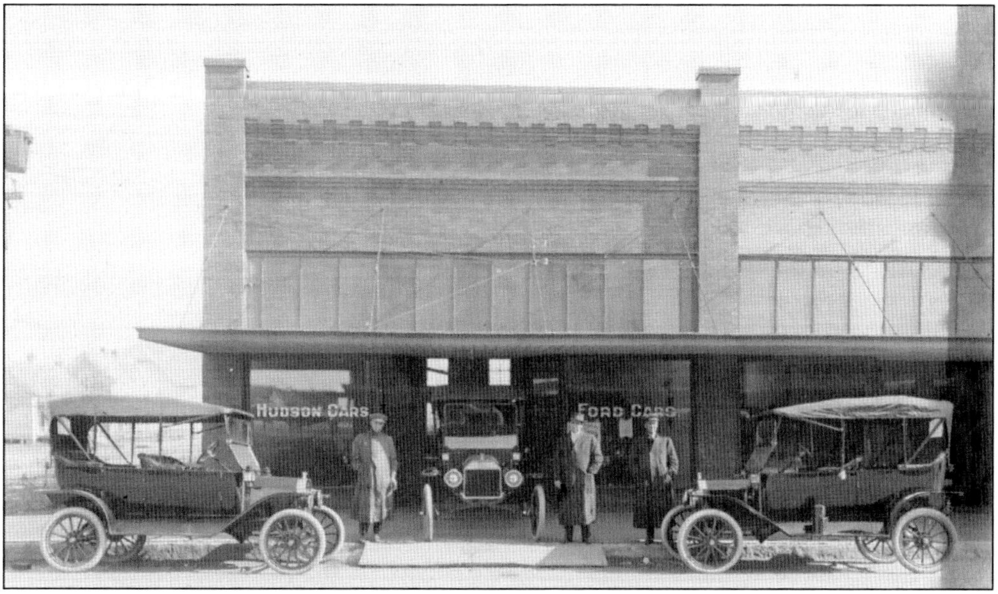

In 1913, Charlie Sammons (right) and Bob Kinard (center) started one of the earliest Stamford automobile dealerships, on Wetherbee Street, selling Hudson and Ford cars. The Hudson Motor Car Company began manufacturing automobiles in Detroit in 1909. The company was named for department store entrepreneur Joseph Hudson. The Ford Model T began production in 1908. The first mass-produced automobile, it changed very little over the next decade. The dealership closed in 1916.

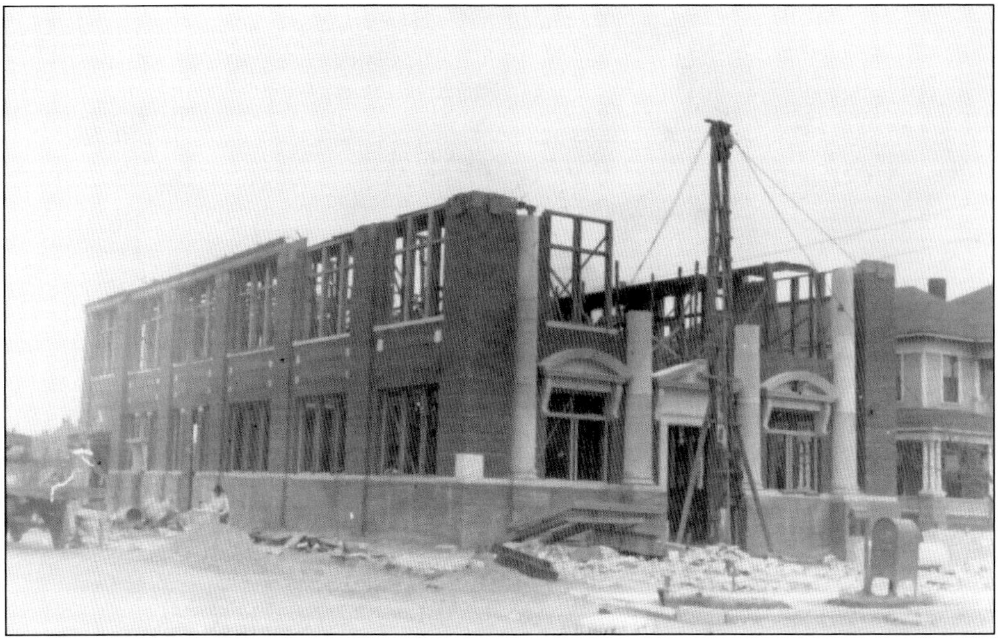

In 1917, the city square underwent a major change. In 1915, city officials had petitioned the federal government for a new, larger post office and offered to provide the center of the square. When their proposal was accepted, a new city hall building, seen here under construction in 1917, was located on the corner of McHarg and Wetherbee Streets, next to the Stamford Inn.

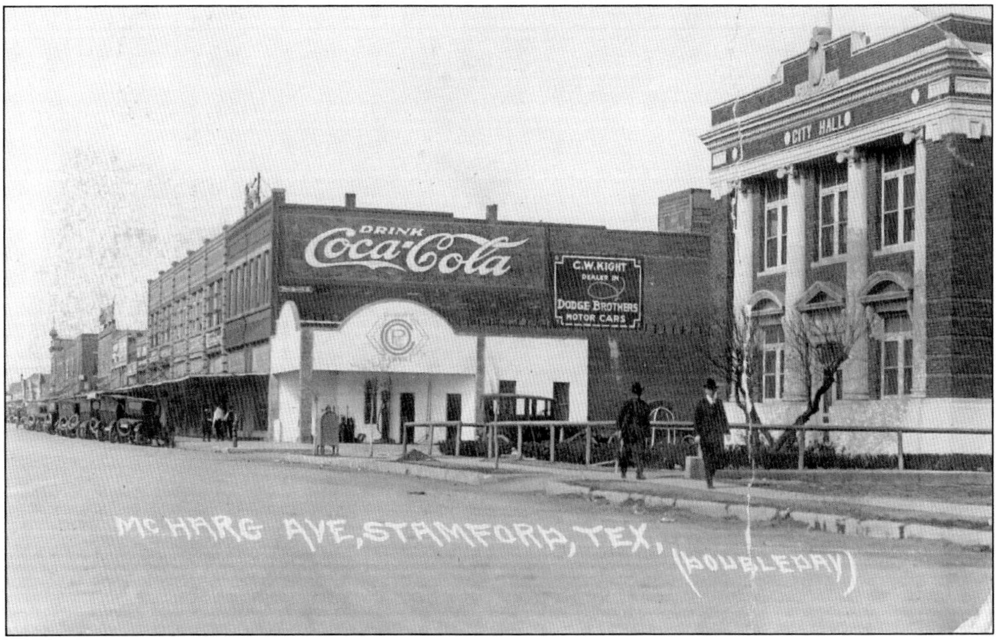

In 1918, the same year the new city hall (right) was completed, Stamford became an incorporated city. A council–city manager form of government was established. R.L. Penick, elected mayor in 1917, presided over the change. The new government had a mayor, five aldermen, and a city manager. This postcard from around 1920 bore the caption "Down on the street in Stamford Texas."

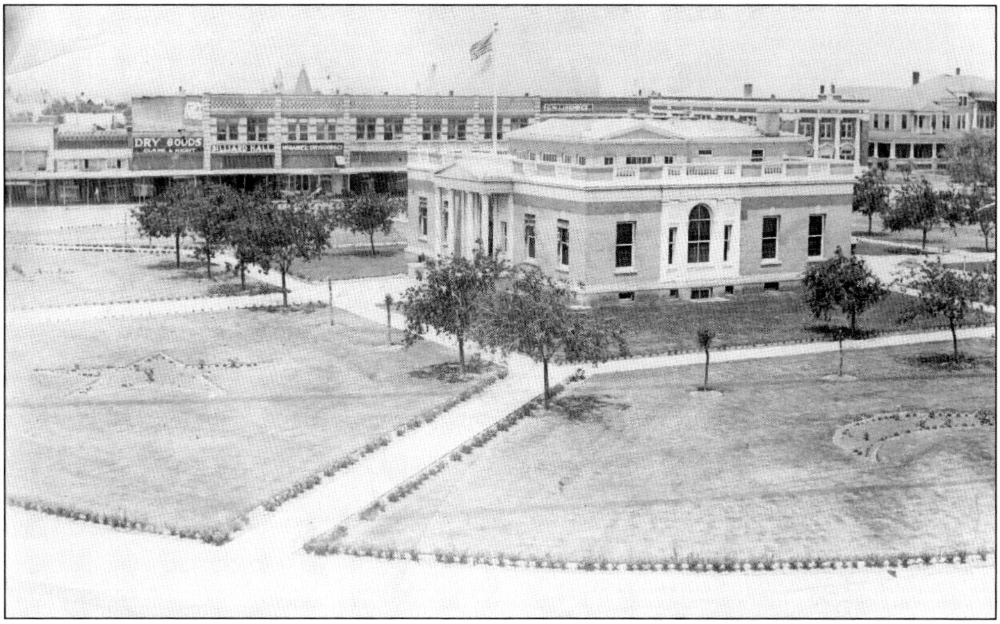

The new post office at the center of the square was completed in 1917 for $40,000. Done in the Beaux Arts style popular at that time, the building has elements from classical architecture, including an entrance with a pediment and ornamentation around windows and the roof. The square was also symmetrically landscaped with trees, grass, and sidewalks, and the horse rails were eliminated.

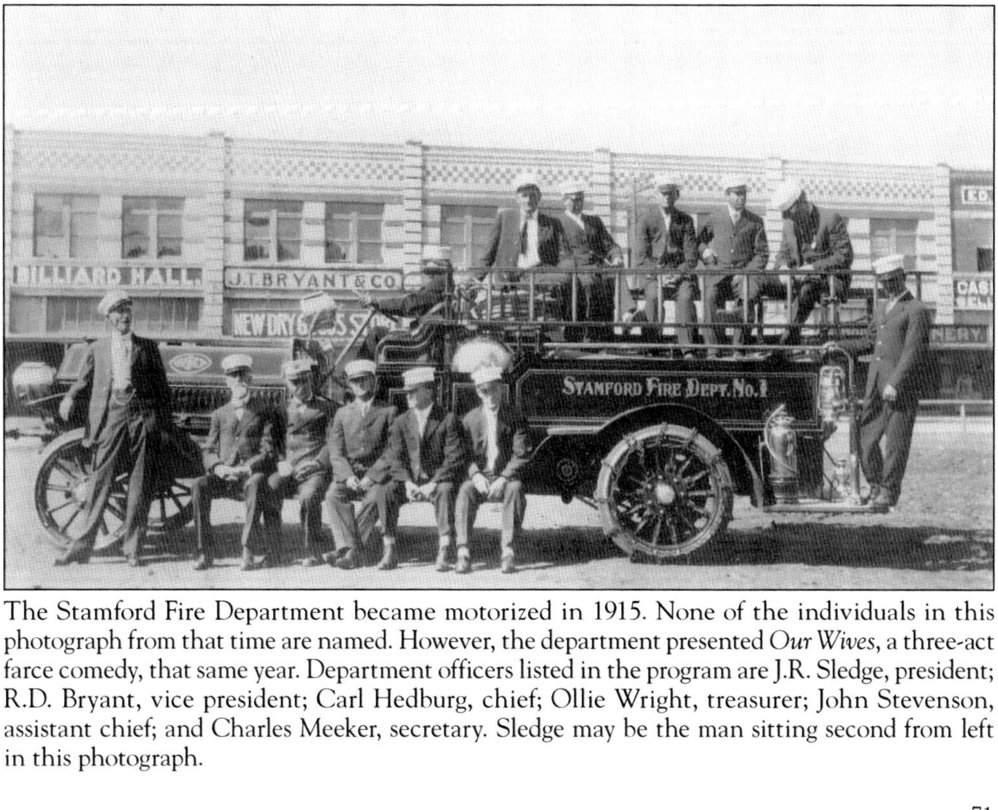

The Stamford Fire Department became motorized in 1915. None of the individuals in this photograph from that time are named. However, the department presented *Our Wives*, a three-act farce comedy, that same year. Department officers listed in the program are J.R. Sledge, president; R.D. Bryant, vice president; Carl Hedburg, chief; Ollie Wright, treasurer; John Stevenson, assistant chief; and Charles Meeker, secretary. Sledge may be the man sitting second from left in this photograph.

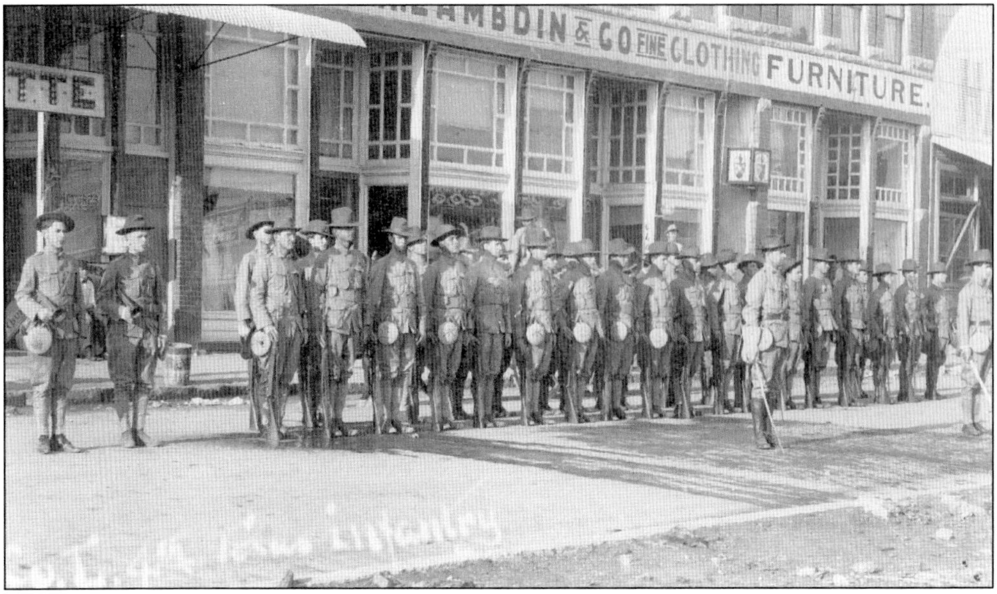

Stamford became home to a state militia force when Company L, 4th Texas Infantry, was based there in 1911. A predecessor of the State National Guard units, the 4th Texas formed in 1898 during the Spanish-American War. In this Ray Rector photograph, the company stands at attention in front of J.A. Lambdin & Co. Lambdin was captain of the company. The unit was comprised of local men, including Rector.

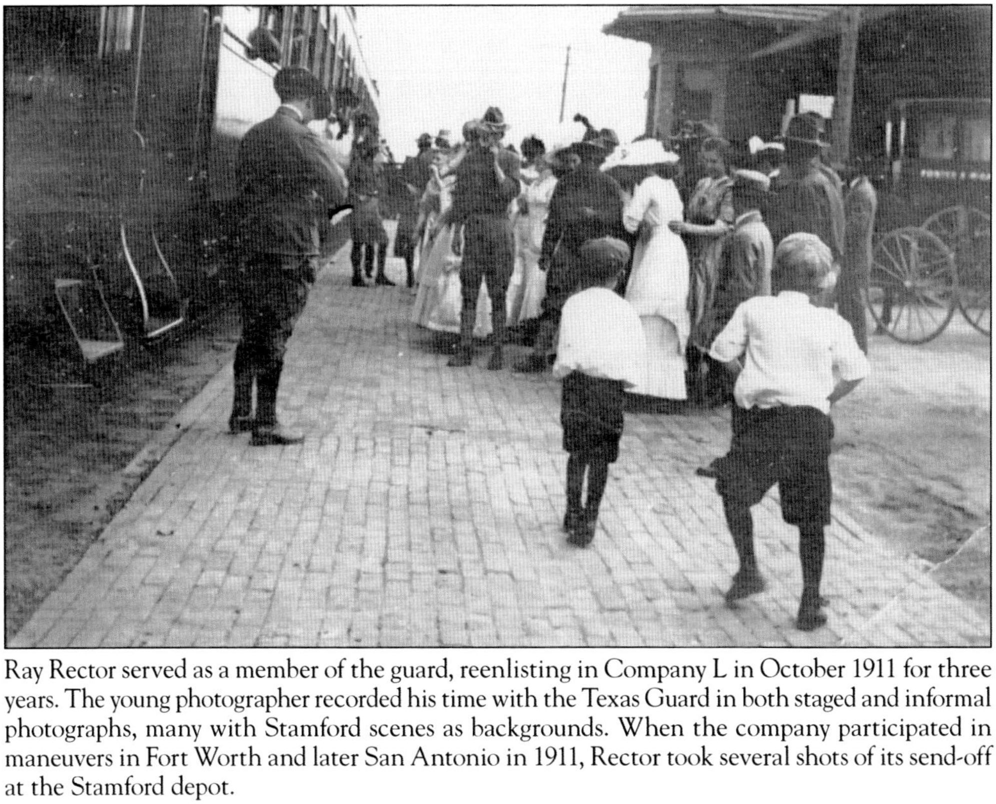

Ray Rector served as a member of the guard, reenlisting in Company L in October 1911 for three years. The young photographer recorded his time with the Texas Guard in both staged and informal photographs, many with Stamford scenes as backgrounds. When the company participated in maneuvers in Fort Worth and later San Antonio in 1911, Rector took several shots of its send-off at the Stamford depot.

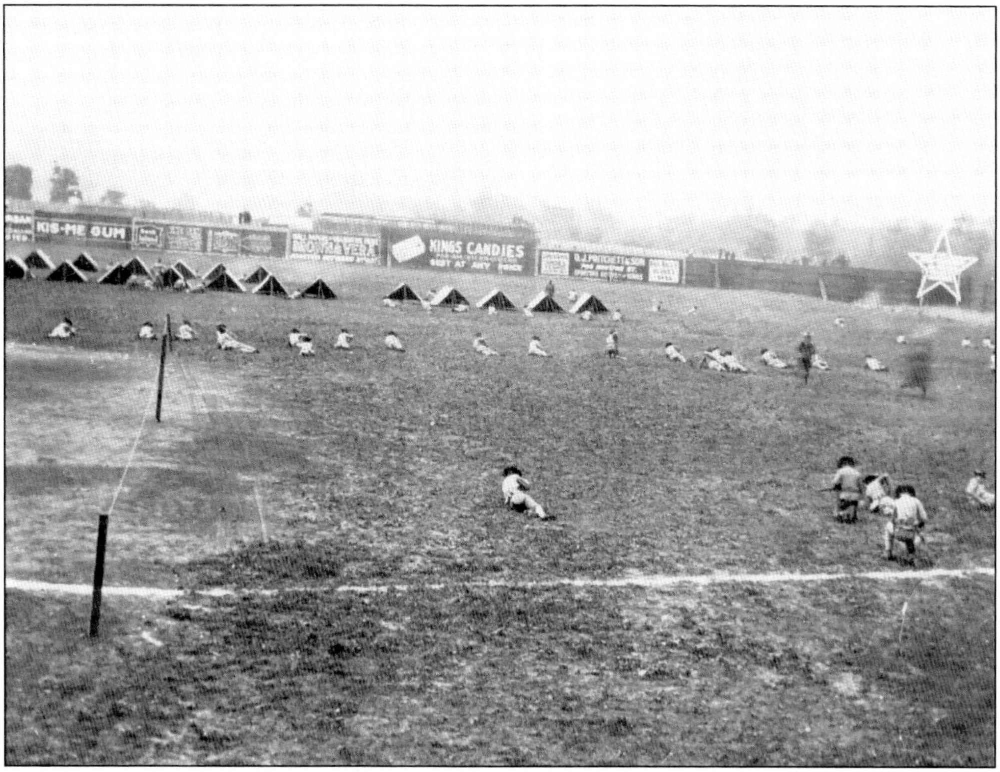

In April 1911, a three-day camp of instruction was held at Fort Worth. Company L was among the troops attending. The camp was under the command of Col. Cecil A. Lyon. Soldier Rector photographed one of the drills at the camp site, which appears to be a baseball field. Records indicate the camp was "without expense to the state" and was funded by the Fort Worth Jobbers and Manufactures League.

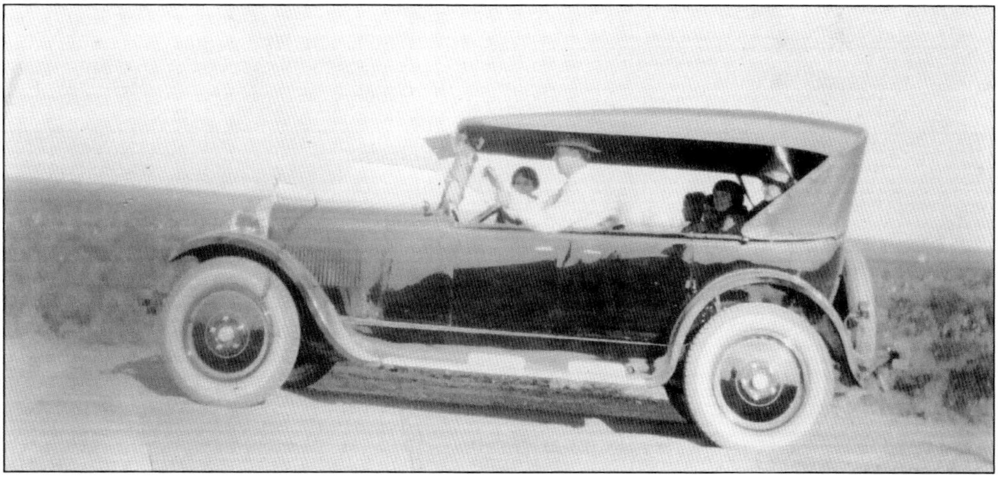

Ray Rector, seen here with his children in the family's Dodge touring car, was active in Stamford from his arrival in 1906. His community work included serving as a St. John's Methodist Church steward, a member of the chamber and the Rotary Club, and a grand master of the Texas Odd Fellows. He was also the tax collector for the Stamford school district. The SMS ranches recruited him to take photographs for their promotional booklets.

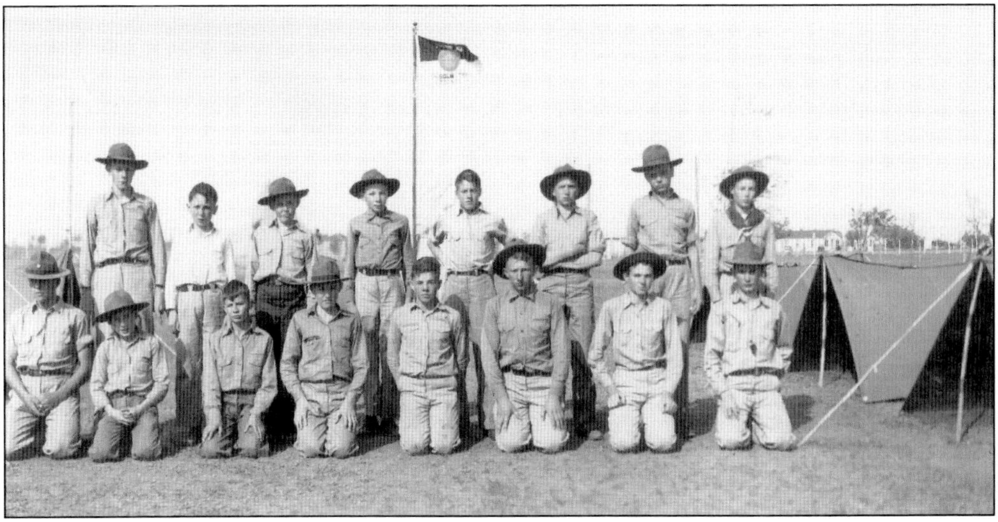

Rector is credited with forming the first organized troop of Boy Scouts in Texas in 1913, when Scoutmaster Rector and his troop affiliated with the US Boy Scouts. In 1919, the Stamford troop, along with others across the nation, withdrew from the US Boy Scouts and formed Boy Scouts of America. This Stamford troop is unidentified, but Stamford eventually had several Scout troops.

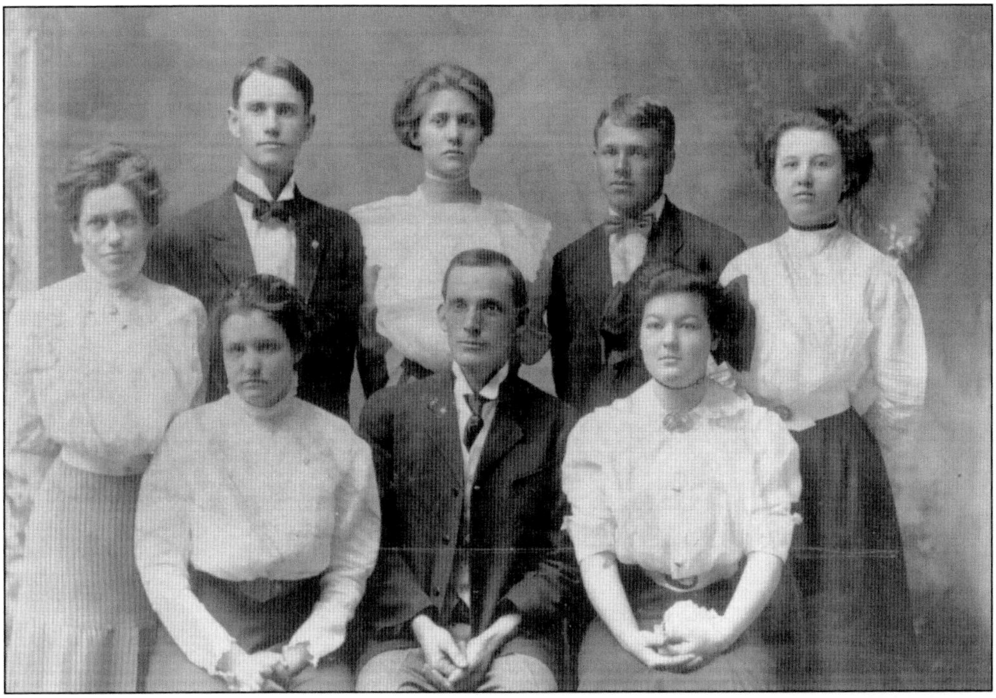

Rector also supported the Methodist-based Stamford Collegiate Institution. By 1909, the three-building campus had 346 students, including 22 ministry students, and 16 faculty members. The 1909 Latin class included, from left to right, (first row) Margaret Whitney, Arrie Barrett, J.N. Brown, and Josie May Griswold; (second row) Ira Kiker, Ester Blackwell, Karl Langford, and Lois Overby. (Courtesy of Southwest Collection/Special Collections Library, Texas Tech University, Lubbock, Texas, SWCPC, 132.)

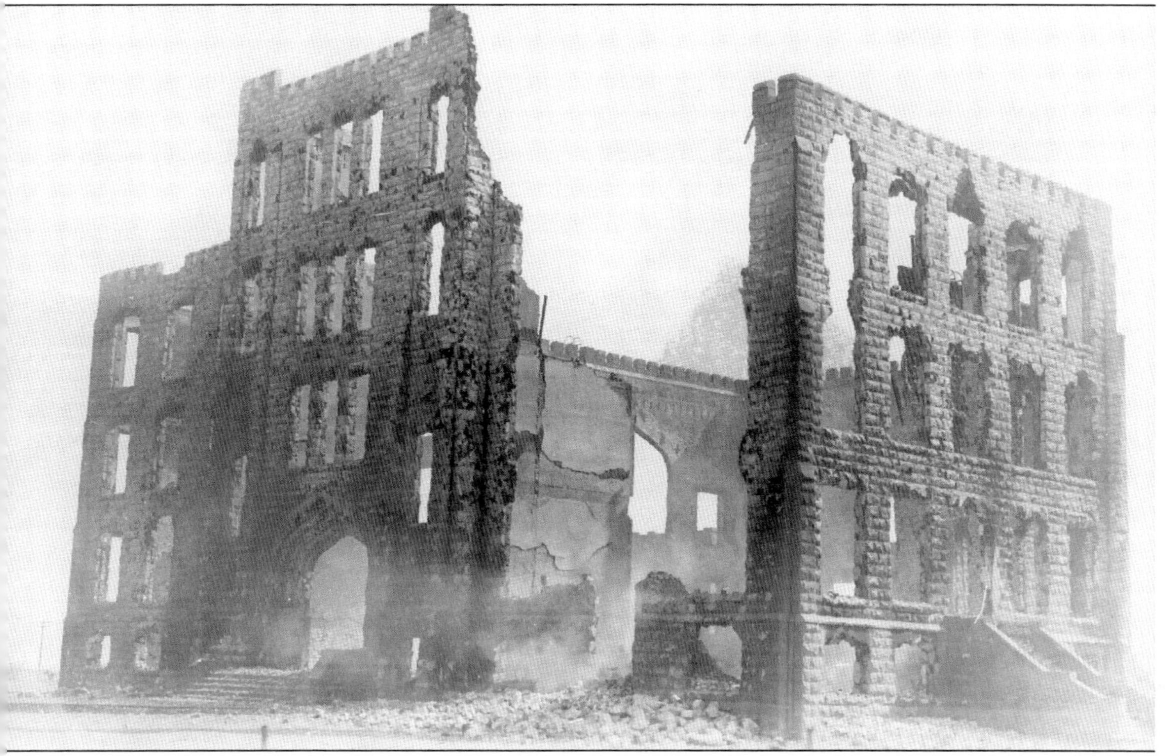

The campus included an administration building of native stone quarried at Leuders, 17 miles southeast of Stamford, and brick dormitories for women and men. The school included a primary and high school department and a two-year college program. The school's baseball team won several pennants for the maroon and white, and clubs included a fine arts club, a student association, and the Young Preachers Association. Renamed Stamford College in 1911, the institution struggled throughout the decade. A drought in 1910 decreased enrollment, and finances became strained. Another drought struck in 1917. World War I enlistment further decreased enrollment. Disaster came in 1918, when the administration building was destroyed by fire (seen here), resulting in $150,000 in losses. The Methodist district annual conference decided the college could not be rebuilt. In 1920, McMurry College was established in Abilene, Texas, as a Methodist school. The *Sphinx*, the Stamford College monthly begun in 1907, published its final issue, and the 20-acre campus was deeded to the Stamford school system.

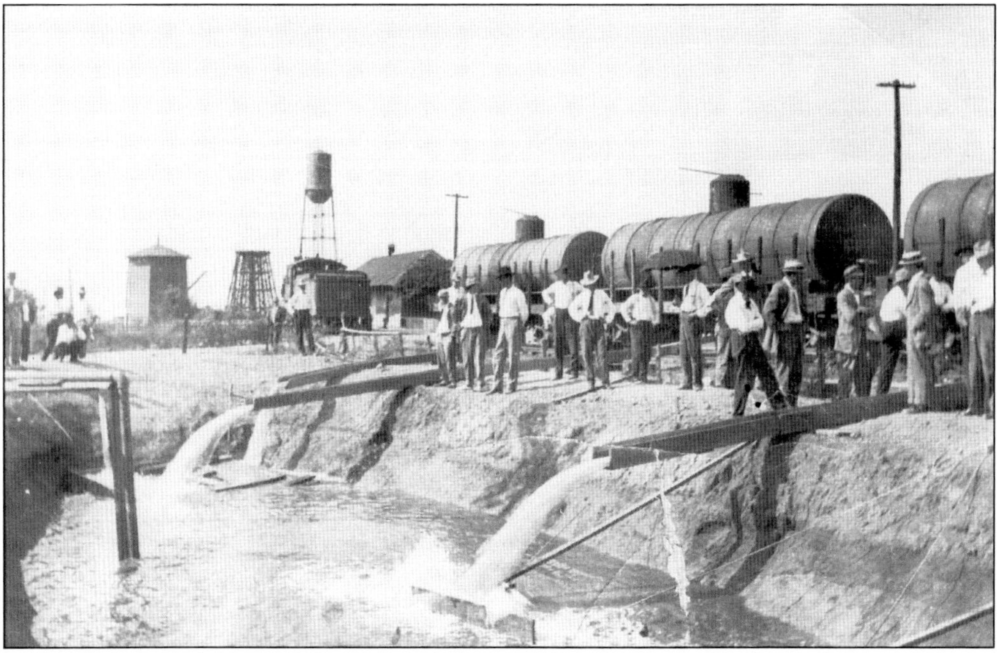

The 1917 drought devastated the Stamford area. The landscape was filled with the empty houses of failed farms as crops scorched and water supplies failed. The city ran out of water, which had to be brought in by railroad tank cars and pumped into muddy main lines (as seen here) and out to the community. The water shortage also scorched Stamford's reputation.

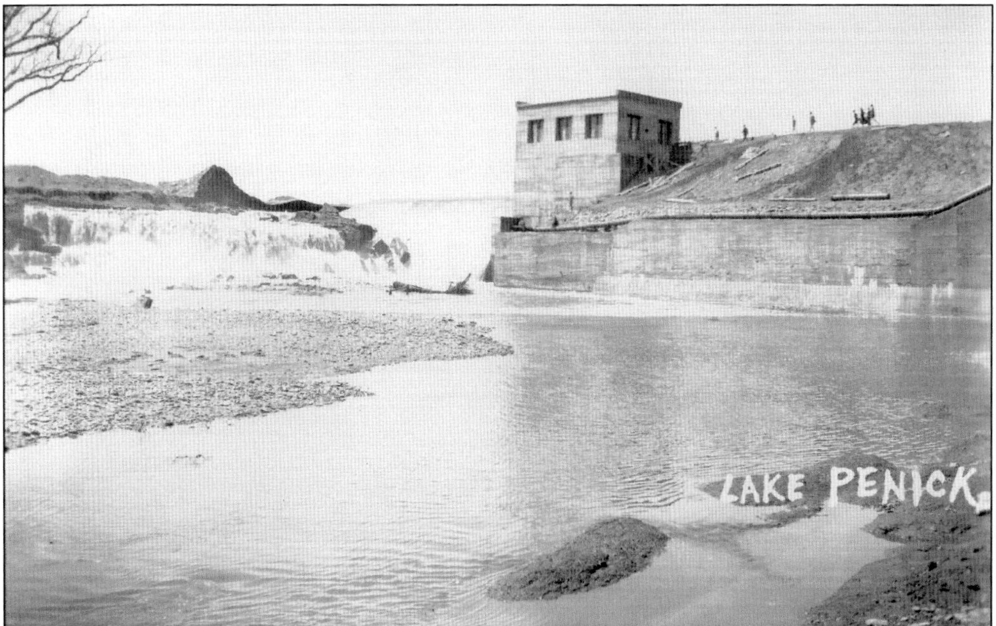

Stamford leaders worked quickly to avoid another embarrassing water shortage. This dam was constructed on the Clear Fork of the Brazos River, 16 miles southeast of Stamford, using rock from the nearby Leuders quarries. Completed in 1919 at a cost of $575,000, the new Lake Penick was the fourth-largest artificial body of water in Texas at the time.

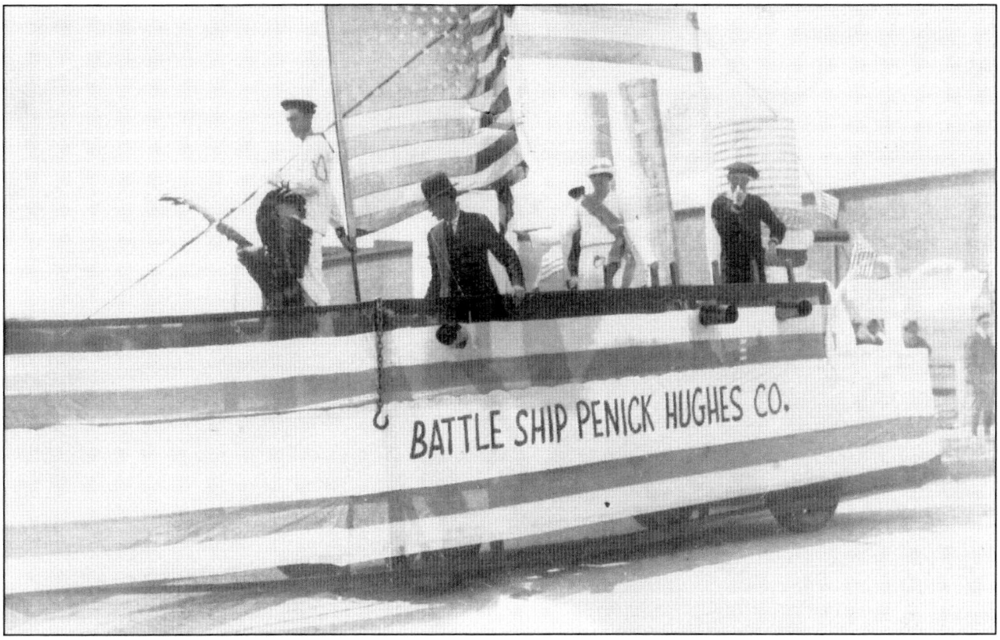

World War I involvement affected more than Stamford College. The United States launched a patriotic campaign in 1917 to support the issuing of war bonds. Stamford held a bond drive in 1918, including a parade with the Battleship *Penick Hughes* sailing down the street. Patriotism had other impacts. The German American citizens of Brandenburg, on the Stamford & Northwestern line, changed the town's name to Old Glory to demonstrate their loyalty.

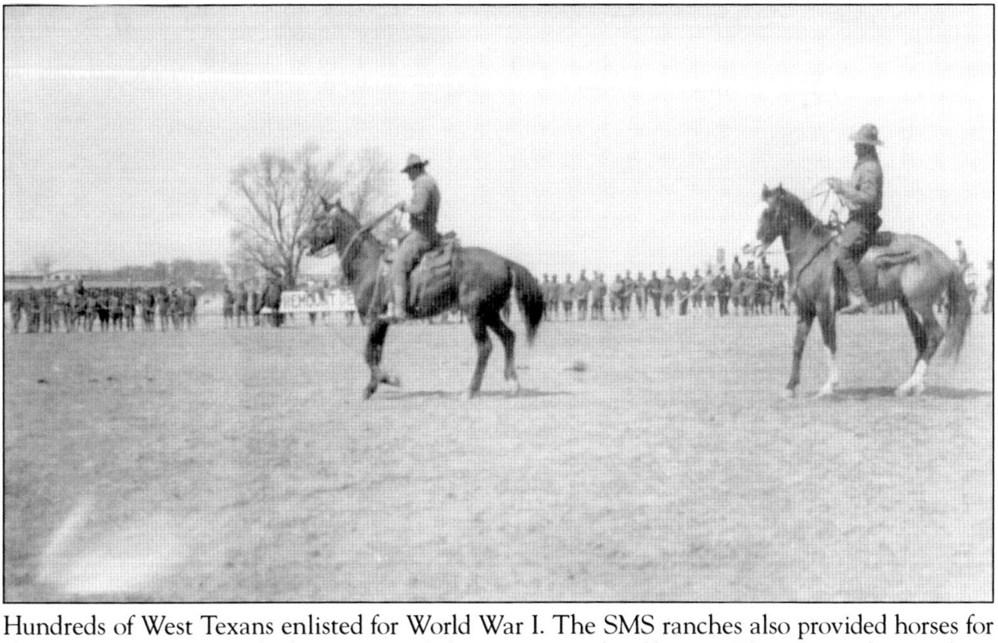

Hundreds of West Texans enlisted for World War I. The SMS ranches also provided horses for the Remount Service, which maintained the army's supply of horses. These animals, seen here at the Third Army Remount Depot in Kripp, Germany, in June 1919, were survivors, but many had died. So had young men like Guy Zinn, the brother of Emma Selmon, who perished at St. Mihiel and lies buried in France. (Courtesy of Swenson Land and Cattle Company.)

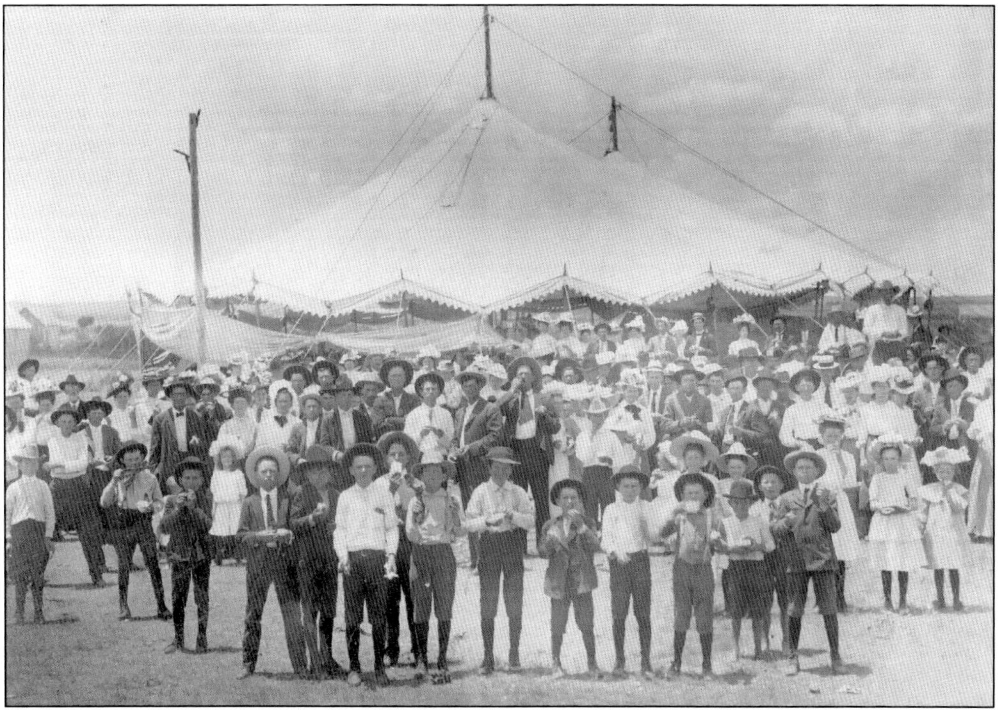

The purpose of this meeting has been lost, but tent-based shows remained an important aspect of Stamford entertainment. William Jennings Bryan returned with a Chautauqua show in 1916. Open-air tent revivals were common around Lake Penick. Harley Sadler brought his tent show annually for years. Sadler played a comic character named Toby before his orchestra performed. Cleo Hughes recalled, "The tent was always full." (Courtesy of the Cleo Shipman family.)

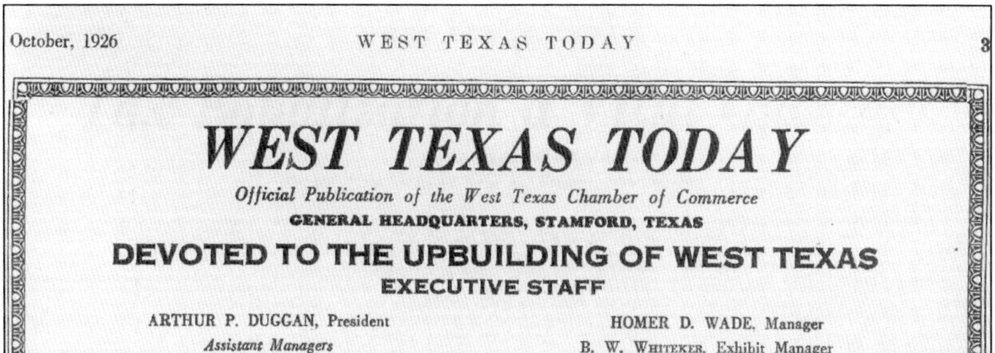

October, 1926 WEST TEXAS TODAY 3

WEST TEXAS TODAY

Official Publication of the West Texas Chamber of Commerce

GENERAL HEADQUARTERS, STAMFORD, TEXAS

DEVOTED TO THE UPBUILDING OF WEST TEXAS

EXECUTIVE STAFF

ARTHUR P. DUGGAN, President
Assistant Managers
RAY LEEMAN, Ft. Worth
B. F. BENNETT, Amarillo

BUSINESS OFFICE
Neil P. Anderson Building, Fort Worth, Texas

HOMER D. WADE, Manager
B. W. WHITEKER, Exhibit Manager
U. S. PAWKETT, Traffic Manager
E. H. WHITEHEAD, Publicity Manager

EDITORIAL OFFICE
Stamford, Texas

The West Texas Chamber of Commerce began in 1918, when representatives from 25 Texas counties met in Fort Worth. Stamford became the headquarters for the organization, which sought to foster the continued development of West Texas and to promote its economic welfare. One important goal was the protection of West Texas water rights. The official chamber publication, *West Texas Today*, began as a quarterly and expanded to a monthly in 1922.

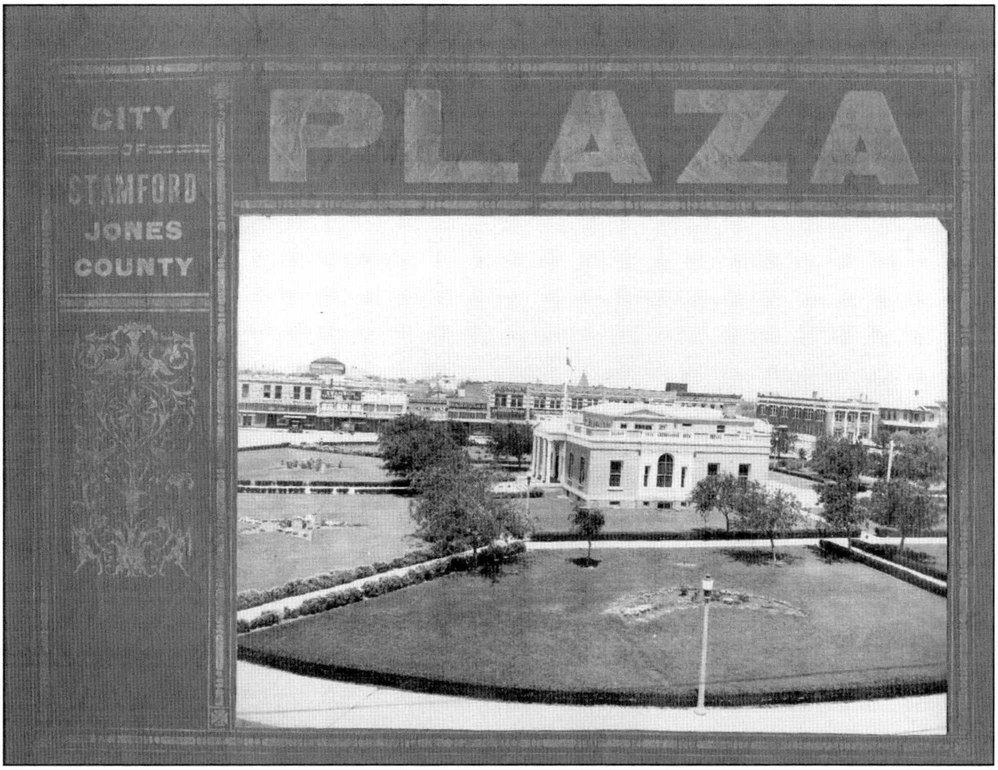

One important chamber project was the campaign for a major regional college, a longtime goal in West Texas. Texas Technological College was founded by Texas Senate Bill 103 in 1923. Stamford was among the 37 towns that submitted briefs to become the college site. The Stamford proposal, seen here, included narrative, statistics, and numerous photographs. The location board chose Lubbock, and the college opened in 1925 with 914 students and six buildings.

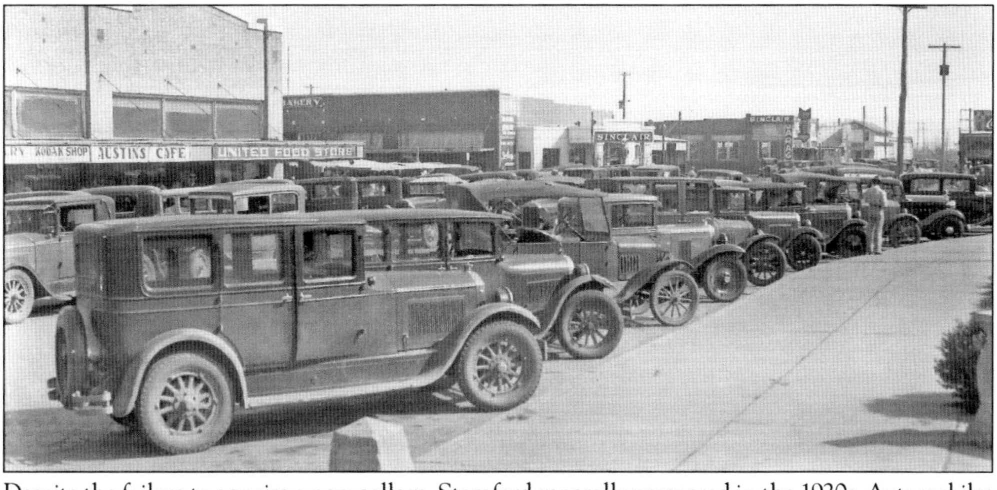

Despite the failure to acquire a new college, Stamford generally prospered in the 1920s. Automobiles replaced horses and lined the square. In this 1920s photograph of Wetherbee Street, Ray Rector's studio is on the left. Gasoline stations were a new phenomenon, like the Sinclair station (right of center). These stations offered a variety of basic services for drivers, as well as selling oil, tires, and batteries. Some even included public restrooms.

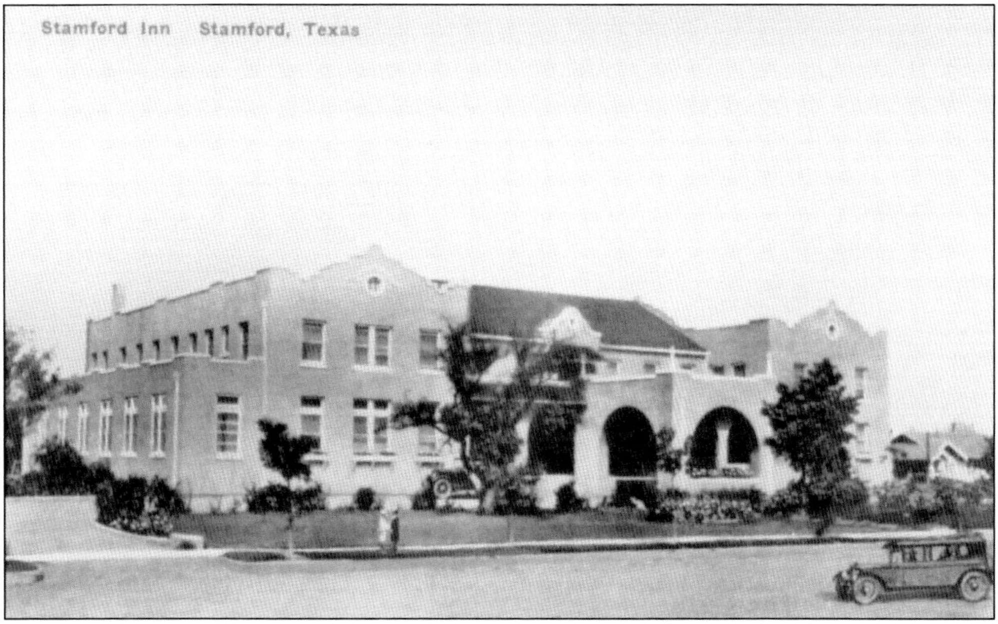

On Christmas Eve 1924, fire completely consumed the Stamford Inn. The intense heat shattered windows in city hall next door and threatened nearby buildings. The fire claimed four lives, including a mother and her two young children traveling for Christmas. A.C. Cooper, who had purchased the inn in 1919, rebuilt a new fireproof, concrete-and-steel building within six months, seen in this postcard. The new motto was, "The House That Service Built."

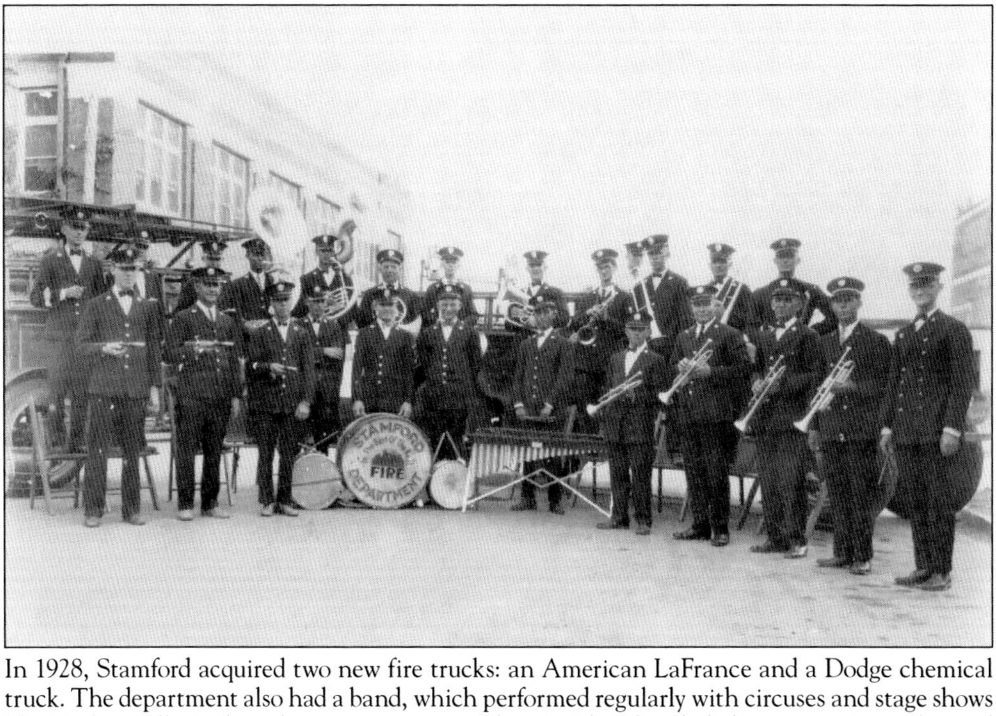

In 1928, Stamford acquired two new fire trucks: an American LaFrance and a Dodge chemical truck. The department also had a band, which performed regularly with circuses and stage shows like Harley Sadler's when they came to town. This 1929 band included Tommie Rector (second row, seventh from left), the son of photographer Ray Rector.

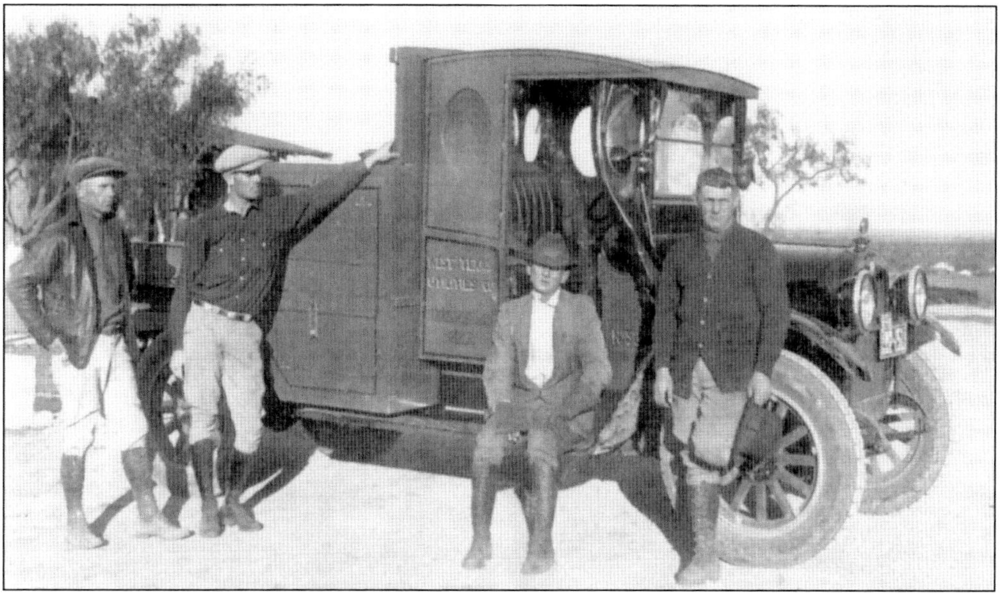

In 1912, the American Public Service Company acquired several utility firms in the Abilene area and began to extend service to nearby towns. Stamford received power in 1916. In 1923, an integrated company emerged, the West Texas Utilities Company. Bill Hale, seated on the fender of this 1923 company pickup, led an earlier crew in 1917 to construct a transmission line to Hamlin in western Jones County.

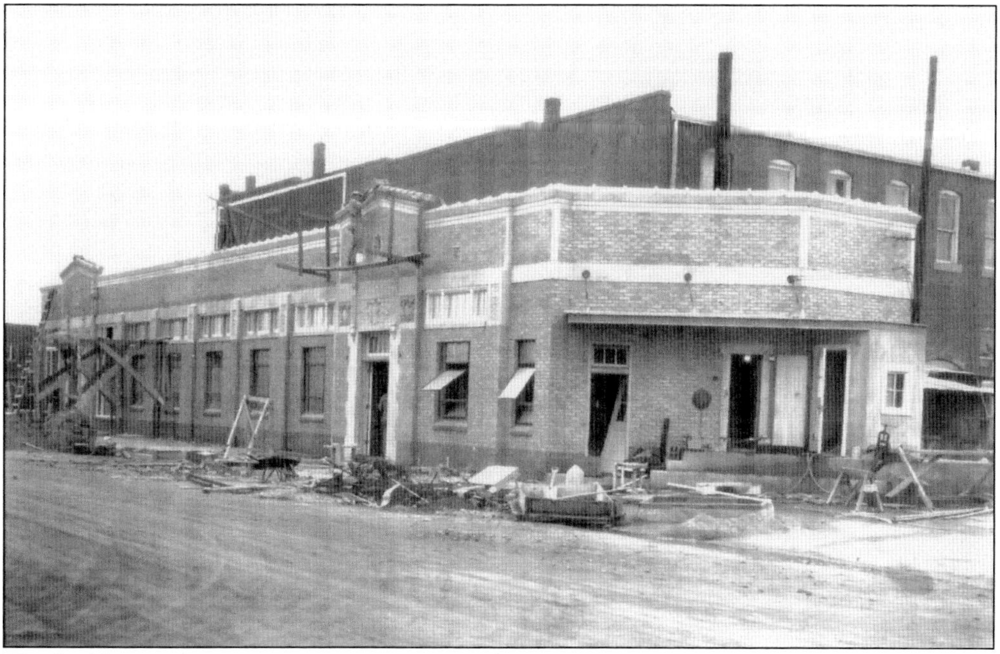

This building under construction at McHarg and Swenson Streets in 1927 was the Stamford office for West Texas Utilities (WTU). The facility served as the headquarters for the Stamford district, part of the expansion of the power company into the major electrical provider across much of West Texas. It included offices, a retail area, and an ice dock at the rear of the building—WTU supplied ice along with electricity.

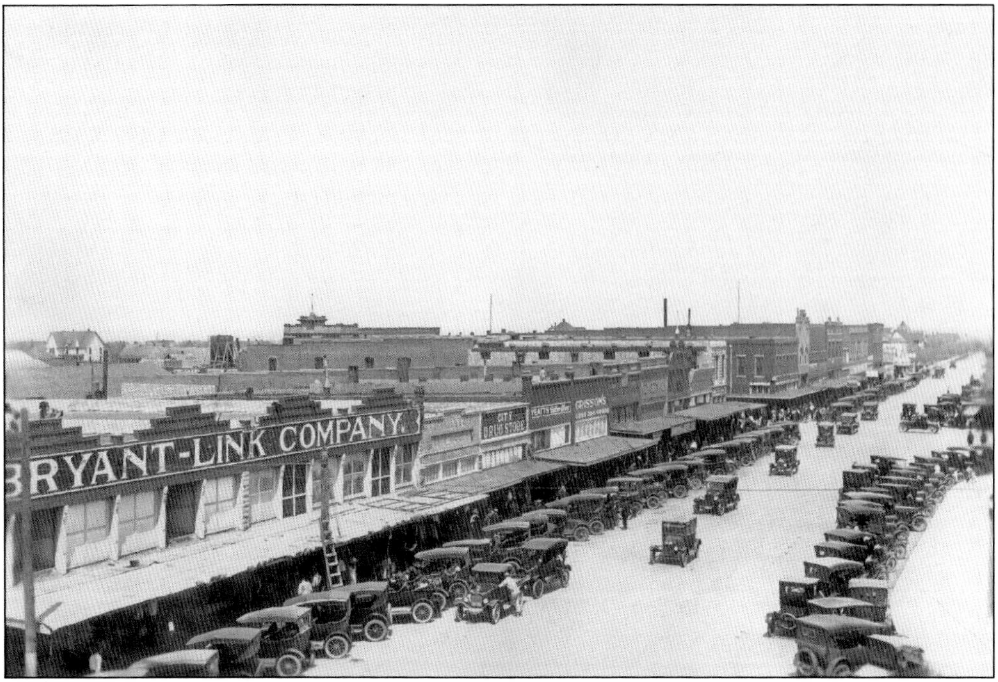

This 1920s view of Swenson Street shows Stamford as a bustling community, especially on Saturdays, when many farm families made the trip to town to purchase necessary materials and supplies. Even as roads improved and automobiles became faster, a trip to town was at least a daylong adventure that often necessitated returning home in the dark.

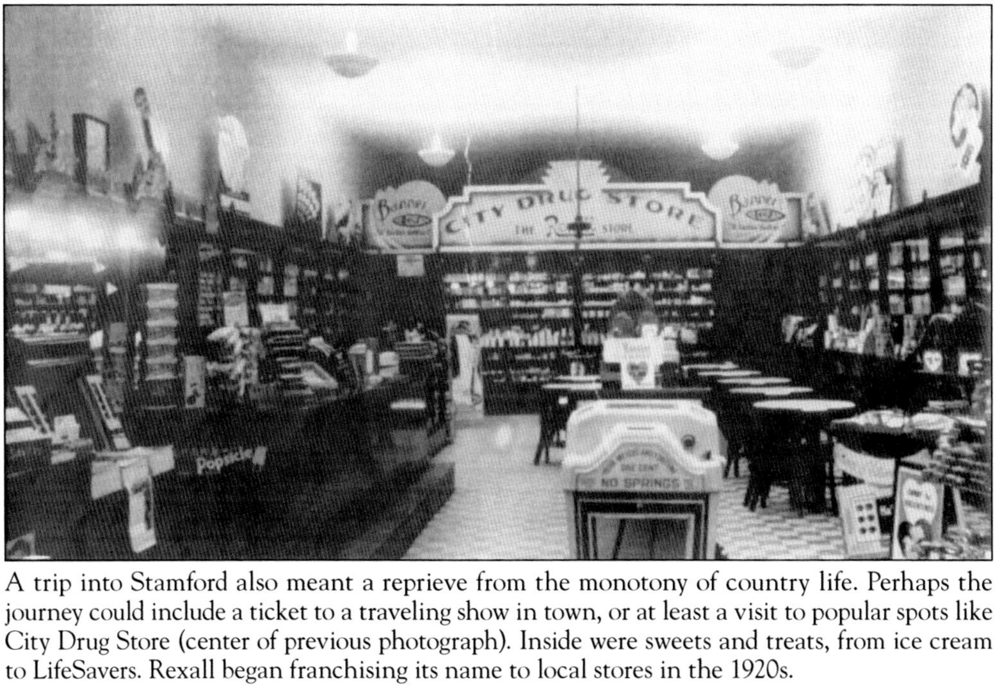

A trip into Stamford also meant a reprieve from the monotony of country life. Perhaps the journey could include a ticket to a traveling show in town, or at least a visit to popular spots like City Drug Store (center of previous photograph). Inside were sweets and treats, from ice cream to LifeSavers. Rexall began franchising its name to local stores in the 1920s.

For those frustrated by the prohibition of alcohol mandated by the 18th Amendment, other remedies were available. This prescription bottle in the Cowboy Country Museum provided medicinal whiskey with a dosage of a half-ounce every four hours. Those with stronger thirsts found other sources. Tommie Rector remembered that most Saturday nights included fistfights and perhaps a shooting. "Stamford was muscle and brawn back then," he recalled.

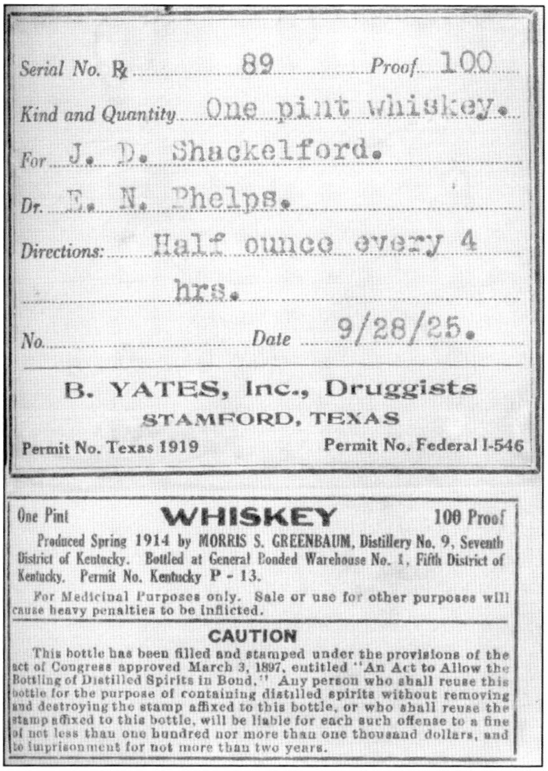

Serial No. ℞ 89 Proof 100

Kind and Quantity One pint whiskey.

For J. D. Shackelford.

Dr. E. N. Phelps.

Directions: Half ounce every 4 hrs.

No. Date 9/28/25.

B. YATES, Inc., Druggists

STAMFORD, TEXAS

Permit No. Texas 1919 Permit No. Federal I-546

One Pint **WHISKEY** 100 Proof

Produced Spring 1914 by MORRIS S. GREENBAUM, Distillery No. 9, Seventh District of Kentucky. Bottled at General Bonded Warehouse No. 1, Fifth District of Kentucky. Permit No. Kentucky P - 13.

For Medicinal Purposes only. Sale or use for other purposes will cause heavy penalties to be inflicted.

CAUTION

This bottle has been filled and stamped under the provisions of the act of Congress approved March 3, 1897, entitled "An Act to Allow the Bottling of Distilled Spirits in Bond." Any person who shall reuse this bottle for the purpose of containing distilled spirits without removing and destroying the stamp affixed to this bottle, or who shall reuse the stamp affixed to this bottle, will be liable for each such offense to a fine of not less than one hundred nor more than one thousand dollars, and to imprisonment for not more than two years.

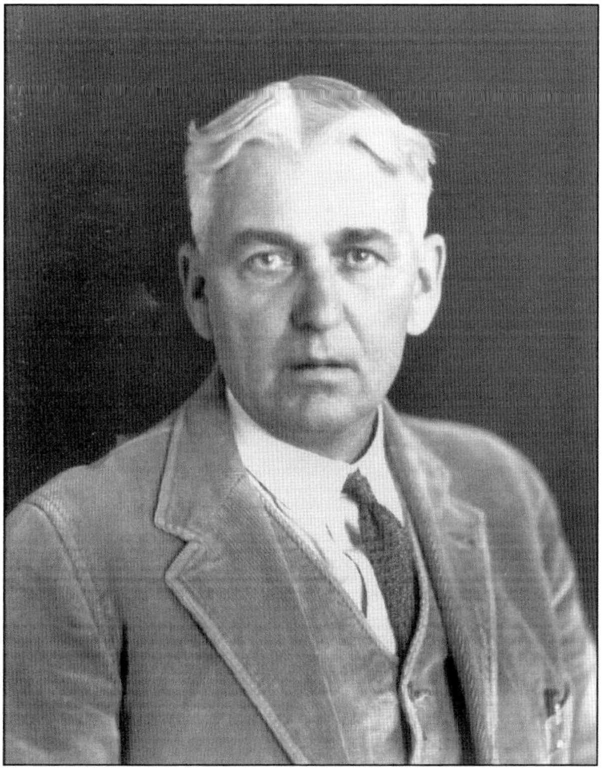

George C. Flourney made certain that the crime rate remained low for more than four decades. Flourney began as city marshal in 1903 and later served as police chief from 1922 until 1951. For years, Flourney began each day by stepping outside city hall, a cigar clenched in his teeth, and firing a shot into a nearby stump. On more than one occasion, the Texas Rangers requested his assistance.

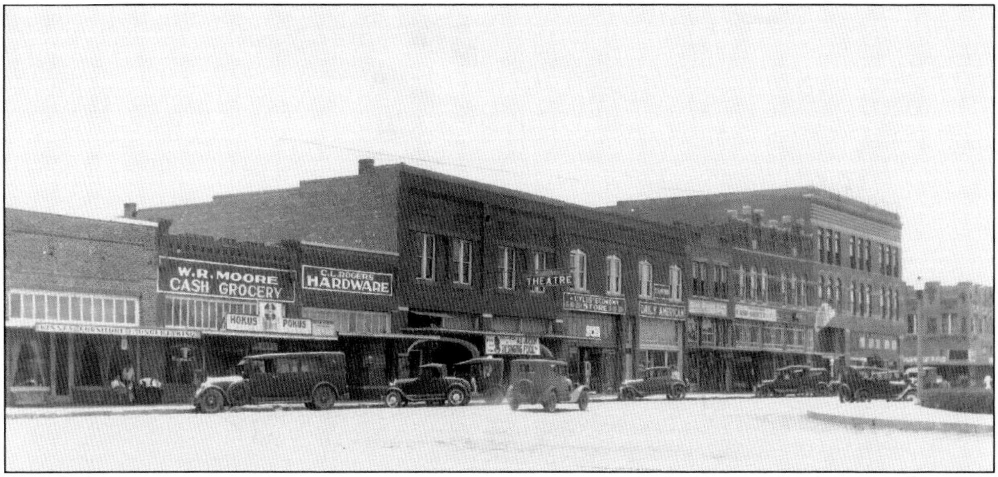

A new form of entertainment competed with fistfights and tent shows. In 1928, the Alcove Theatre (center) offered Al Jolson's new film, *The Singing Fool*. Like his earlier feature *The Jazz Singer*, the movie included talking segments. As in the rest of the nation, "talkies" and musicals quickly became popular with Stamford citizens and the farmers and cowboys who came to town.

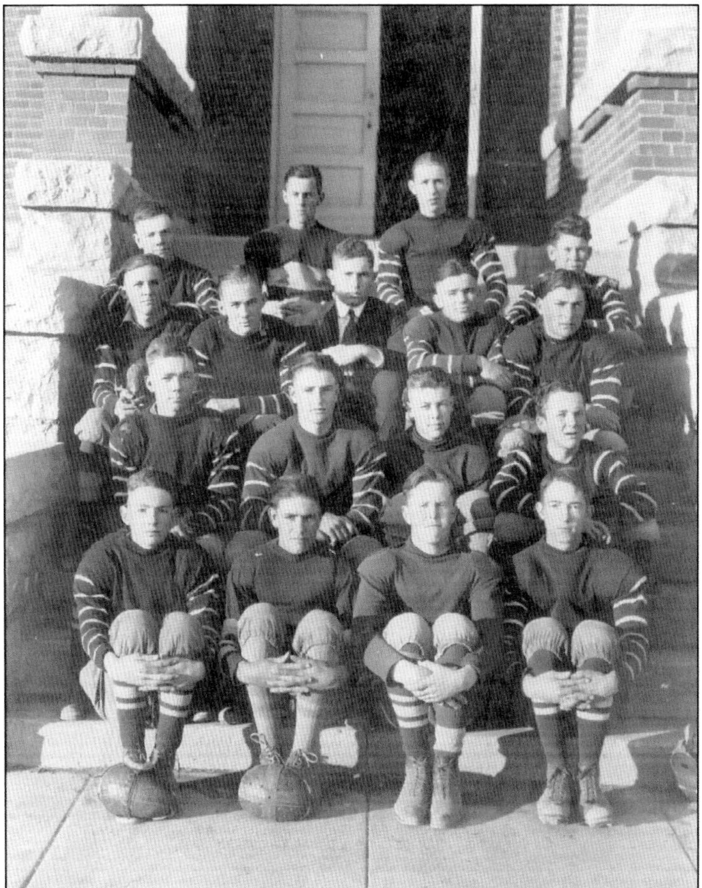

Stamford High School initiated another popular form of West Texas entertainment when high school football began in 1915. The Stamford Bulldog team won the West Texas Championship that first year. Baylor University graduate T.R. Tinsley, seated in the center of the third row with an early-1920s team, came to Stamford in 1915 and served as a principal and coach for three generations of students.

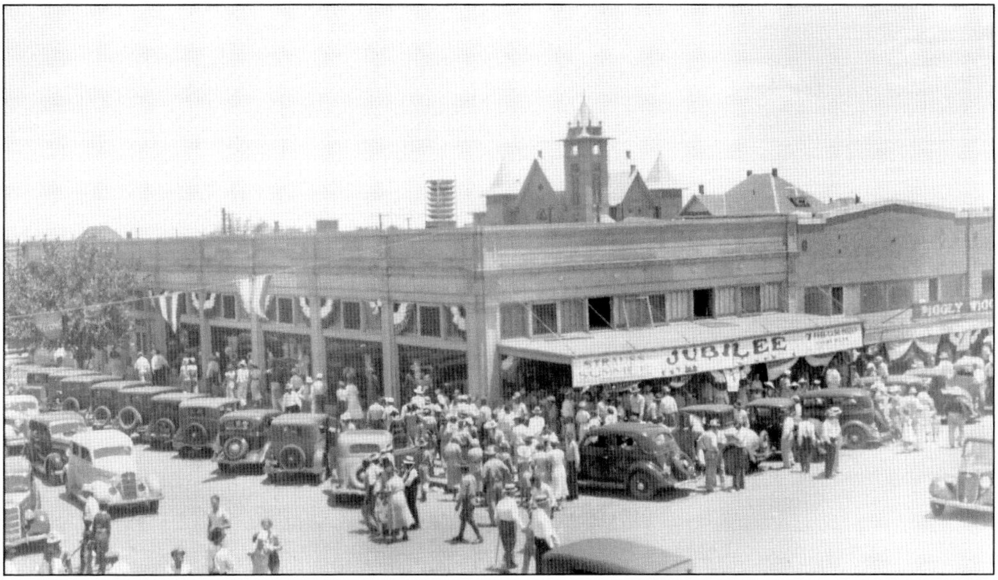

A scrawny Jewish boy, Robert "Bobby" Strauss did not play football, but he did gain popularity by cultivating a witty tough-guy persona. In 1928, the Strauss family moved to Stamford from nearby Hamlin, seeking a larger market for their dry goods business. Here, their Summer Jubilee Sale draws a crowd. One of only 10 Jewish families in Stamford, the Strausses never felt discriminated against for their faith.

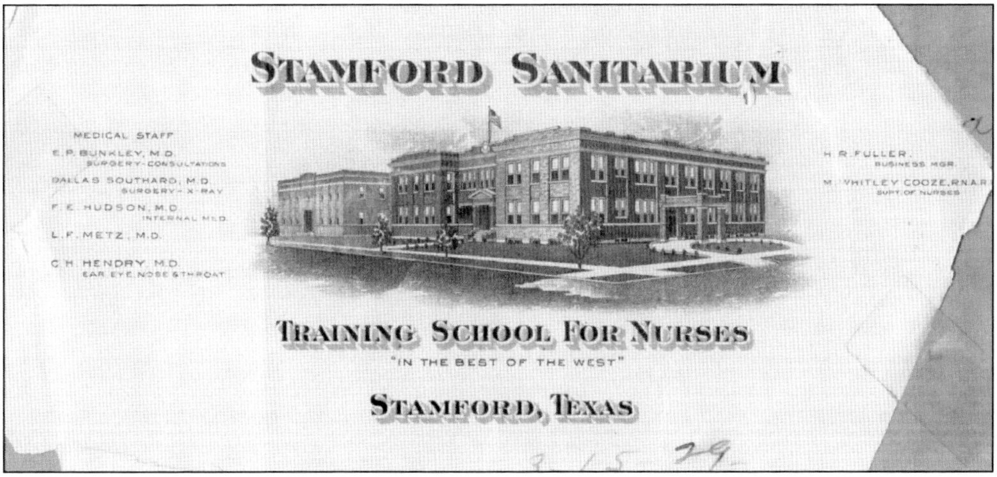
STAMFORD SANITARIUM

MEDICAL STAFF
E. P. BUNKLEY, M.D.
SURGERY-CONSULTATIONS
DALLAS SOUTHARD, M.D.
SURGERY - X-RAY
F. E. HUDSON, M.D.
INTERNAL MED.
L. F. METZ, M.D.
C. H. HENDRY, M.D.
EAR EYE NOSE & THROAT

H. R. FULLER,
BUSINESS MGR.
M. WHITLEY COOZE, R.N.A.R.
SUPT. OF NURSES

TRAINING SCHOOL FOR NURSES
"IN THE BEST OF THE WEST"

STAMFORD, TEXAS

Stamford medical facilities expanded in 1929, when a 15-bed wing was added to the original sanitarium. This stationery included a sketch of the new facility. Replacing the founders, Dr. Sam Webb and Dr. M.E. Lott, were Dr. Eustus Bunkley, Dr. Dallas Southard, and Whitney Cooze, the superintendent of nurses. Earlier improvements included a clinic, a nurse's home, and expanded x-ray and clinical laboratories.

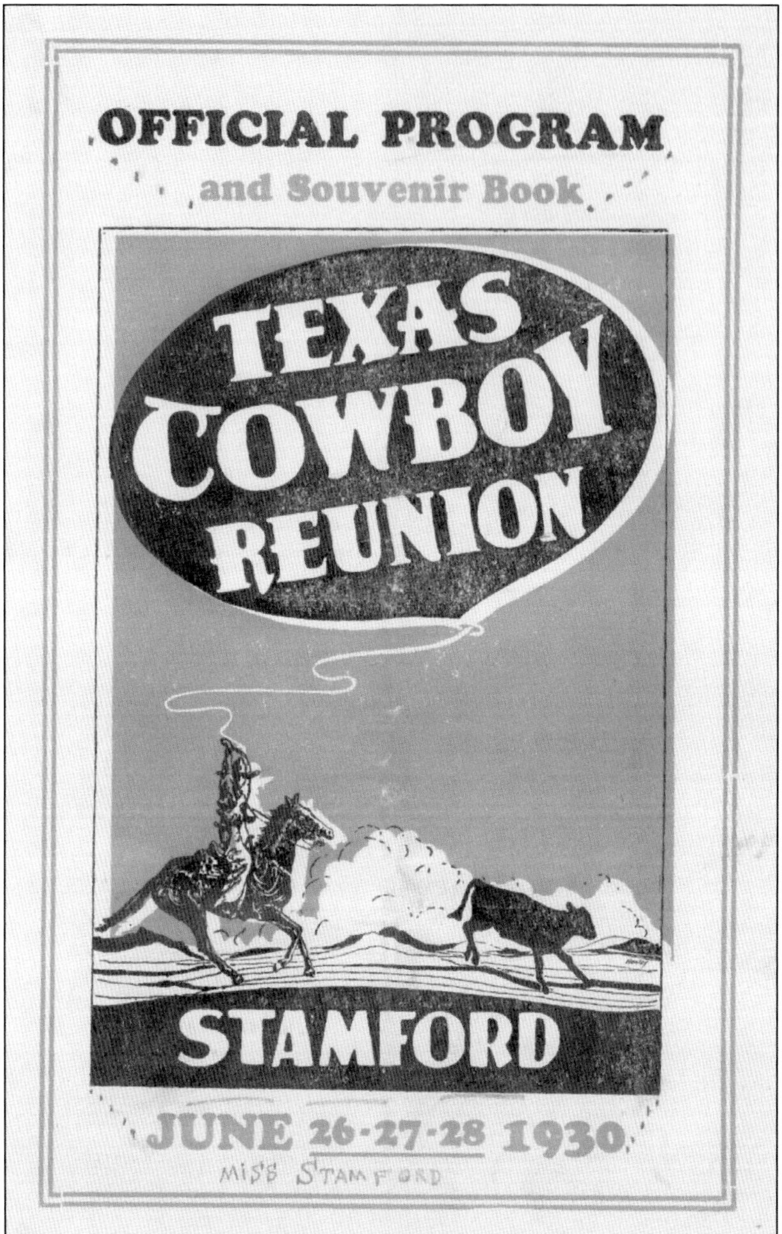

In 1930, a lean year at the beginning of the Great Depression, a group of Stamford men decided to create something to bring people and money to the community. They wanted an annual event where cattlemen and cowboys could bring their gear and chuck wagons to camp and relive the early days of life on the range. No professional rodeo performers could participate, only cowboys, competing in contests showcasing their ranch skills and being judged by cowboy judges. The 13 founders included A.J. Swenson, Bill Swenson (A.J.'s son), R.M. Swenson, R.V. Colbert, A.C. Cooper, Ray Rector, H.F. Goble, Gent Owsley, R.B. Bryant, Roy Arledge, L.M. Hardy, Charles E. Coombes, and John Selmon. The event was set for June 26, 27, and 28. They wanted a new business enterprise, but they also sought "to perpetuate the memory of the West." Throwing a wide loop for their ambitions, they named it the Texas Cowboy Reunion.

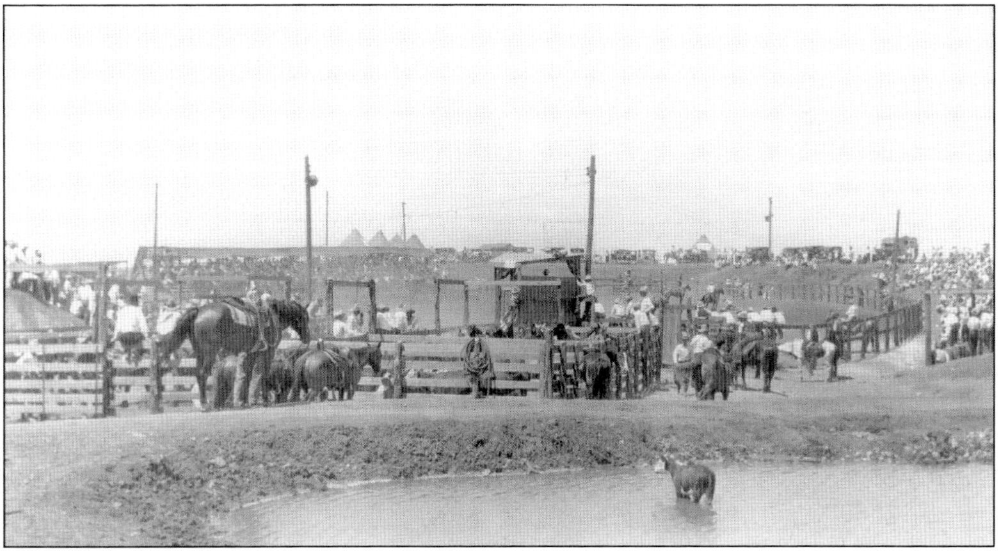

The Swenson Land and Cattle Company provided the site for the Texas Cowboy Reunion, a draw west of town that formed a natural amphitheater. For the first reunion, an arena was constructed and wooden bleachers were erected on the west bank. Automobiles parked along the north and east, and ranch "outfits" with chuck wagons and camp tents filled in the surrounding countryside. This photograph captures a moment of the action at the inaugural reunion.

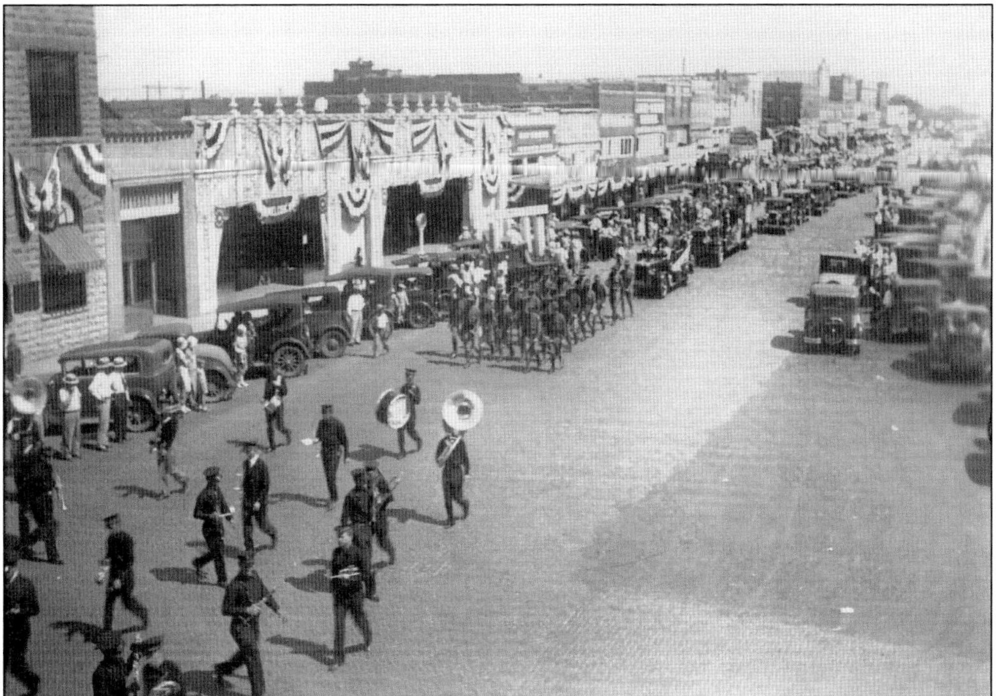

The reunion included a parade through downtown. The Camp Fire Girls won a prize for the best float. The Stamford Fireman Band played, marching behind a mounted police unit. Ray Rector photographed the band from atop Penick-Hughes Hardware. His son, Tommie, is on the right in the band, with his bugle under his arm.

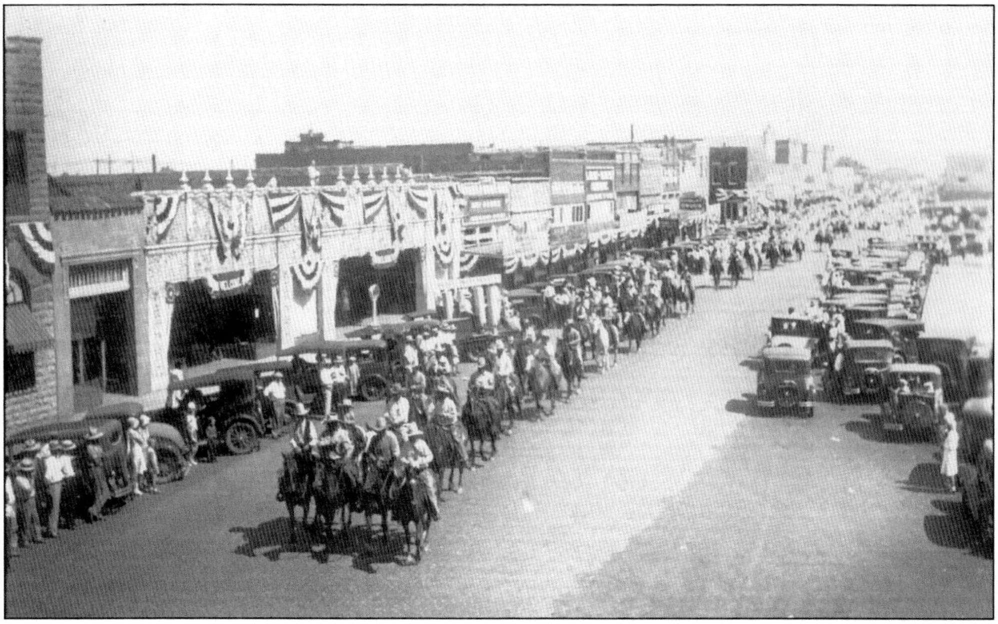

Ray Rector also took this 1930 Reunion parade photograph of a line of cowboys and pioneer cattlemen. Those who had worked ranches before 1895 received special passes to events. In all, 335 pioneers met to create the Texas Cowboy Reunion Association. Col. R.L. Penick became the organization's first president. In their by-laws, written the following year, officers included a range boss, a horse wrangler, and a wagon cook.

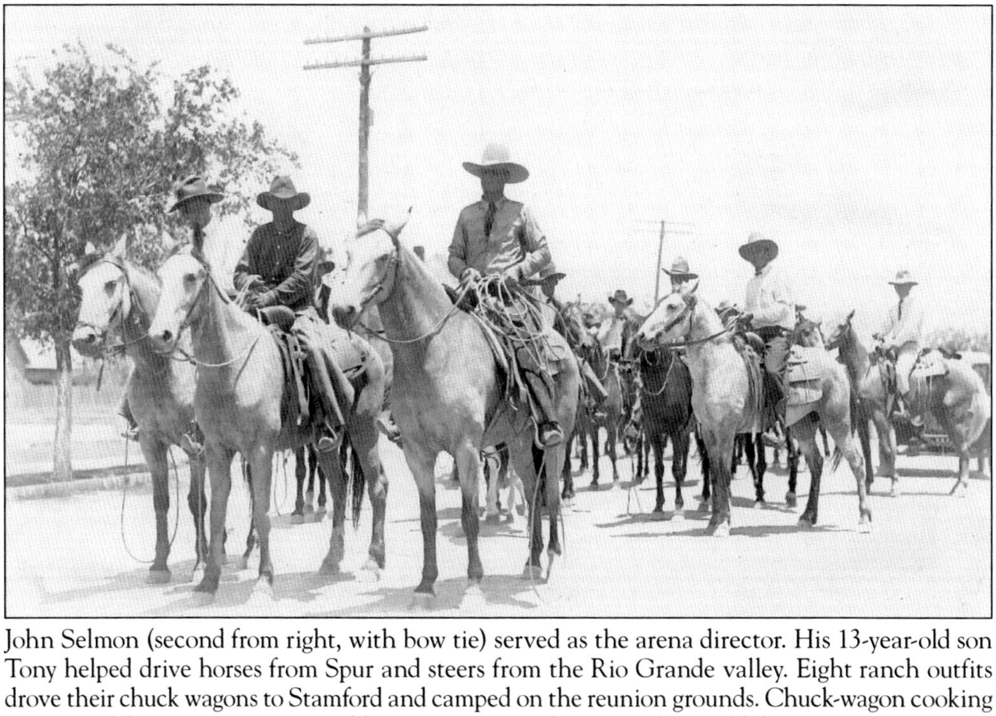

John Selmon (second from right, with bow tie) served as the arena director. His 13-year-old son Tony helped drive horses from Spur and steers from the Rio Grande valley. Eight ranch outfits drove their chuck wagons to Stamford and camped on the reunion grounds. Chuck-wagon cooking was one of the competitions. In addition, 50 Comanches came from Oklahoma to provide tribal war dances and other entertainment. (Courtesy of the Cleo Shipman family.)

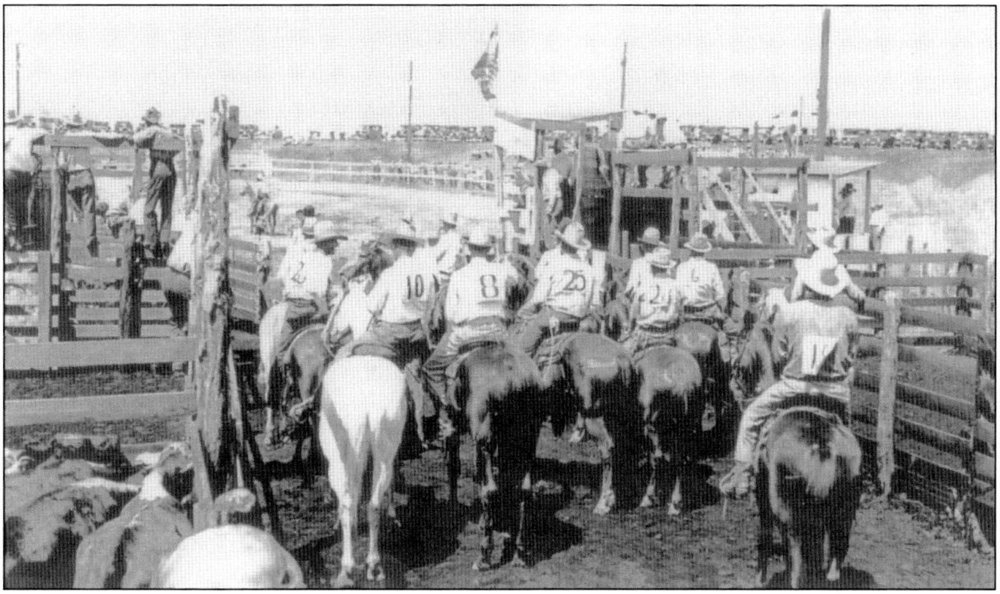

Reunion registration exceeded expectations, with people coming from across Texas as well as from Arizona and New Mexico. In all, 98 cowboys signed up for four events. Here, contestants wait their turn at calf roping, which proved the most popular event. Fewer dared to brave steer and bronc riding. The reunion also pioneered a new timed competition: wild cow milking. Colonel Penick, wearing a derby hat, delighted the crowd when he roped a runaway steer.

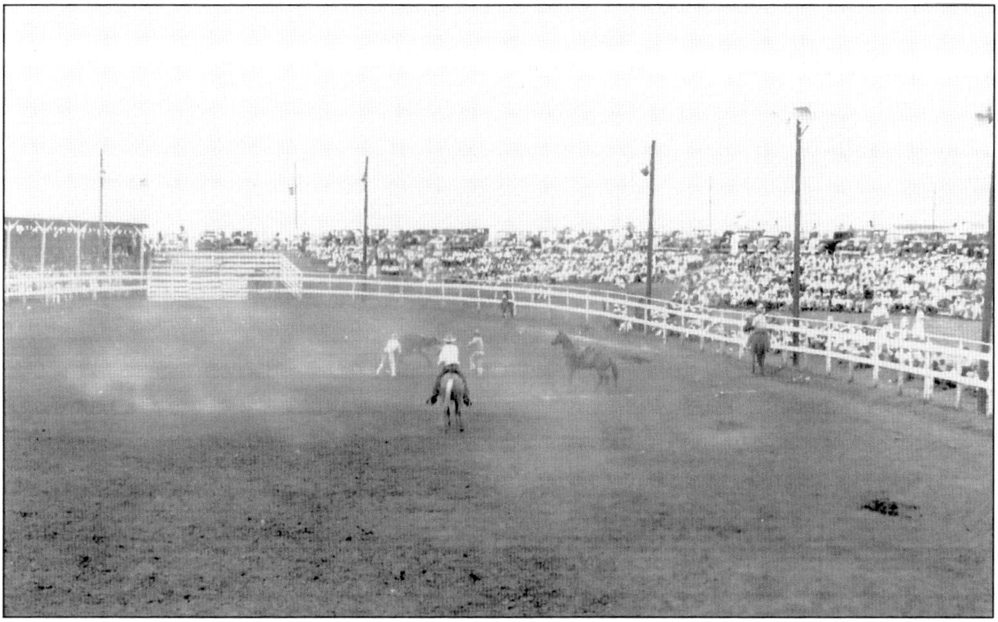

Wild cow milking, seen here at a later reunion, involved a team of two cowboys. A mounted contestant had to rope the cow with a loop over the head. He then dismounted and helped his partner on foot, who had to milk the cow into a bottle, run to the judge's stand, and pour the milk on the judge's boot, stopping the time clock. The best time won.

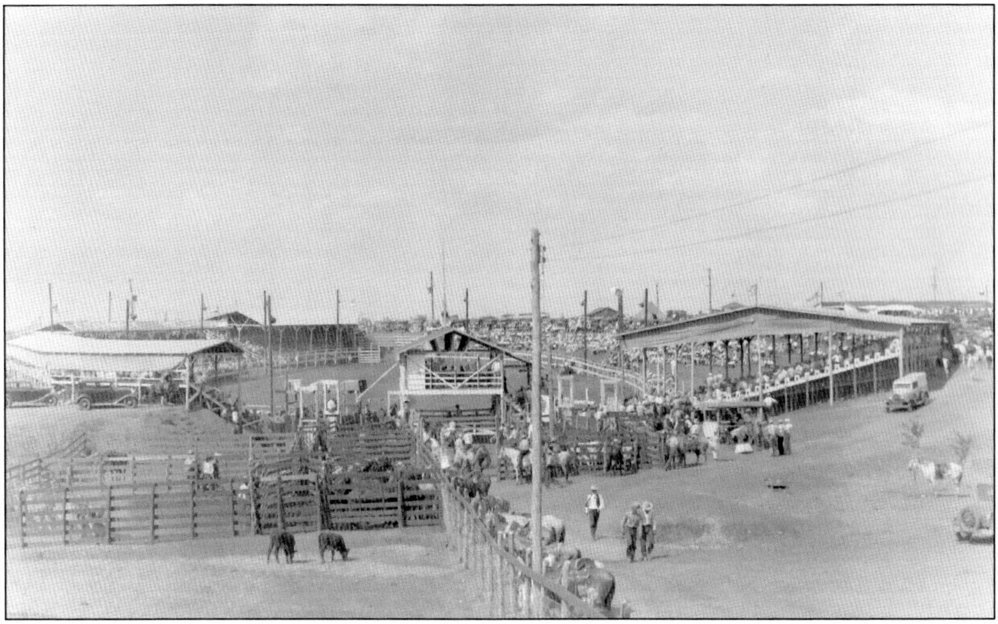

The reunion was a phenomenal success and became an annual event. The reunion grounds were upgraded, with new fencing and more grandstands. In 1931, its second year, 15,000 people attended the three-day event. Texas Ranger Capt. Tom Hickman served as head judge of the rodeo, which included 198 contestants competing for cash prizes totaling $1,215. He pronounced the reunion better than shows he had judged in Chicago, New York, and London.

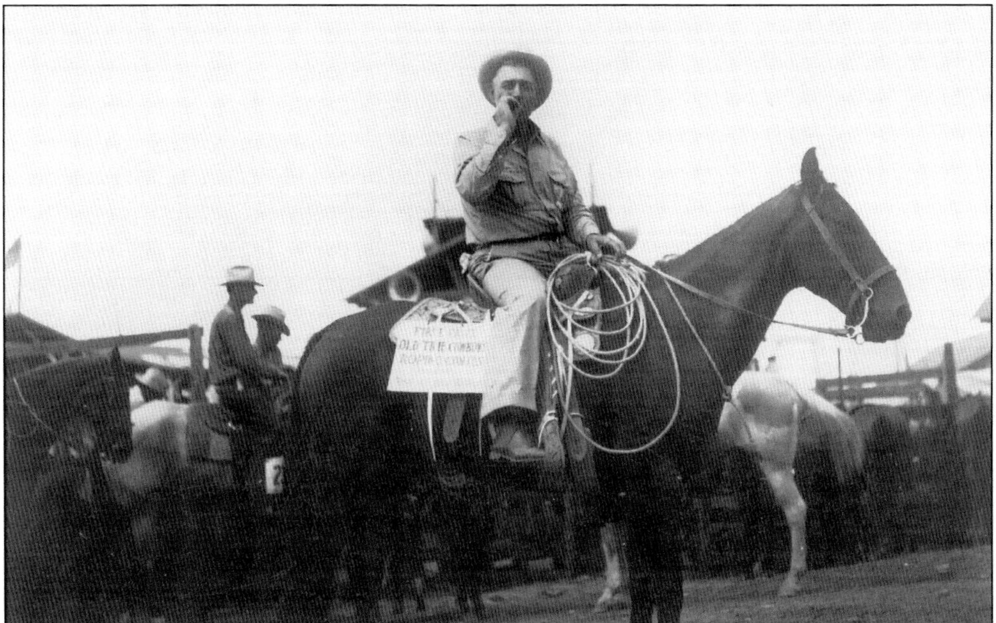

More than 500 pioneer cattlemen registered for the event, and many joined the Reunion Association. A special calf-roping contest was added for cowboys over 55 years of age, with a saddle as the first-place prize. "Uncle Bob" Weatherby of Rotan won the first saddle. This old-timer and his winning year have been lost, but the pride of winning is evident on his face.

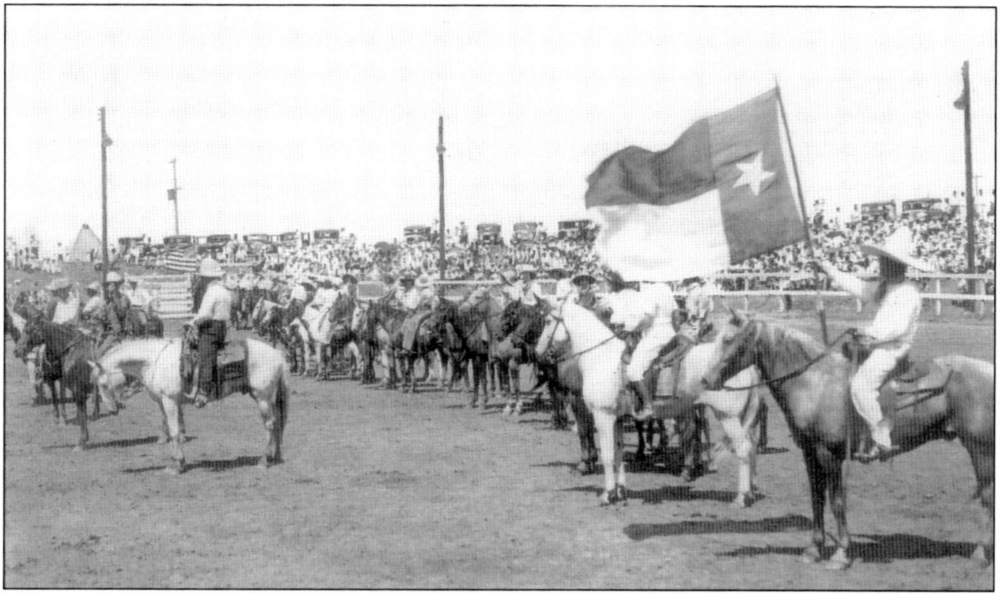

Another 1931 innovation was the creation of a sponsor program. Surrounding communities were invited to select young ladies over age 16 to sponsor their area. Sponsors led the parade and took part in rodeo events. In this 1932 photograph, the sponsors line up between the flags. The culminating event was a Sponsors' Ball. Other rodeos adopted this tradition, which evolved into rodeo queen competitions.

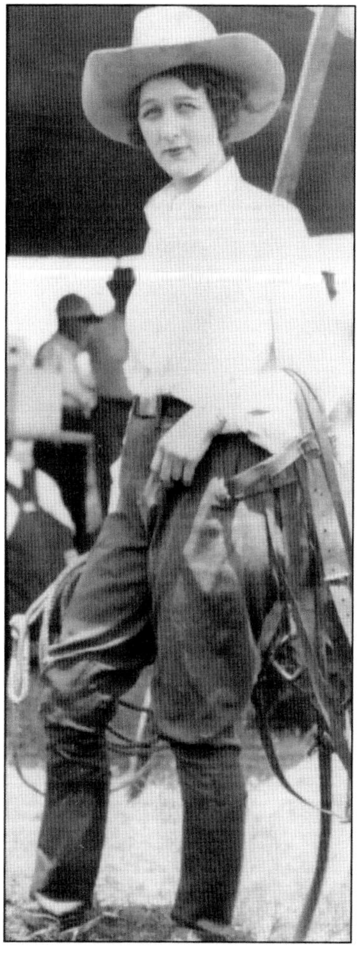

In 1932, the sponsor contest became competitive. Prizes were given to the girl with the most attractive riding outfit and for the girl who showed the best horsemanship by riding in a figure-eight fashion around a set of barrels. Clothes were the dominant element, but the roots of women's barrel racing were laid. Lois Perkins, seen here, represented Stamford in 1932, but Curley Seale of Baird, Texas, won the initial competition.

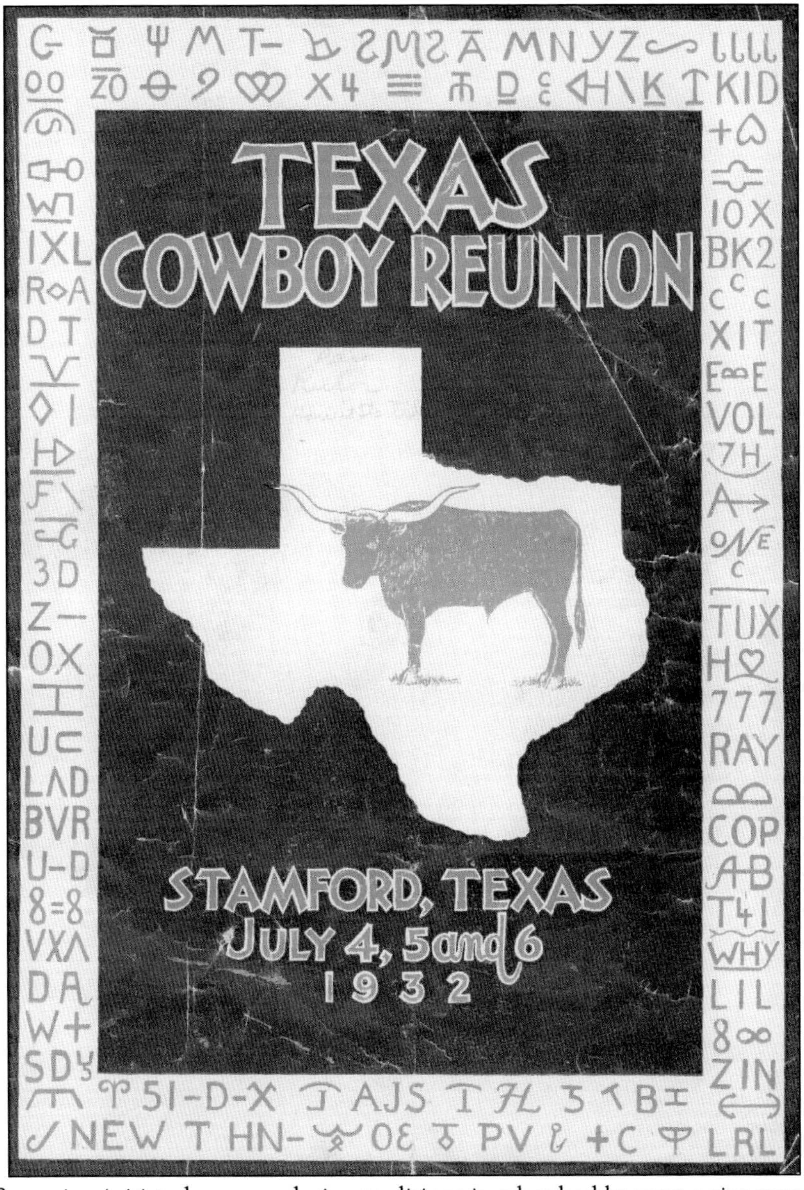

The 1932 reunion initiated many enduring traditions in what had become a signature event in Stamford. Besides the sponsor's barrel-riding contest, a cutting horse contest was also added. Highly trained horses and their riders demonstrated the special skill of separating a cow from a small herd and then preventing its return in a timed event. John Selmon was disappointed that he was prohibited from demonstrating the talents of his cutting horse because he served as arena director. The program cover for that year included brands of participating outfits. The Swenson SMS occupied top center and A.J. Swenson's own brand (AJS) the bottom center. Other prominent outfits included the Four Sixes (upper right corner), the Pitchfork (third from top left), and the XIT (eighth from top right), a three-million-acre ranch in the Texas Panhandle built on land given in exchange for constructing the state capitol building. One legend of the XIT brand's origin claims that trail boss Abner Blocker drew it with his boot when asked to create a design that rustlers could not easily change.

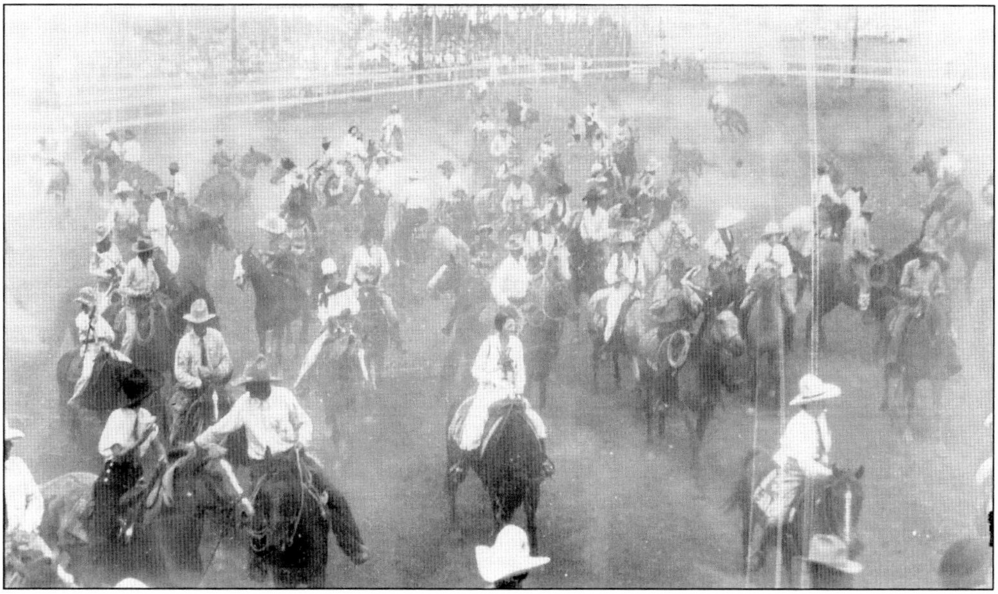

The opening procession also began in 1932. As seen in this undated photograph of the event, reunion officials, pioneer cattlemen, contestants, and sponsors all rode in an exciting and dusty melee. That first year, a circle formed around the pioneers in the center and hats were raised in salute to them. Other rodeos adopted this procession, which became known as the Grand Entry.

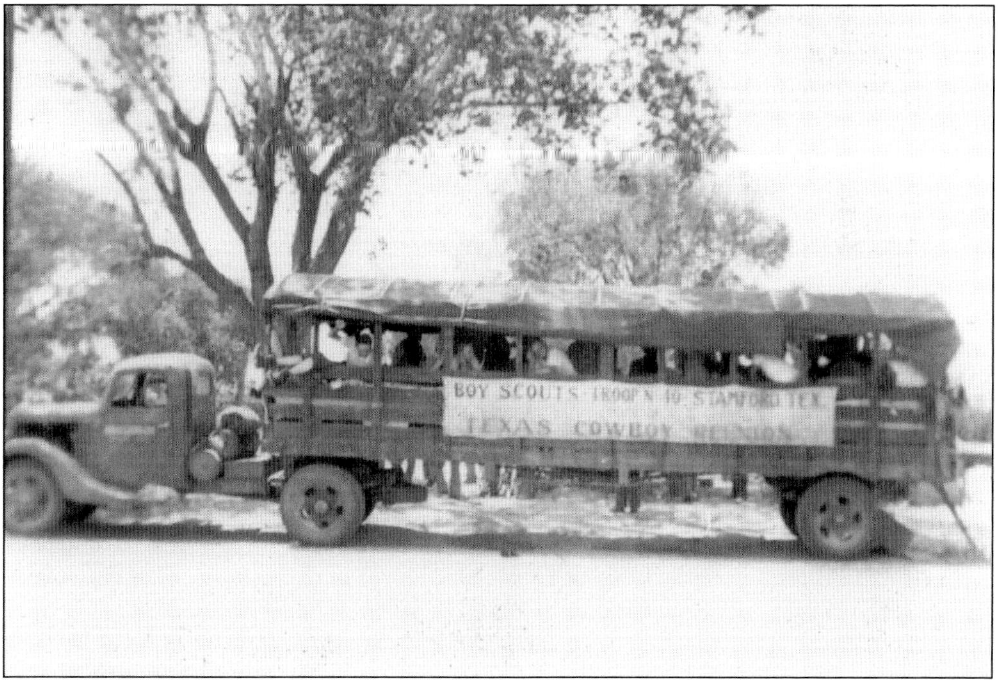

The Tuxedo Boy Scout troop found the reunion a profitable market. In 1933, the troop of around 30 boys sold refreshments at the reunion to raise money. With their earnings, they converted this old cattle truck, adding benches and a tarpaulin top. They traveled to the Grand Canyon, carrying their food and gear and camping out along the way. (Courtesy of Dwaine Stephens family, Tuxedo Reunion files.)

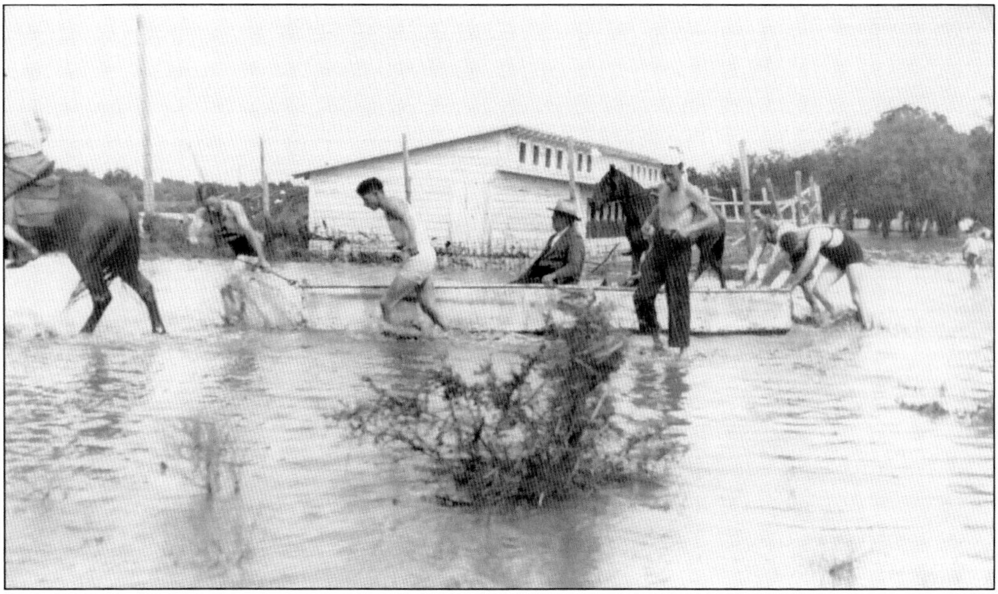

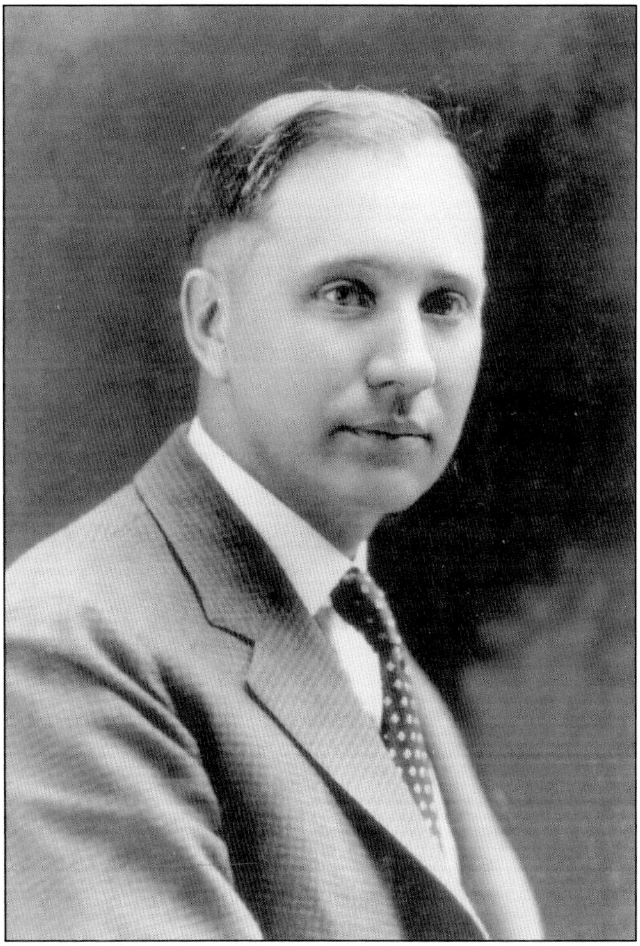

Even annual rodeo crowds could not prevent Depression-era problems. Penick-Hughes Company failed in the early 1930s, after Colonel Penick had retired to Leuders. A 1932 flood of the Clear Fork of the Brazos inundated his home, requiring his rescue—he is seen here seated in the boat. Penick lost a toupee he had worn undetected for years. He never replaced it, remaining bald for the rest of his life.

Tragically, and for reasons that remain mysterious, 48-year-old Ray Rector took his own life in January 1933 with a shotgun blast to his heart. His wife, Mamie, concerned with his unexplained absence, launched a search that led to the discovery of his body. He left a note that read, "Good-bye all, not afraid to go. See you all in the morning." Rector left behind his son, Tommie, and five daughters.

Tommie Rector, seen here with his mandolin, had begun helping his father with photography work at age 12. After graduation, he moved to California to work in a cannery. With his father's death, he returned to Stamford and took over the photography business. He continued to use his musical talents, even when he later enlisted in the military.

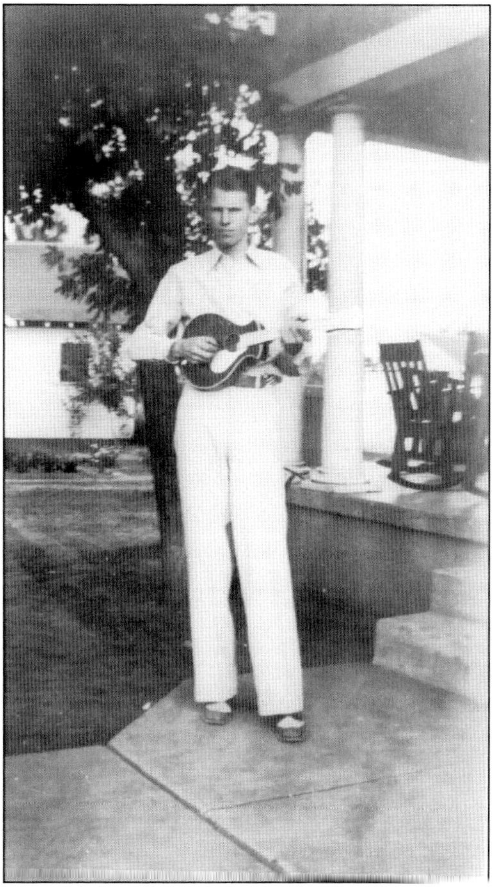

Despite the hard times, Stamford was a bustling city in 1933. The north side of the square included the J.C. Penney Company, which celebrated its 32nd anniversary with a sale. The Davenport law offices were located above Penney's. Next-door was the Kinney Furniture Store, established by O.A. Kinney in 1932. Continuing along the street were Martin Jewi, optometrist; the Texas Café; Conant's Barber Shop; and city hall (far right).

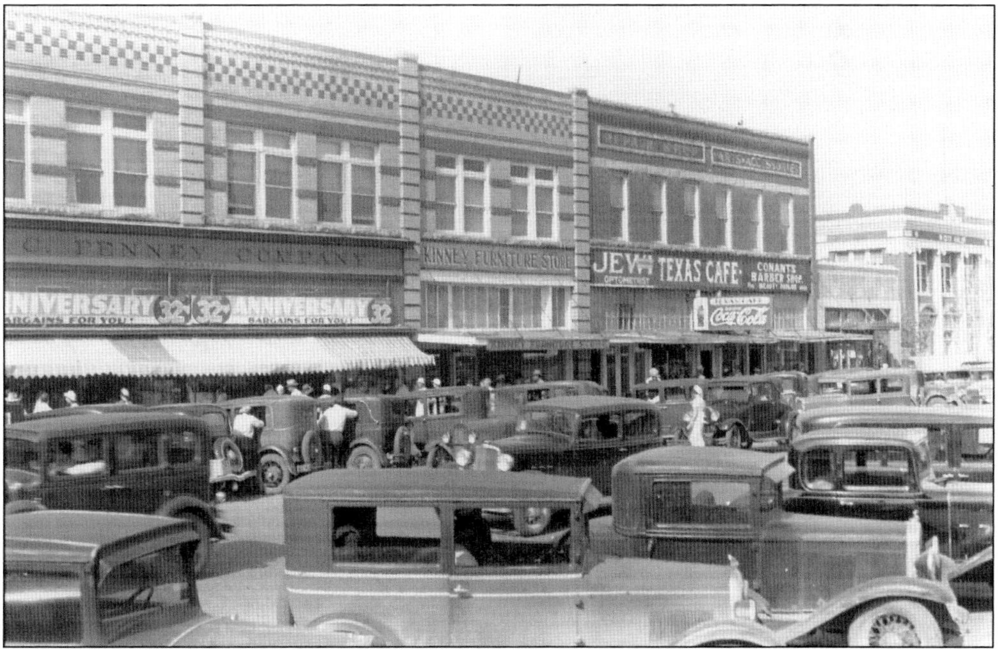

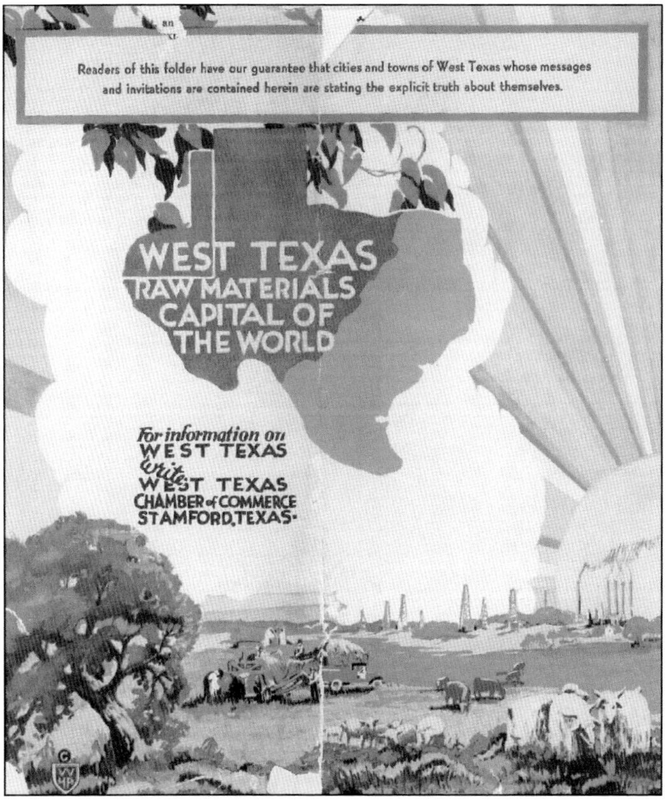

The Century of Progress Exposition, also known as the World's Fair, took place in Chicago in 1933 and celebrated America's scientific and economic growth. The West Texas Chamber of Commerce produced this booklet for distribution at the Texas exhibit in the Court of States exhibition at the fair, extolling the strengths of the region. Stamford, with a population of 4,000, was described as the best-paved small city "in the best of the west."

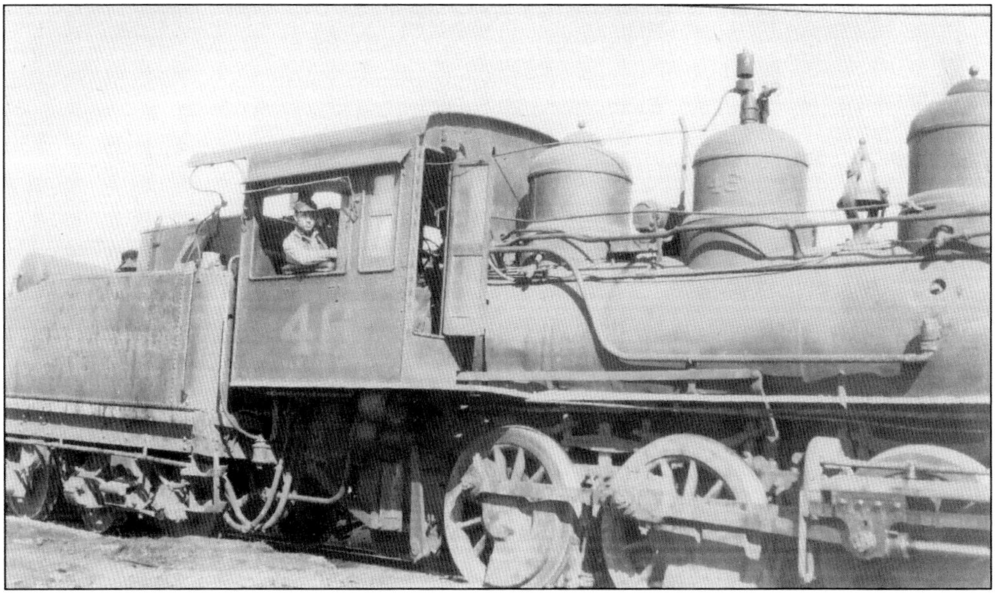

The economy had diversified somewhat. Oil was discovered in southern Jones County in 1926, and production of it helped maintain the local economy. In 1930, the Flat Top Ranch developed a gravel enterprise and a 10-mile spur line to the Texas Central at Hamlin. Cleo Shipman (in engine) took the engineer's job, carrying gravel to the freight yards. With nowhere to turn around, he backed the 10 miles home. (Courtesy of the Cleo Shipman family.)

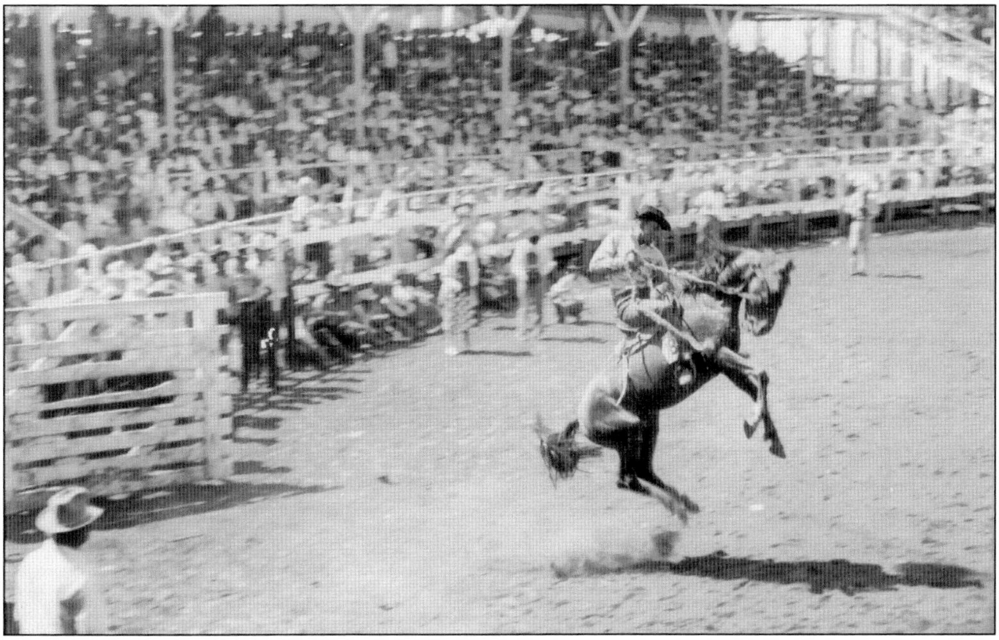

The reunion gained national attention for its unique nature. It had all the excitement of a traditional rodeo, with events like bronc riding, seen here, and a host of other things, from fiddle contests to chuck-wagon cooking. At its heart, however, it was a true reunion. Cowboy humorist Will Rogers called it "a real celebration in a real cowtown by real old-timers."

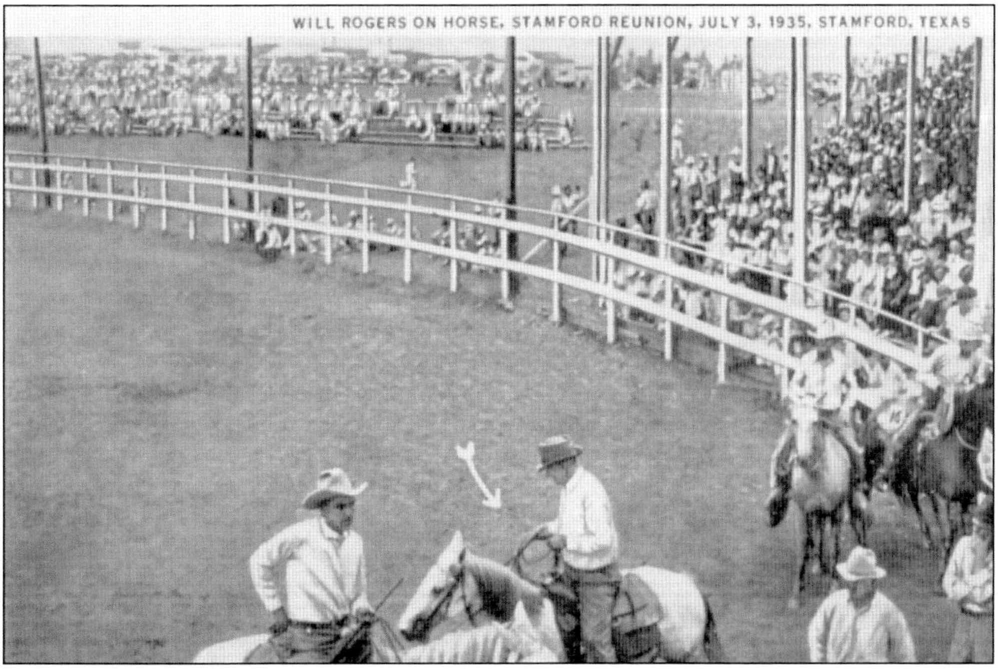

In July 1935, Will Rogers decided to attend the event, flying into Abilene and taking a taxi north to Stamford. When the celebrity was discovered, he was asked to participate. This old postcard shows Rogers on a horse named Tommy (owned by a young Tony Selmon) at the event. He was a crowd favorite. Rogers died the following month in a plane crash near Point Barrow, Alaska.

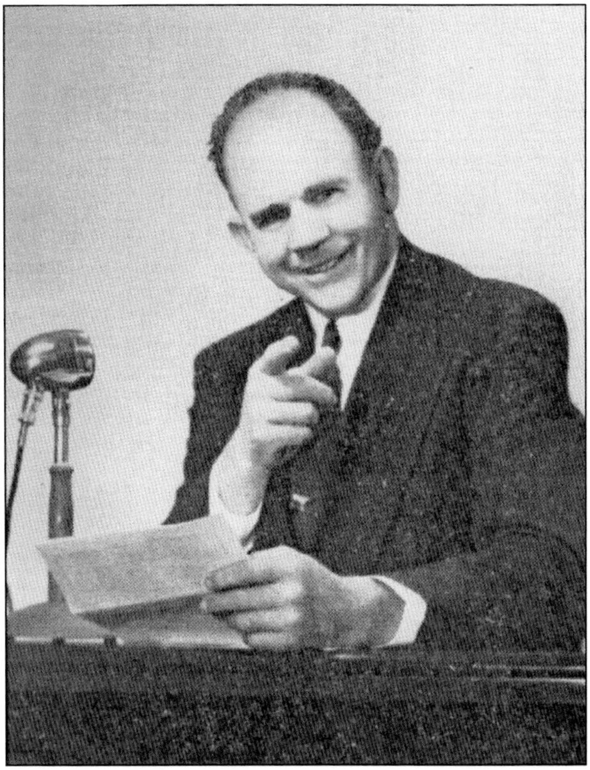

Stamford also played a role in the development of national radio broadcasting. Sam Morris, the pastor of Stamford First Baptist in the early 1930s, began using radio to extend the reach of his anti-liquor campaign. Frustrated with regulations, Morris moved to the Rio Grande border to utilize Mexican stations with signals strong enough to cover much of the United States. From there, the "Booze Buster" preached on "the Ravages of Rum."

Stamford had a newspaper within months of its founding, and others soon began publishing. Most were short-lived. The *Stamford American*, seen here in the 1940s, opened in 1925. Cleburne Huston, with a journalism degree from the University of Texas, purchased it in 1925 and made it the primary paper in Stamford for the next two decades.

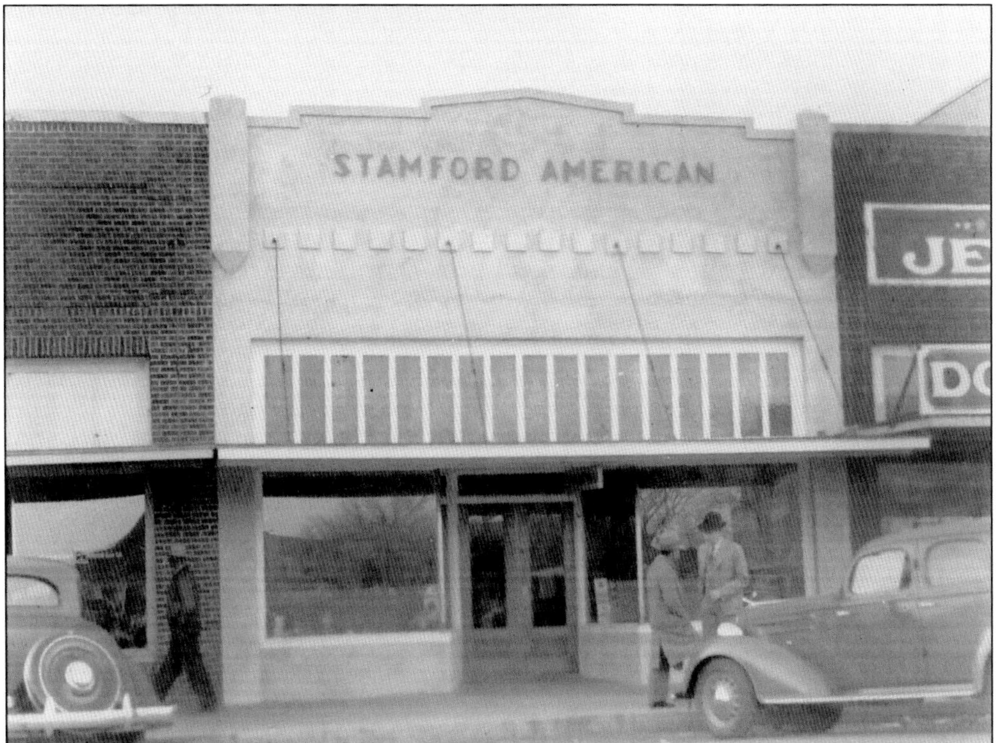

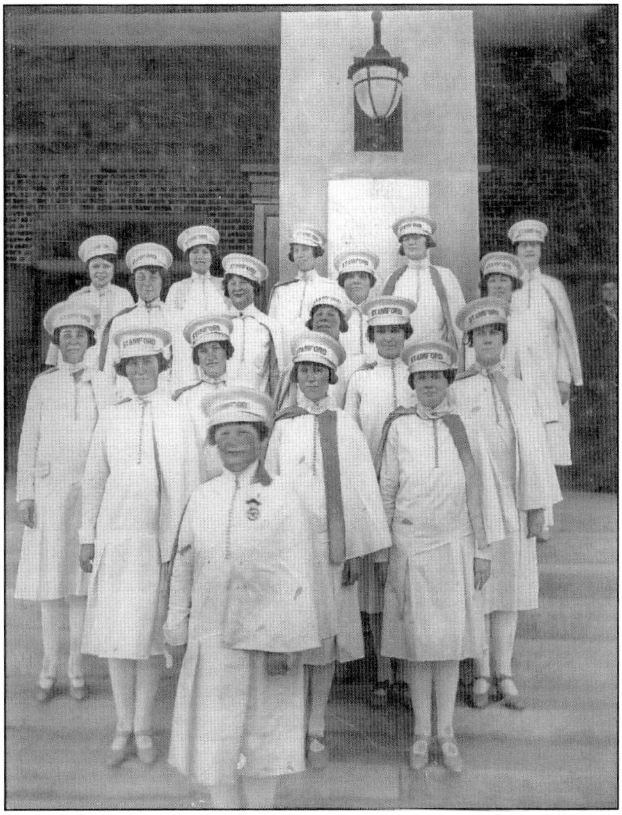

The nursing school organized in 1910 when the Stamford Sanitarium was built closed in 1939. The Texas Nurses Association ruled that no graduate of a nursing school with less than 100 beds would be eligible to take the state board examination. Over the years, the school had successfully graduated many classes of nurses, including this unidentified group.

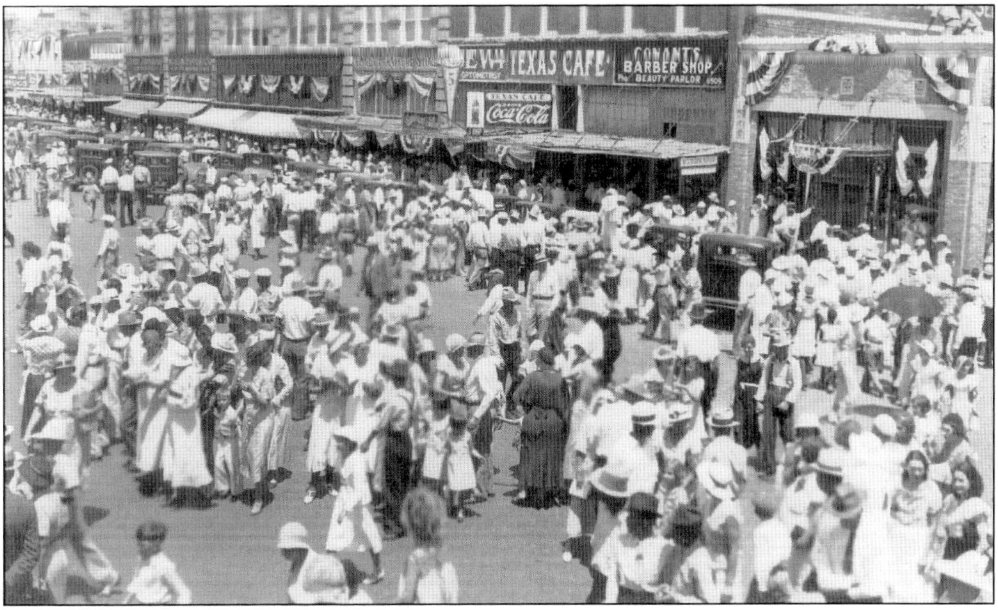

This photograph may have been taken during reunion days, but Stamford was busy on any Saturday, when the farmers came to town. Farm boy Ralph Shanafelt recalled how his family drove in early to find parking on the square. The stores opened early and remained open until 11:00 p.m. Everyone also wanted time to visit with other farmers and walk up and down the streets.

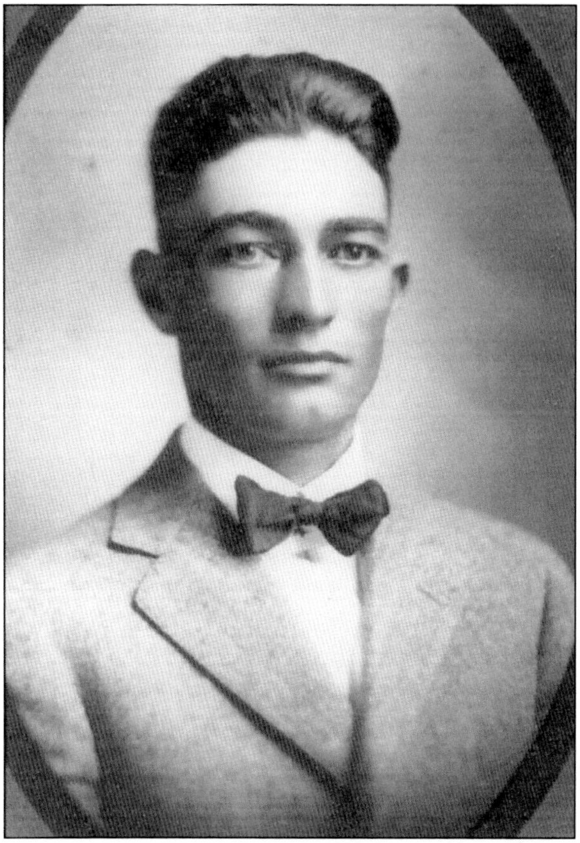

Ralph Otto Shanafelt raised his family, including his son Ralph, on his father's farm, six miles west of Stamford. He tried tenant farming and later worked a farm with several family members. When a family fight destroyed the partnership, Shanafelt sold his livestock and bought a small country filling station and grocery, but he kept his tractor in case the business failed.

The value of West Texas farms dropped 40 percent between 1930 and 1940, and there were 700 fewer farms at the decade's end. Lee Roy Nauert's family farmed in those times, burning kerosene for heat in their three-room home and living without electricity until 1941. Nauert started at Flat Top School (seen here) a year early because his older brother cried to have him along. His teacher, Ernestine Romas, roomed with a family that still spoke German. (Courtesy of Lee Roy Nauert.)

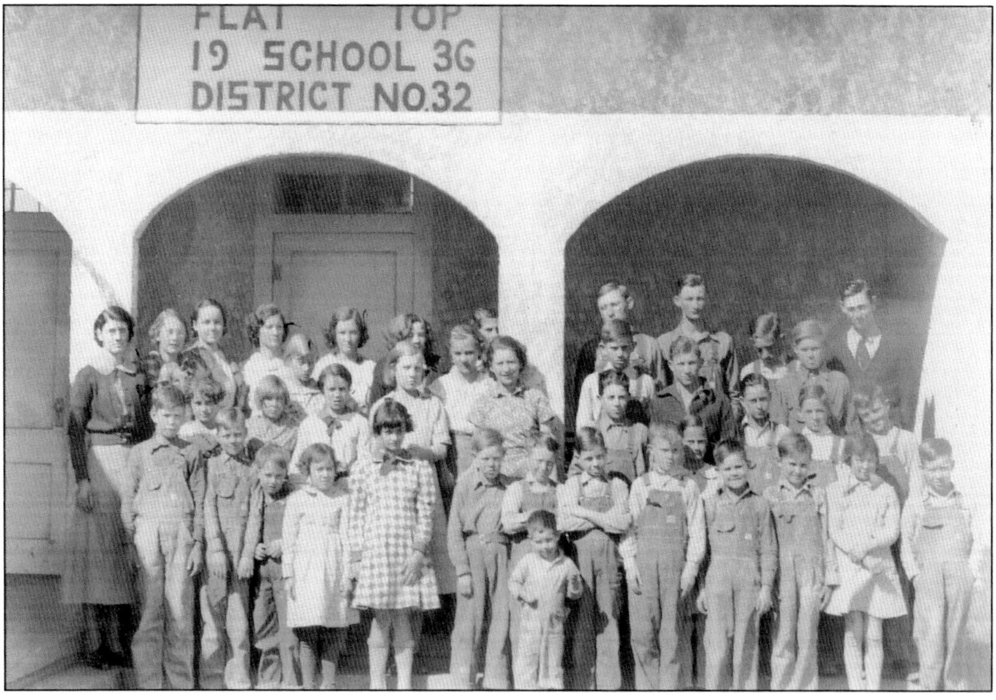

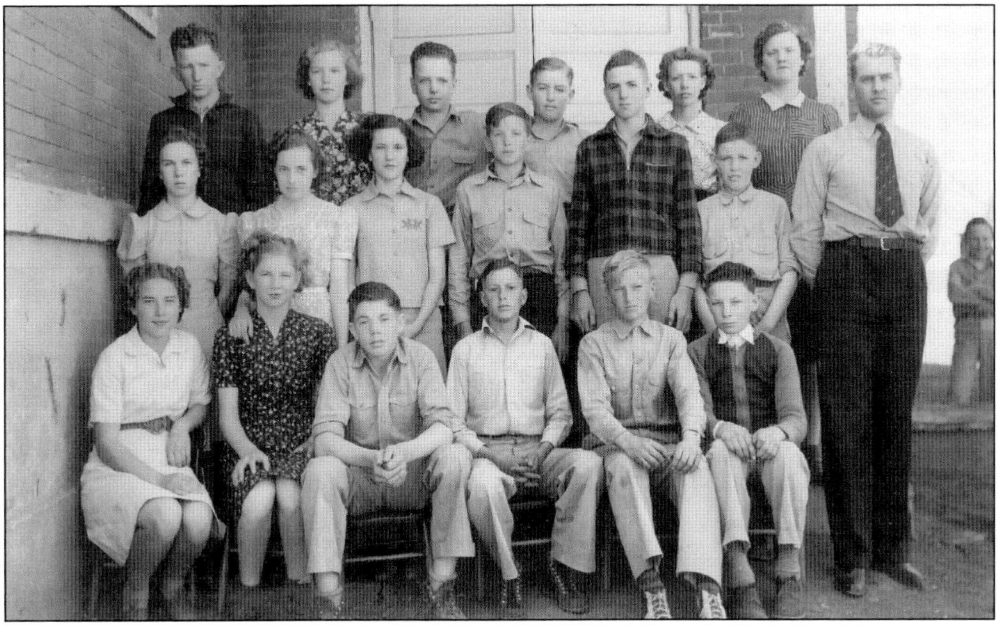

The 1940 Tuxedo High School students represented the survivors of the Great Depression. Their families had managed to hang on to their own farms or work as tenants on someone else's land. Tuxedo remained a small but active farm community. In 1923, the old brick schoolhouse was remodeled into a three-room school, and a new redbrick auditorium with one classroom was constructed.

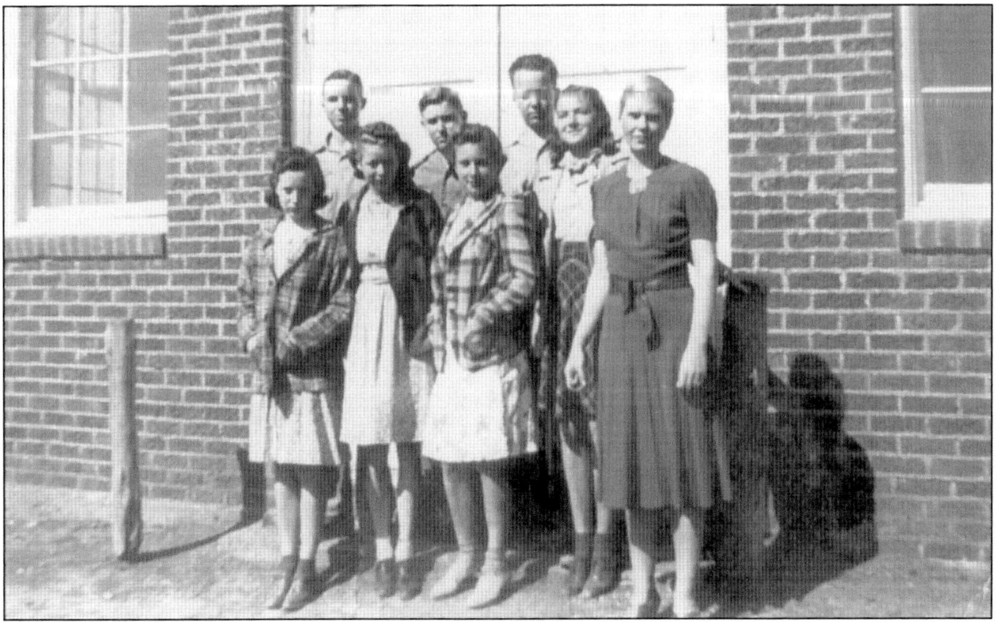

The cast and director of the 1941 annual Tuxedo school play, *Aaron Slick of Punkin Crik*, posed for *Round-Up*, the handmade school yearbook, unaware of the dramatic change their lives would take on December 7 of that year. In the less than half-century prior, their world had gone from open prairie to a landscape with paved highways and electric lines, all spread outward from the city that brought them all here.

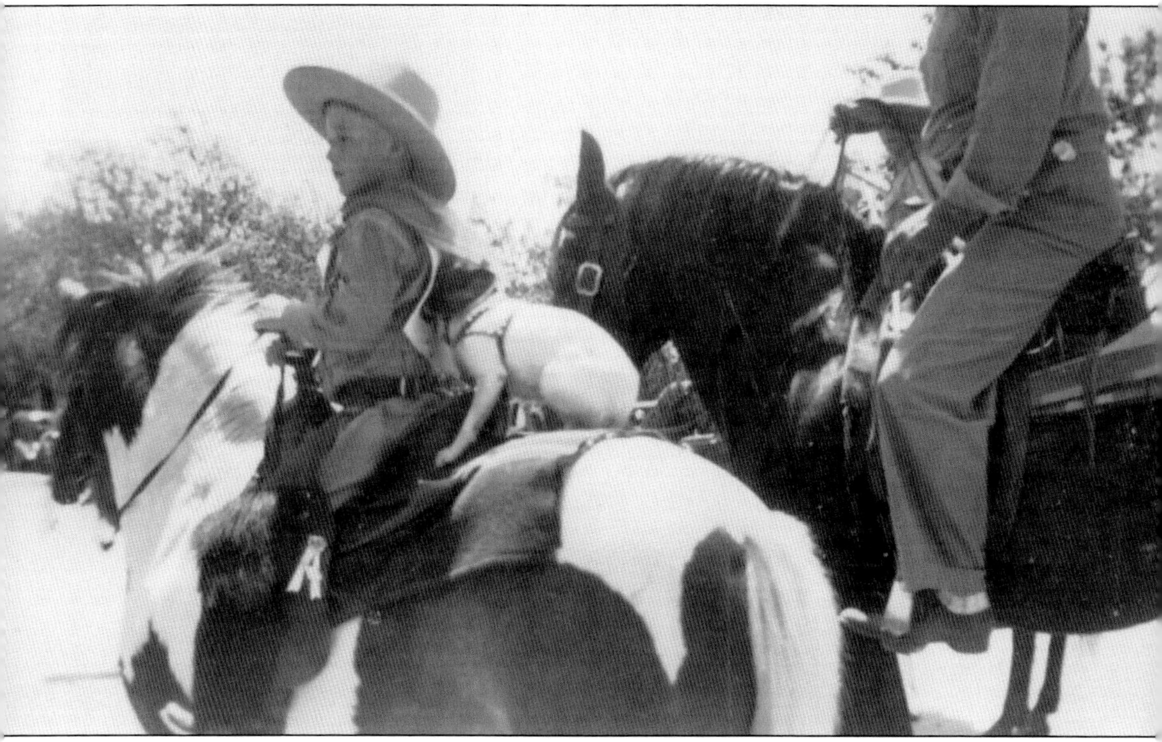

In 1941, the Hardin-Simmons University cowboy band came from Abilene to bring their colorful costumes and spirited music to the Texas Cowboy Reunion parade. The American Quarter Horse Association held its second Quarter Horse Show in conjunction with the reunion. The association was founded in 1940 in Fort Worth and chose the reunion as the site for its first approved show that same year. The quarter horse was the ideal cow horse, with quick speed for short distances and great ability to maneuver and live off the land when necessary. Del Rio Joe became the first Quarter Horse grand champion. The news in Europe was growing darker, but it was reunion time in Stamford. This unidentified young rider exemplified the reunion spirit. He wore a contestant number for an event, and even his dog wanted to participate. Writer Walt Cousins of Dallas stated the feeling best, writing, "Pards, we hope to see you there this year for the best and biggest show we have ever had."

Five

A Changing World

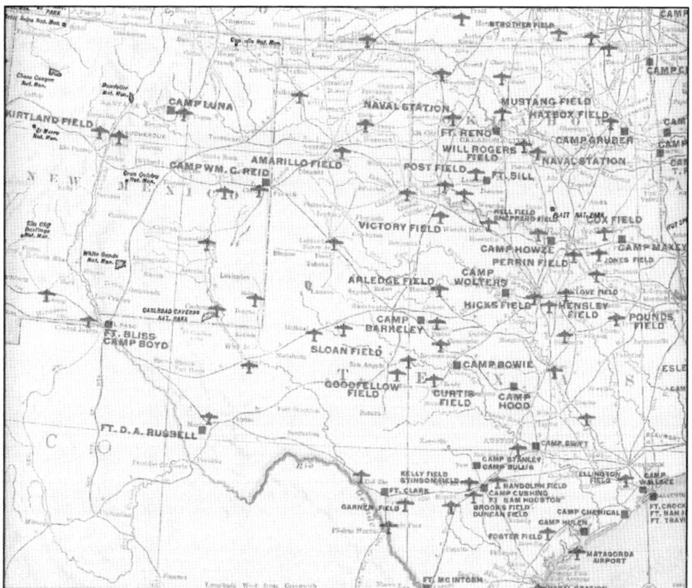

The coming of World War II dramatically changed the United States and Stamford. Many local boys quickly enlisted. The local airfield brought others to Stamford. This Union Pacific Military Map provided the locations of airfields, naval bases, and army posts. Arledge Field (near center) was established at Stamford in March 1941.

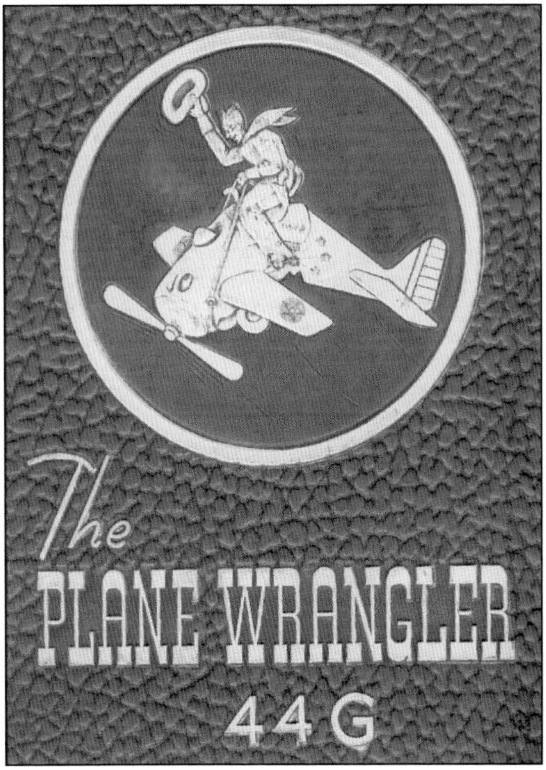

Arledge Field was a contract flying school. Preparing for war, the Army Air Forces contracted with a number of civilian flying schools to train pilots. The flight instructors were civilian contractors, but the cadets still experienced the school as a military duty. Arledge Field was first operated by Stamford Flying School. This is the cover of the *Plane Wrangler*, the 44-G class album.

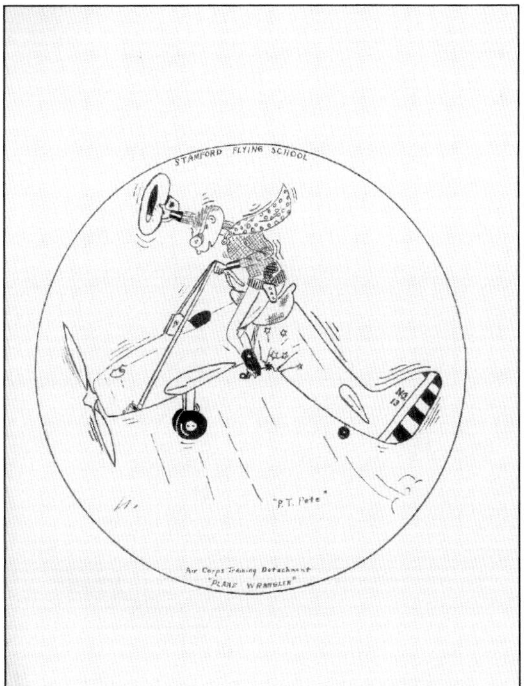

Each class of cadets training as pilots was assigned a designation based upon the year and their order within the year. Every class selected a staff of cadets to produce an album, much like a school yearbook, to record their time at Arledge Field. The school mascot became P.T. Pete, the "plane wrangler," seen here in the original version created by 42-G, the first graduating class.

The community warmly embraced the cadets. When not on duty, they were entertained in homes. The youth center area at the Carnegie library became a cadet club. City Drug Store, with its soda fountain and Wurlitzer jukebox, was a popular spot. This photograph collage is from the 42-G *Plane Wrangler.* Stamford Flying School was replaced by Lou Foote Flying School, followed by Coleman Flying School.

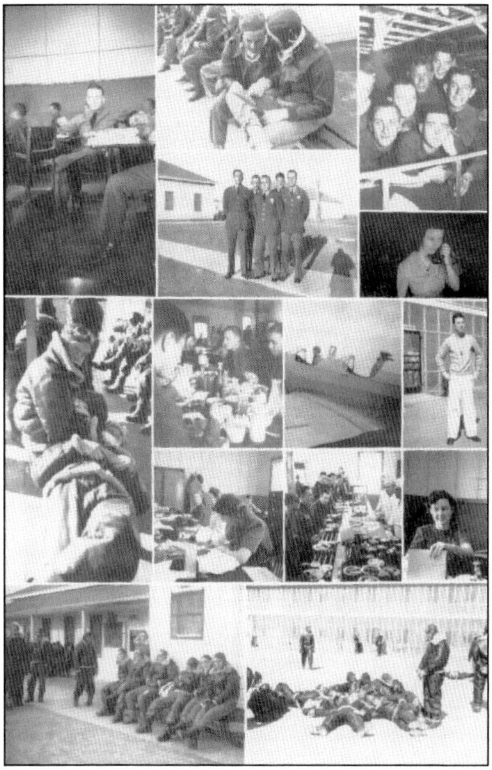

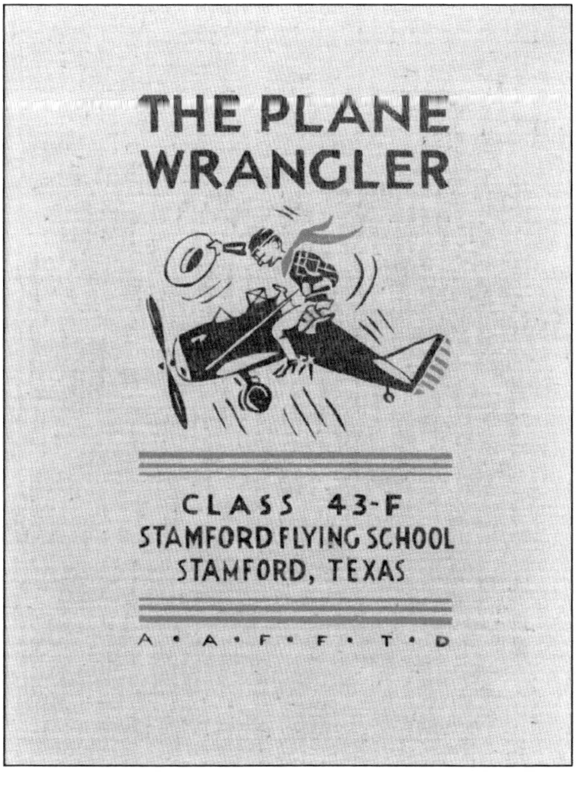

P.T. Pete underwent several changes during the flying-school years. The Army Air Corps paid the school $1,170 for each graduate. The Arledge School was deactivated in September 1944. After the war, Arledge Field became a civil airport. Weldon Crawford, a Stamford native, perished in a plane crash while training at the Eagle Pass Advanced Flying School in 1943.

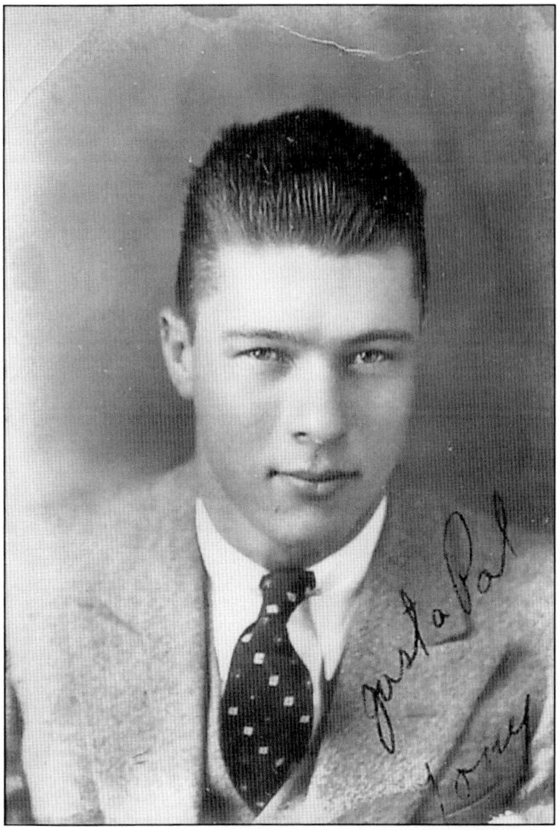

Many young men from Stamford enlisted for the war. Tommie Rector joined the Army and served in Italy. He applied his musical skills, serving as the bugler for 5,000 troops. Tony Selmon, seen here in his high school graduation picture, was in Texas Tech Medical School in Galveston when the war broke out. In 1942, he joined the Navy and interned at San Diego Naval Hospital, which had 10,000 patients at a time.

Not all was solemn on the home front. In 1942, the Stamford square dance team won the state championship. It later went to Washington, DC, to represent Texas at the National Folk Festival. The team included, from left to right, (first row) John Braswell, Johnnie Gray, Judge Charles E. Coombes, Lawrence Crider, and Joe Benton; (second row) Lillian Crider, Les Gray, Floy Benton, and Lou Williams.

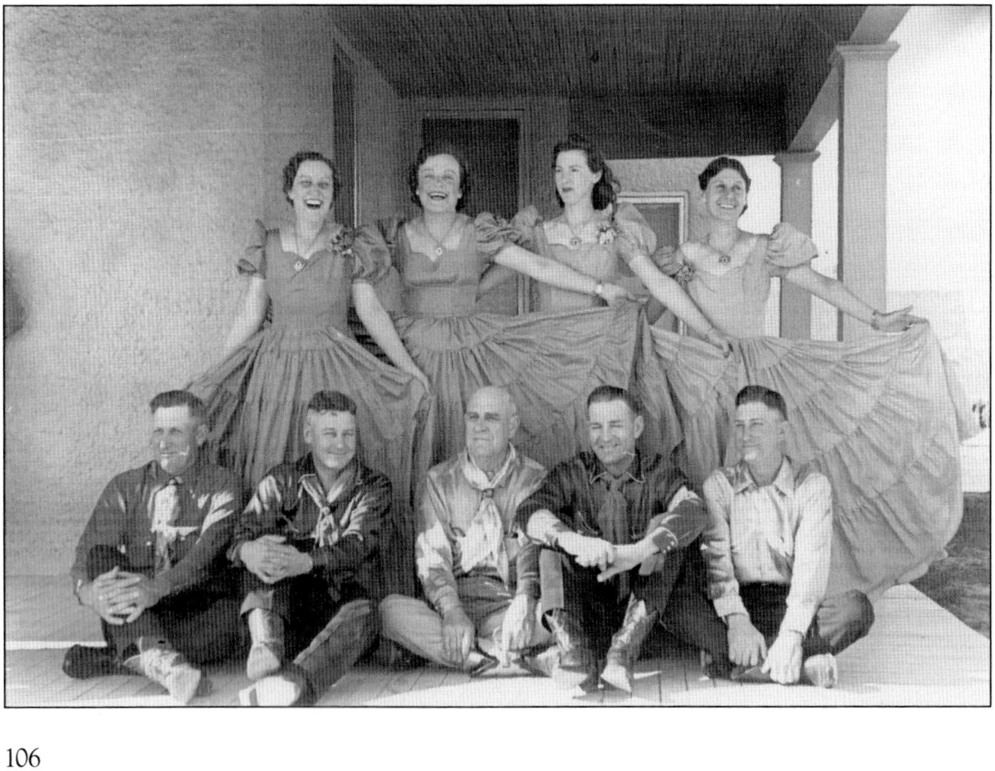

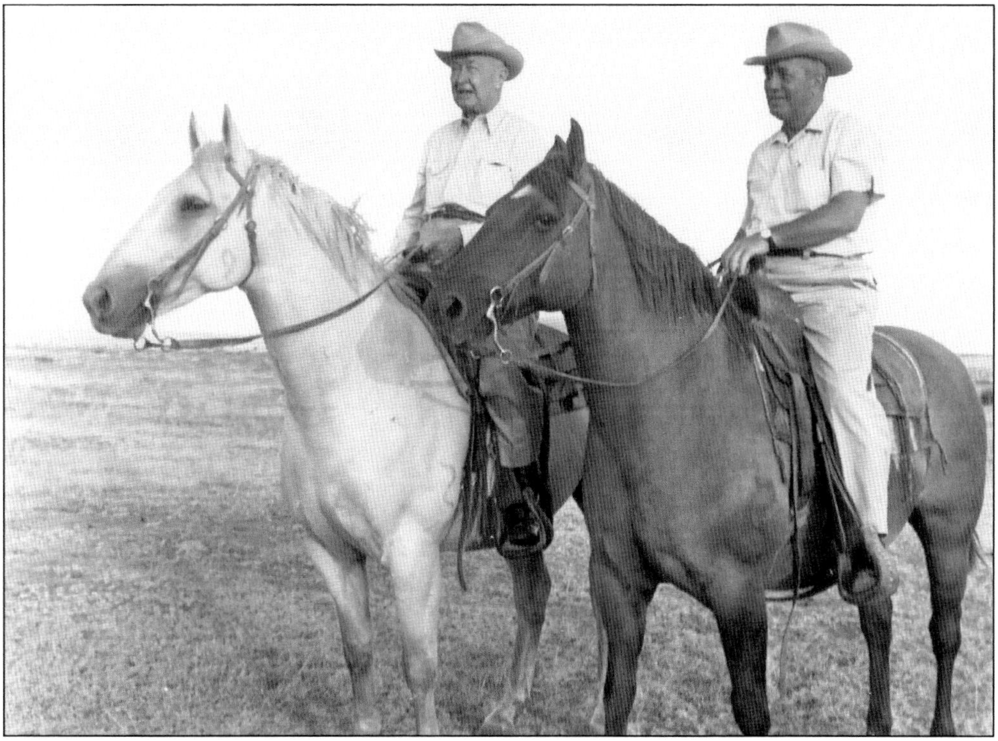

In 1947, A.J. Swenson handed over management of the SMS ranches to his sons, W.G. "Bill" and A.M.G., nicknamed "Swede," who served as comanagers until 1972, when Bill's sons Gene and Carl assumed comanagement. In this 1965 photograph, Swede is on the left, and Bill may be the man on the right. In 1978, the ranch was divided, and Gary Mathis was hired to manage the remaining SMS land. (Courtesy of Swenson Land and Cattle Company.)

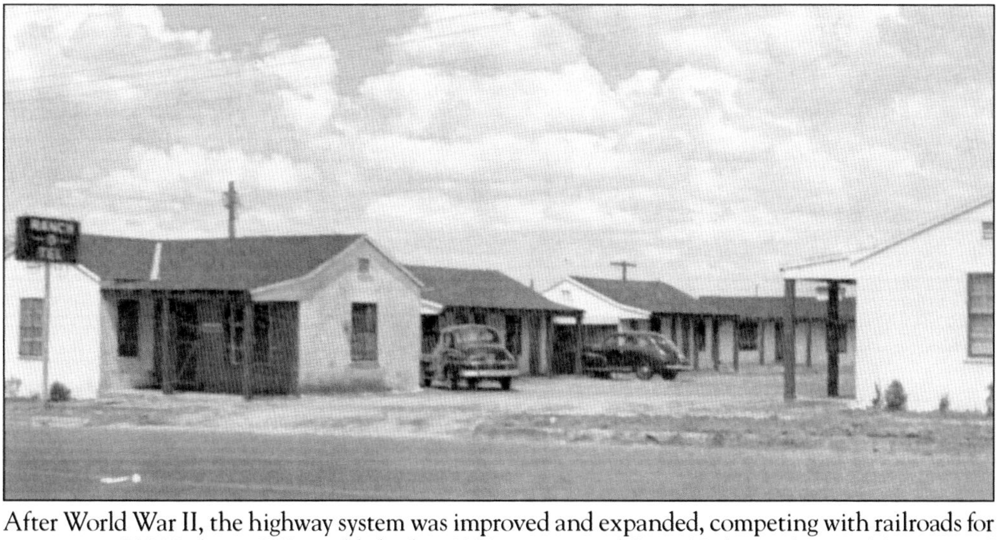

After World War II, the highway system was improved and expanded, competing with railroads for commerce. US Highway 277, established in 1930, intersected State Highway 6, one of the original 26 state highways proposed in 1917, at Stamford. As travel and tourism increased, motor hotels, or motels, became common. This postcard of Ted Schaefer's Ranch O'Tel in Stamford promised "completely modern, tile bath, air conditioned, inner spring mattresses, hotel service."

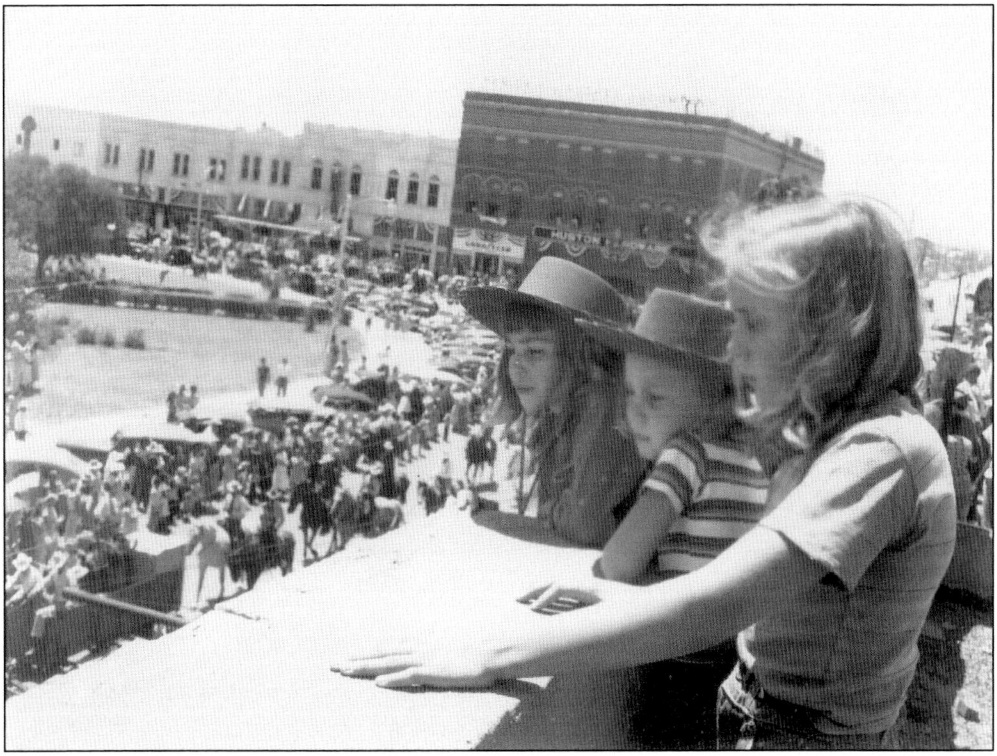

The July 2, 1949, issue of the *Saturday Evening Post* included a two-page photographic story on the Texas Cowboy Reunion, described as "the biggest amateur rodeo in the world." Crowds of 15,000 were normal, though an estimated 70,000 attended in 1937. This parade photograph, probably taken in the 1950s, shows that the rooftops of the square were still the best parade-viewing spots.

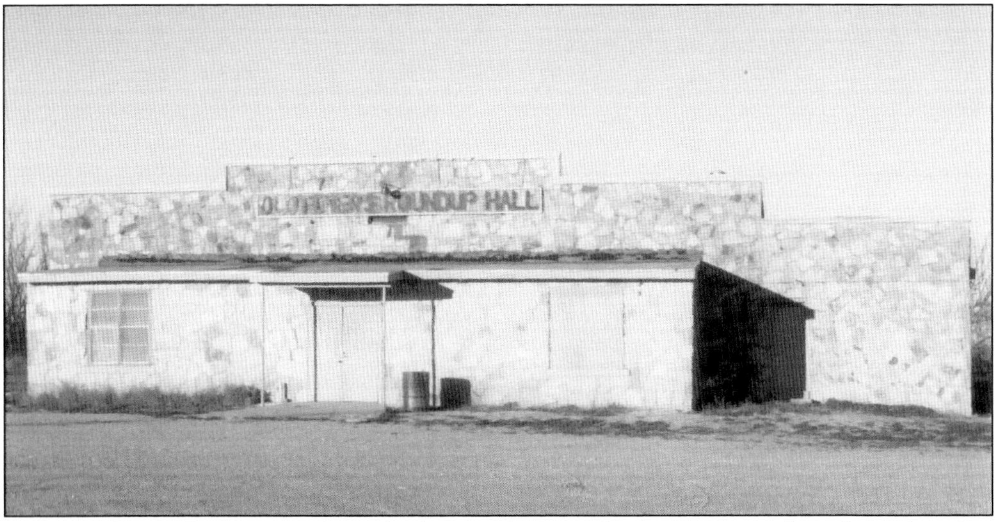

The Roundup Hall, a spacious dance facility, was built on the reunion grounds in the early 1930s. In 1939, it was renamed the Coombes Roundup Hall in honor of Charles Coombes, who served for many years as secretary of the Oldtimers Association. The hall burned in 1951. A new air-conditioned hall was quickly built, which hosted many Stamford events in addition to the reunion activities. (Photograph by James Collett.)

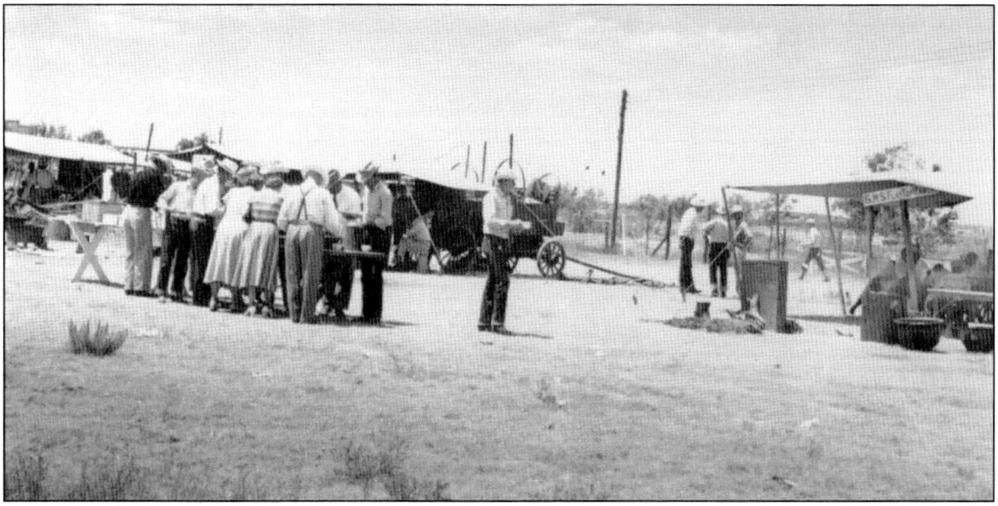

Chuck wagons remained an increasingly nostalgic reunion feature. Meals like this one, by the Flat Top Ranch wagon, still tasted special, and children enjoyed unique treats. Old-timer Dub Harrison recalled, "The cook would pour a box of Post Toasties and a half gallon of milk in a washtub, beat on the side of it and kids would come with spoons like rugrats to eat breakfast out of that washtub."

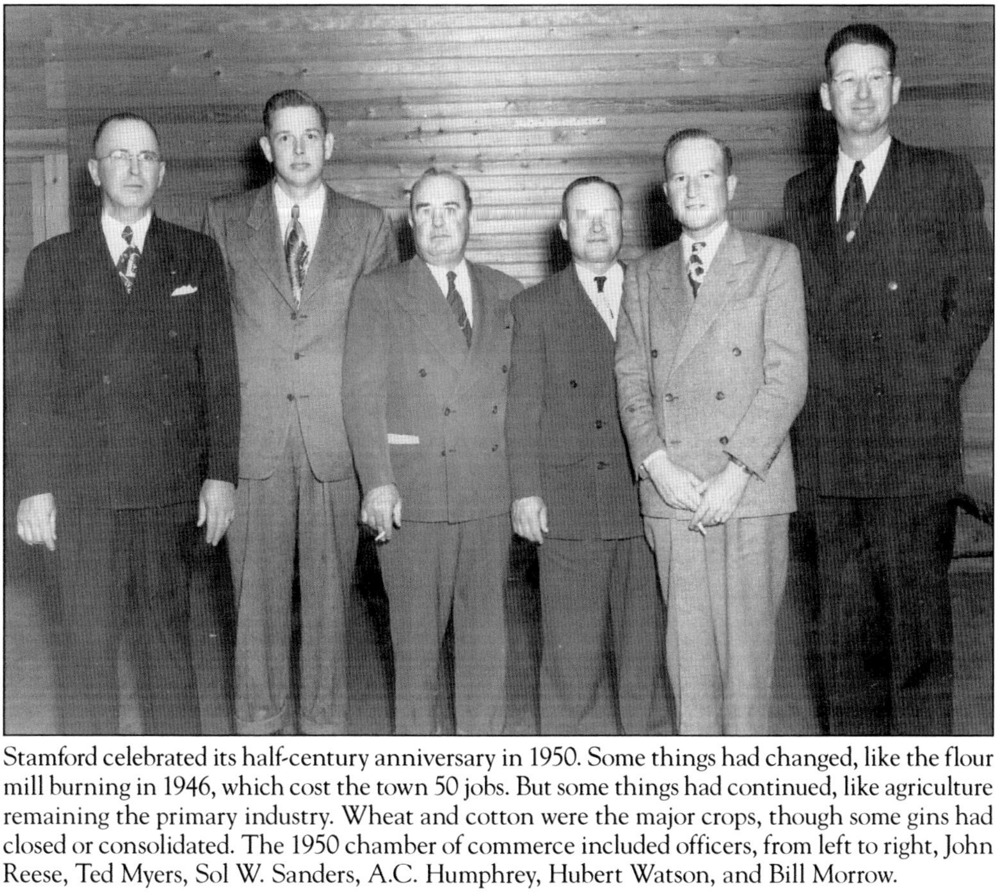

Stamford celebrated its half-century anniversary in 1950. Some things had changed, like the flour mill burning in 1946, which cost the town 50 jobs. But some things had continued, like agriculture remaining the primary industry. Wheat and cotton were the major crops, though some gins had closed or consolidated. The 1950 chamber of commerce included officers, from left to right, John Reese, Ted Myers, Sol W. Sanders, A.C. Humphrey, Hubert Watson, and Bill Morrow.

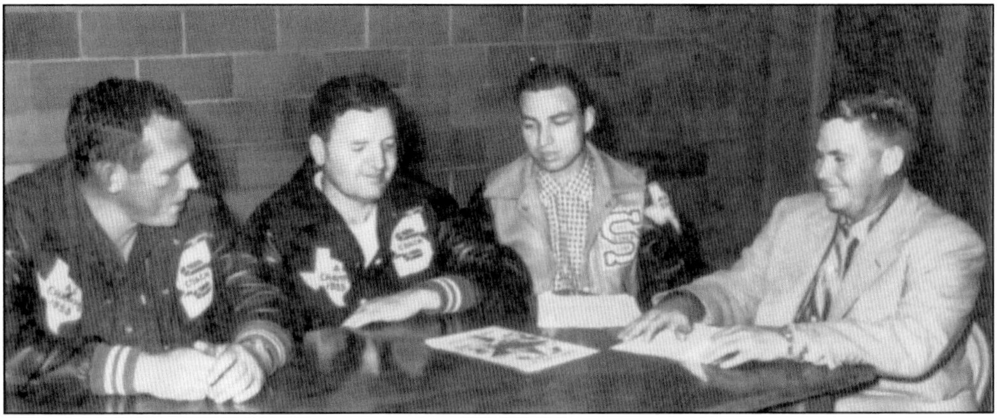

Coach Gordon Wood began coaching at Stamford High School in 1951. Over the next seven years, Wood led Stamford football teams to 80 wins and six losses, a winning percentage of 93. Seen here in the 1957 *Bulldog* annual are coaches, from left to right, Bill Anderson, Gordon Wood, Larry Wartes, and O.M. Isabell. Wood's success continued after he left Stamford in 1958. In 43 seasons as a head coach, he won or shared 25 district championships and nine state championships.

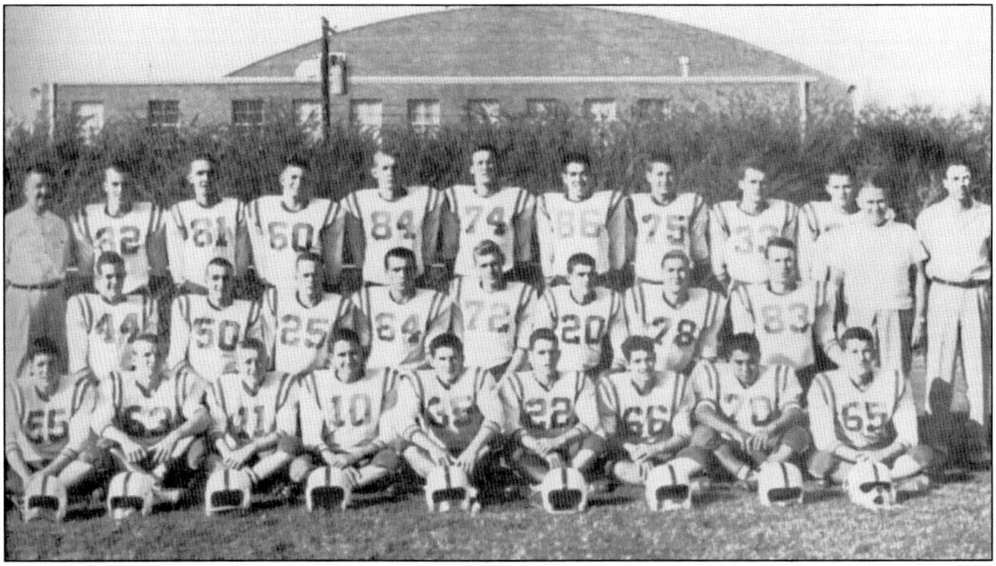

The Stamford Bulldogs won class AA state championships in 1955 and 1956. The 1956 team included, from left to right, (first row) Arche Pardue, Wilbur Cox, Darryl Schoonmaker, Nickey Jackson, Donald Davis, Kenneth Ivy, T.C. Rice, Romeo Garcia, and Jimmy Payne; (second row) Larry Don Ivy, Walter Hood, Stanley Hill, Douglas Monzingo, Delton Ake, Robert Hardin, Jack Magness, J.B. Tabor, coach O.M. Isabell, and coach Larry Wartes; (third row) coach Gordon Wood, Charlie Stenholm, Gayle Ward, Royce West, Dallas Christian, Dale Robinson, Rufino Escobedo, Andy Swenson, Mike McClellan, and Bobby Nelson.

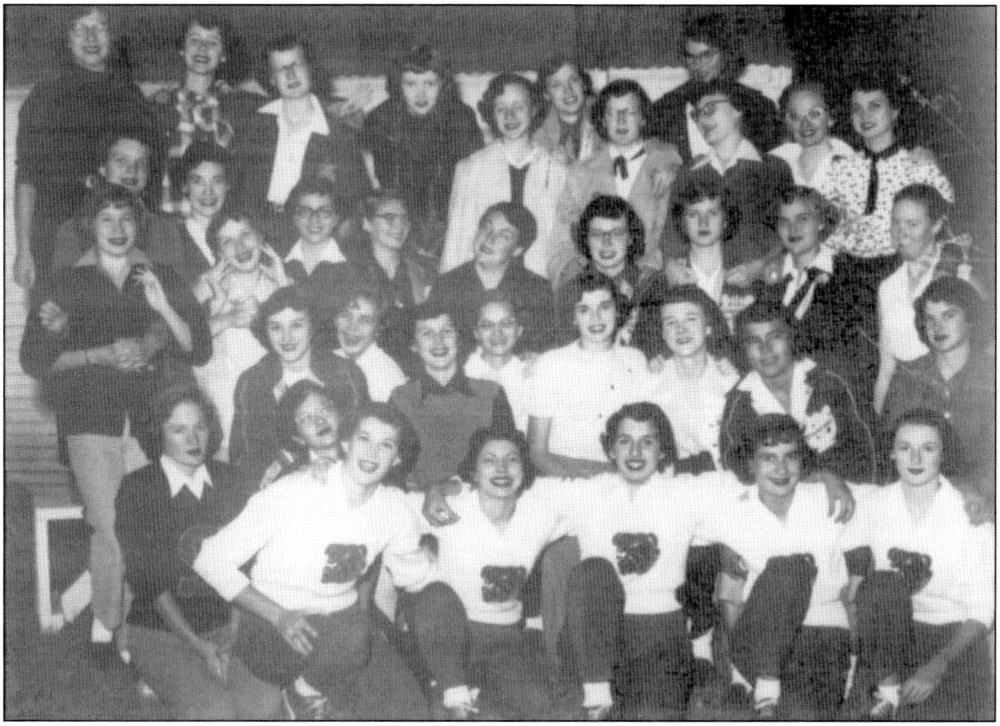

On April 15, 1955, Stamford High School students Judy Metz and Sue Ann McKnight gave relatively unknown performer Elvis Presley a ride from the local radio station to his hotel. Presley was scheduled to perform at the Roundup Hall. At the hotel, Presley offered the ladies thank you kisses. Metz declined; she had a steady beau. In this 1955 yearbook photograph, cheerleader Judy Metz is in the first row, second from the right.

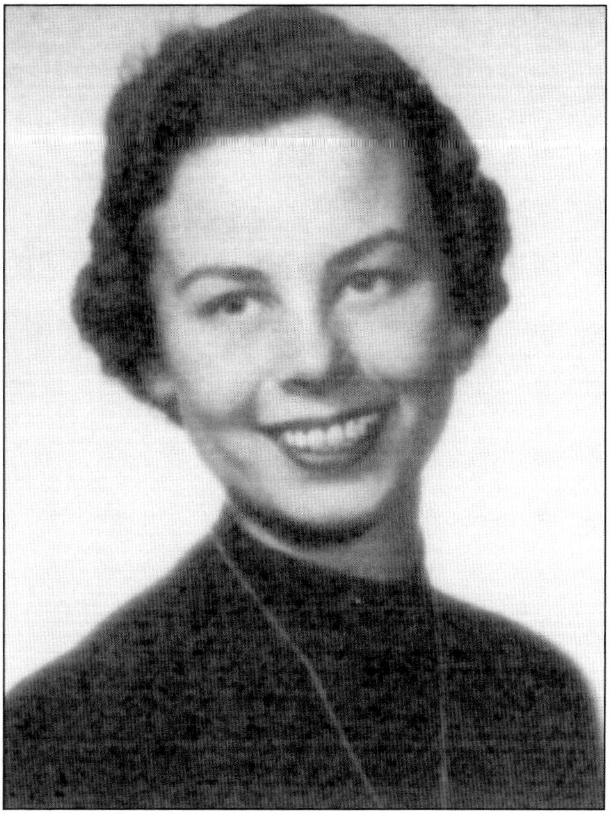

Sue Ann McKnight, seen here in her 1955 school photograph, gladly accepted Elvis's offer of a kiss. She was likely among the group of girls who started the first Elvis fan club after his visit in May 1955. The girls were incredulous when the lady at the *Stamford American* office who took their order for membership cards had never heard of Elvis Presley. The Stamford fan club helped change that.

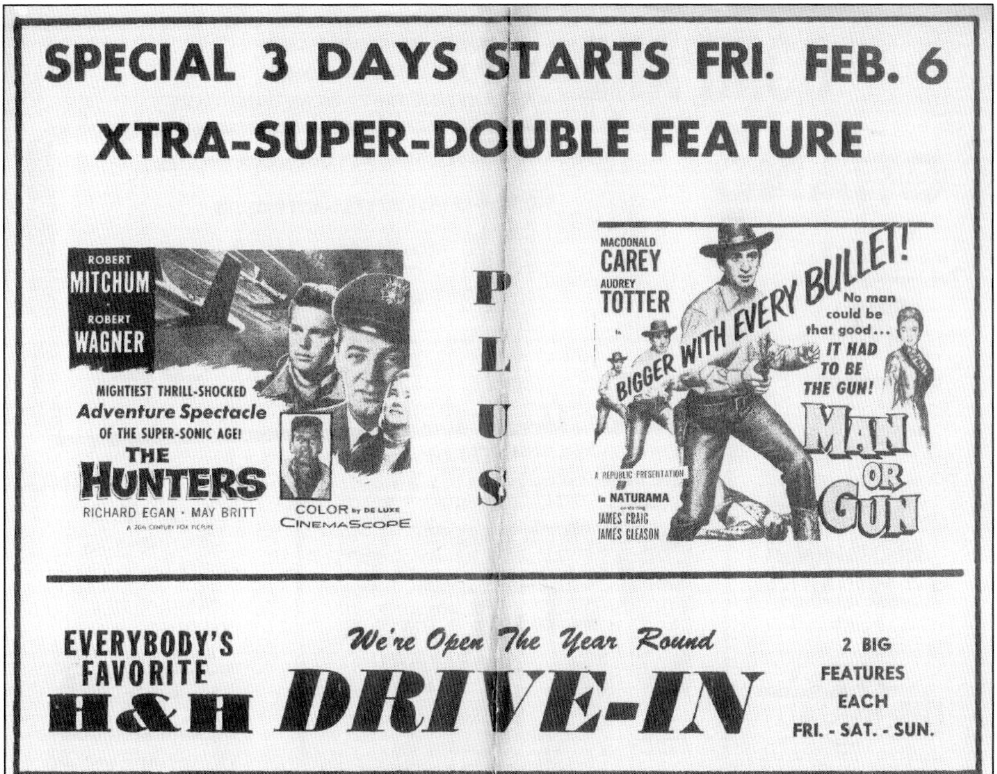

Stamford had movie houses from its early days, and automobiles created a new variation of them in the 1950s with the drive-in theater. The H&H partnered with the downtown Grand indoor movie theater to provide entertainment and a place for weekend dates. This 1958 flyer promised an "xtra-super-double feature" combining a Western and a Korean War film.

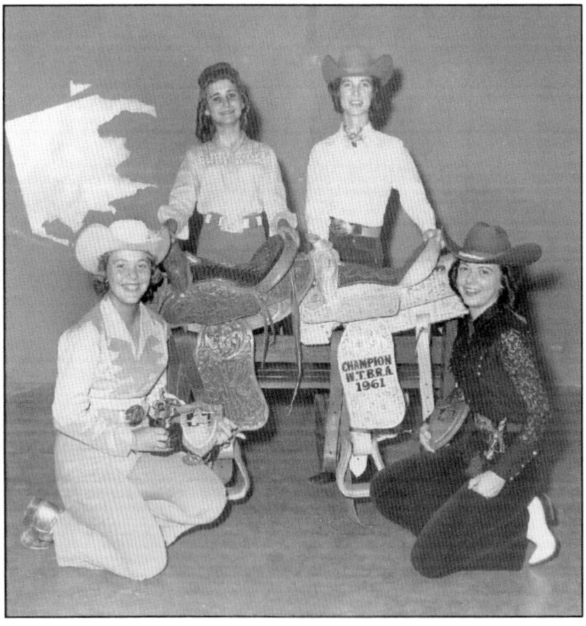

At age 12, Brenda Foster (standing, left) entered the Texas Cowboy Reunion barrel-racing event, placing third and winning a pair of spurs. That same year, she became the Junior West Texas Barrel Racing Champion, winning this saddle. Foster became the youngest girl to receive a Girls Rodeo Association permit. In 1965, she rode the famous Appaloosa stallion Joker B. in the Cotton Bowl parade in Dallas.

Stamford continued its role as a regional center into the 1960s. As this map indicates, West Texas Utilities (WTU) provided service to 49 counties in West Texas, managed through seven districts, each with separate headquarters and personnel. The Stamford district included a gas-fired electric-generating power plant at Lake Stamford. The lake, 10 miles north of the city, was created in 1953.

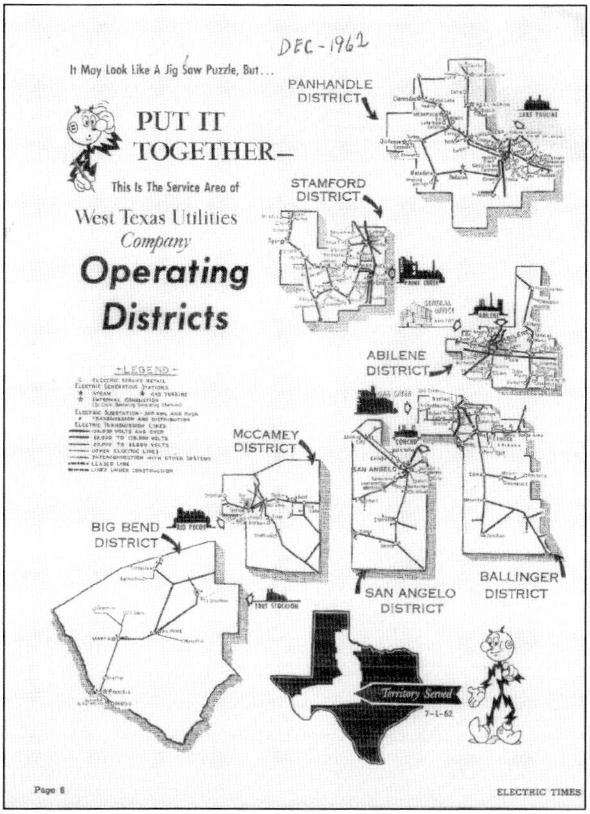

Stamford also successfully attracted several small manufacturing companies to the area, though some were short-lived. Stamford had several bottling plants, including a Coca-Cola plant, for a number of years. A variety of textile manufacturing plants operated here, producing clothing from western shirts to ladies' lingerie and apparel. Cox Tractor, seen here, produced farm equipment in the 1960s.

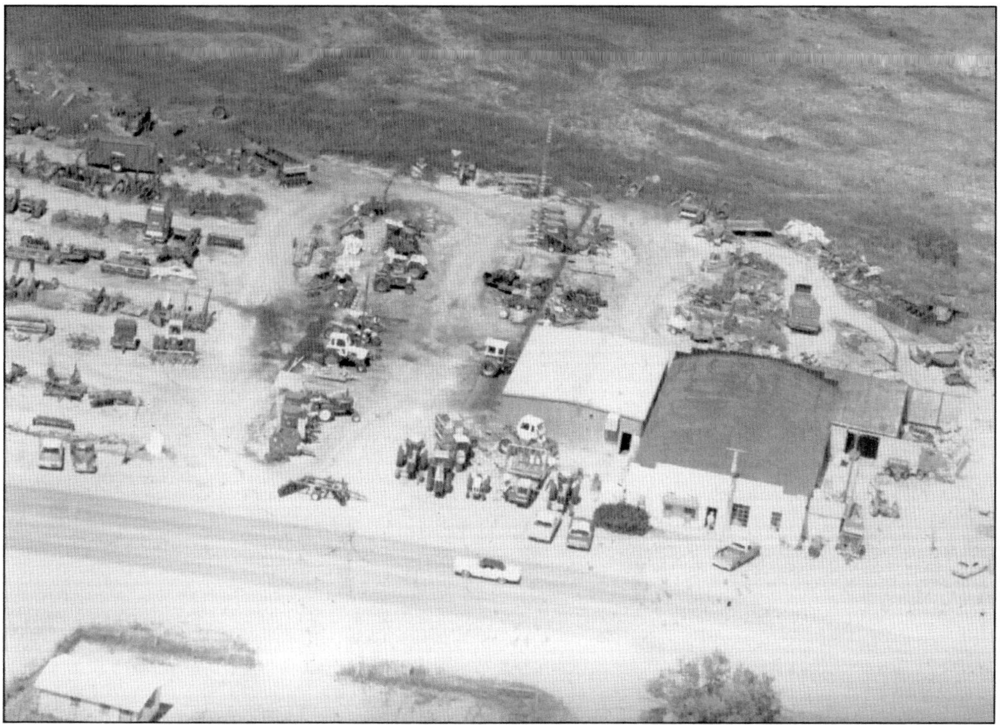

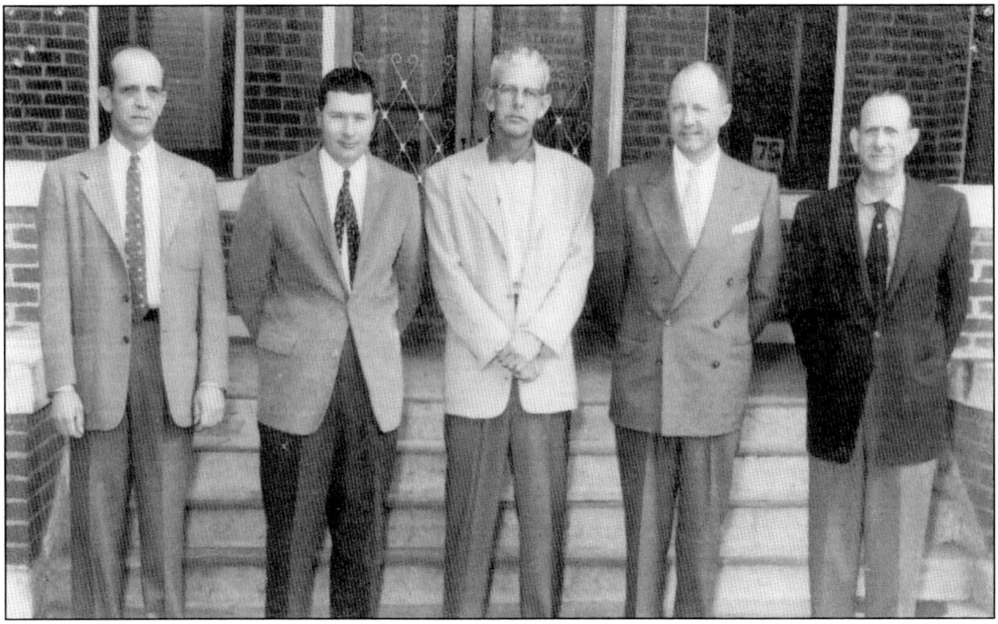

Tony Selmon returned from his military duty and joined other Stamford doctors in the ownership and operation of the Stamford Sanitarium. The doctors included, from left to right, Dr. Tom Bunkley, Dr. Tony Selmon, Dr. George Pryor, Dr. Ike Hudson, and Dr. Louie Metz. They served Stamford's 5,000 residents and the broad surrounding area. Dr. Selmon often ended up with baby-delivery duties. He retired in 1983 after 38 years in practice.

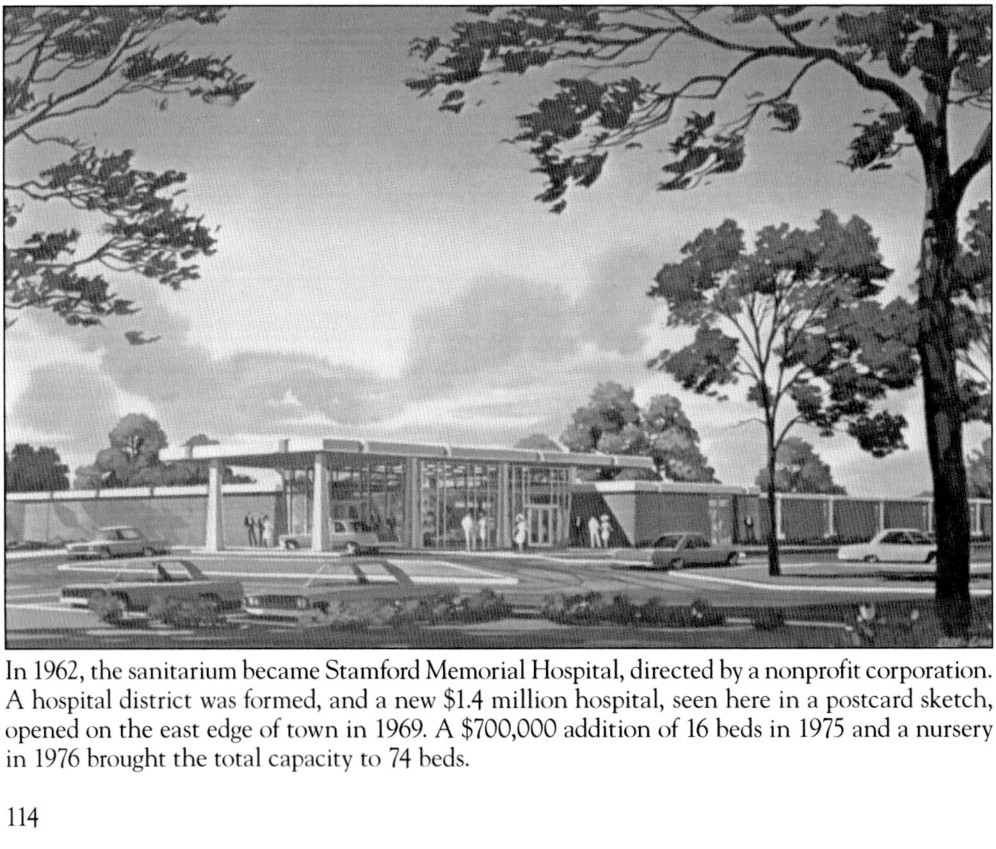

In 1962, the sanitarium became Stamford Memorial Hospital, directed by a nonprofit corporation. A hospital district was formed, and a new $1.4 million hospital, seen here in a postcard sketch, opened on the east edge of town in 1969. A $700,000 addition of 16 beds in 1975 and a nursery in 1976 brought the total capacity to 74 beds.

By the 1960s, Stamford's population stabilized around 4,500 after reaching almost 6,000. The square, as seen in this aerial view from that time, maintained the basic outline defined 50 years before and remained the heart of the city. Many different businesses have occupied those buildings lining the square. One constant was Kinney's Furniture, which opened in 1932. Ray Kinney joined his father in managing the store in 1959.

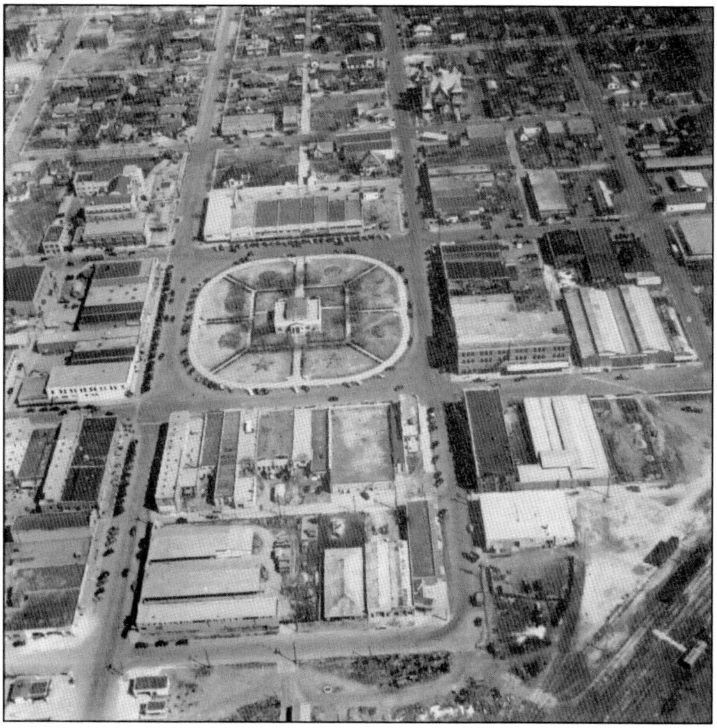

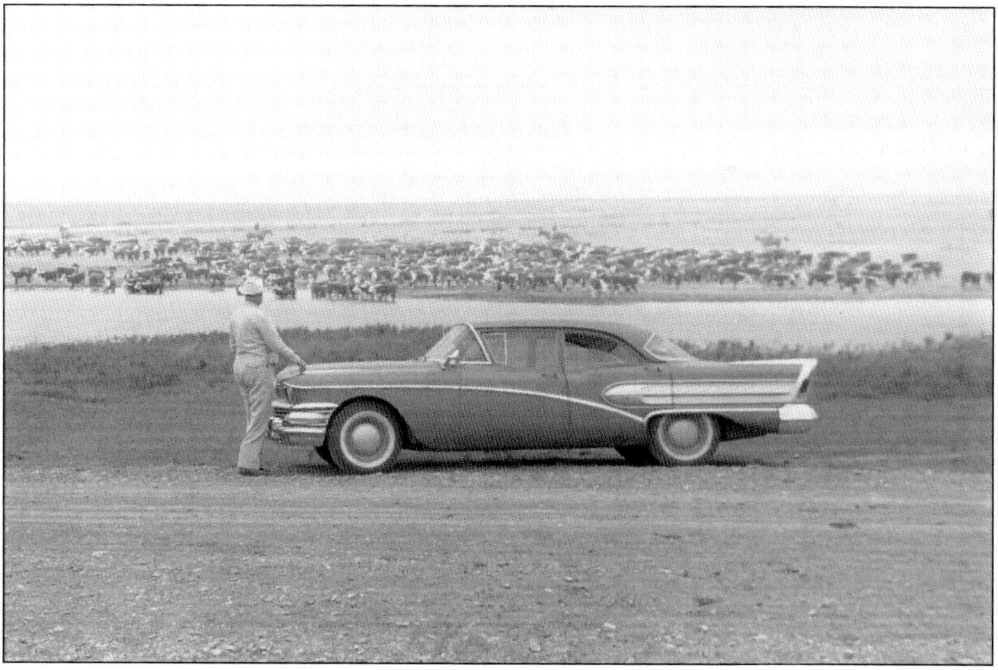

This convertible, driven by W.G. Swenson in 1960, was quite different from his father's car, but the view on the Throckmorton Ranch looked similar to both. Farming had changed considerably, however. The numerous small farms consolidated into larger enterprises, requiring bigger equipment to successfully manage them. Many farmers now worked on rented land, some still paying in shares. (Courtesy of Swenson Land and Cattle Company.)

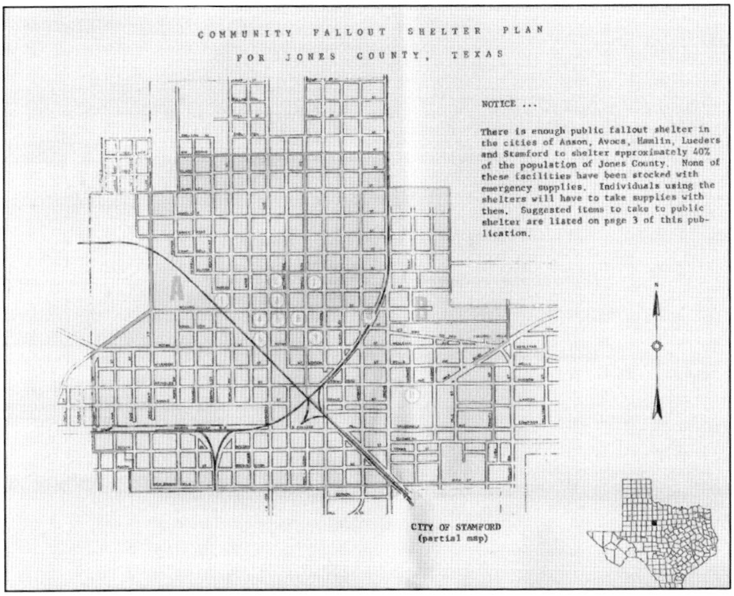

There were other reminders that the world was different. A newspaper insert in the 1960s reminded citizens that the community was prepared for the threat of nuclear war. The insert contained maps of each city in Jones County, including this one of Stamford that identified the designated fallout shelters. People were informed they would have to carry their own supplies to the shelters.

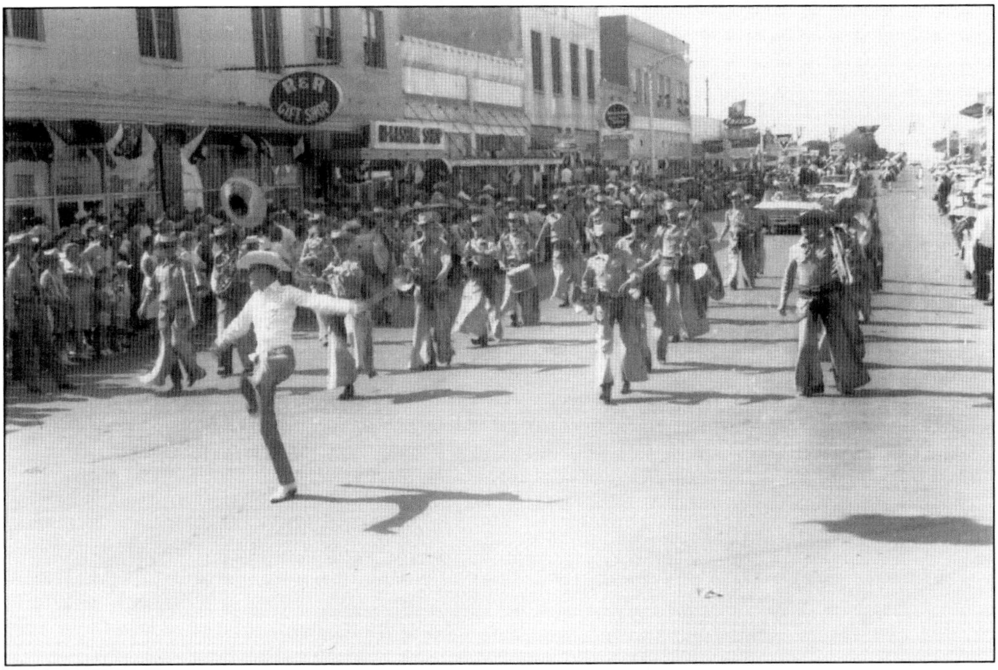

This view along Swenson Avenue shows the Hardin-Simmons University cowboy band marching in the 1960s and reflects the increasing influence of the modern highway-based economy. National brands related to transportation fill the background, including Western Auto, Conoco, Shamrock, and Goodyear. In 1987, a bypass around Stamford was constructed for Highway 277. Designed to relieve trucks from having to navigate the square, it dramatically changed the downtown business community.

A reporter once asked John Selmon what happened to his hand, which was damaged by ranch and arena mishaps. Selmon replied, "Oh, I wore it out trying to play the guitar." Selmon (left) retired as the Flat Top Ranch foreman in 1968. He also served as the reunion arena director for 35 years. He referred to his wife, Emma (right), as "that widow woman" because he spent so much time away from the house. (Courtesy of the Cleo Shipman family.)

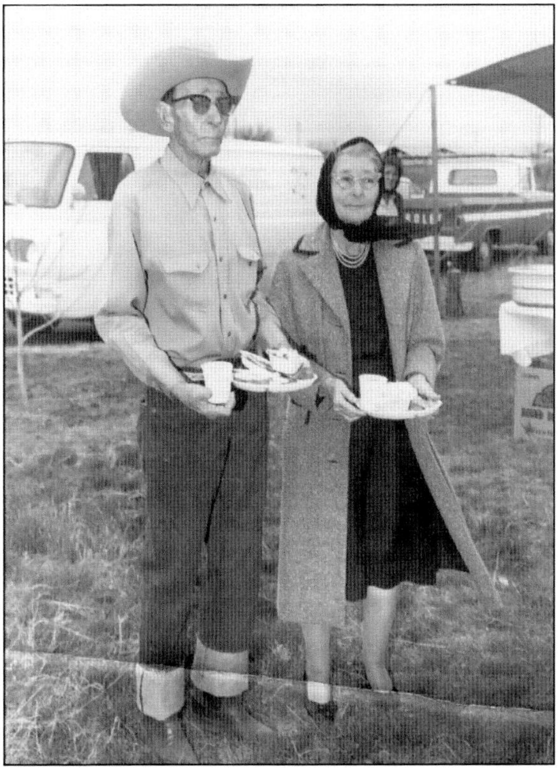

The Cowboy Country Museum opened in July 1977 as a project commemorating the national bicentennial. Dr. Ike Hudson (left), the museum's founder and president, also became the first curator. With Dr. Hudson at the open house were, from left to right, Paul Corley, Dorothy Pryor, Mrs. Paul Corley, and Mrs. C.A. Corley. Dr. Hudson successfully acquired donations of farm and ranch antiques, serving as museum curator until 1988.

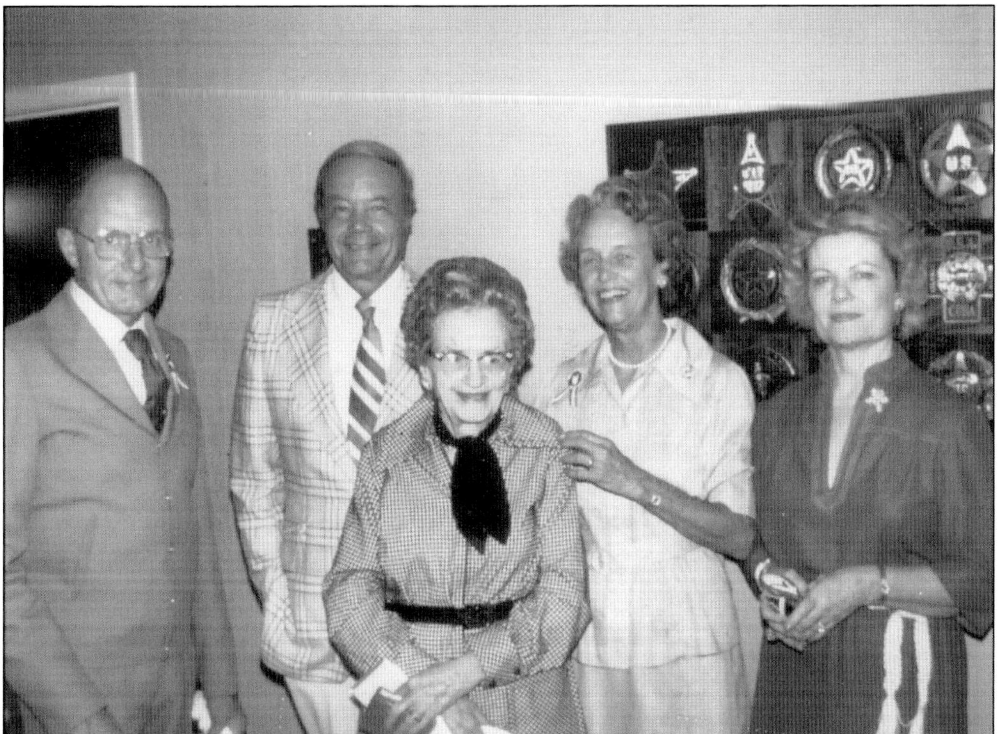

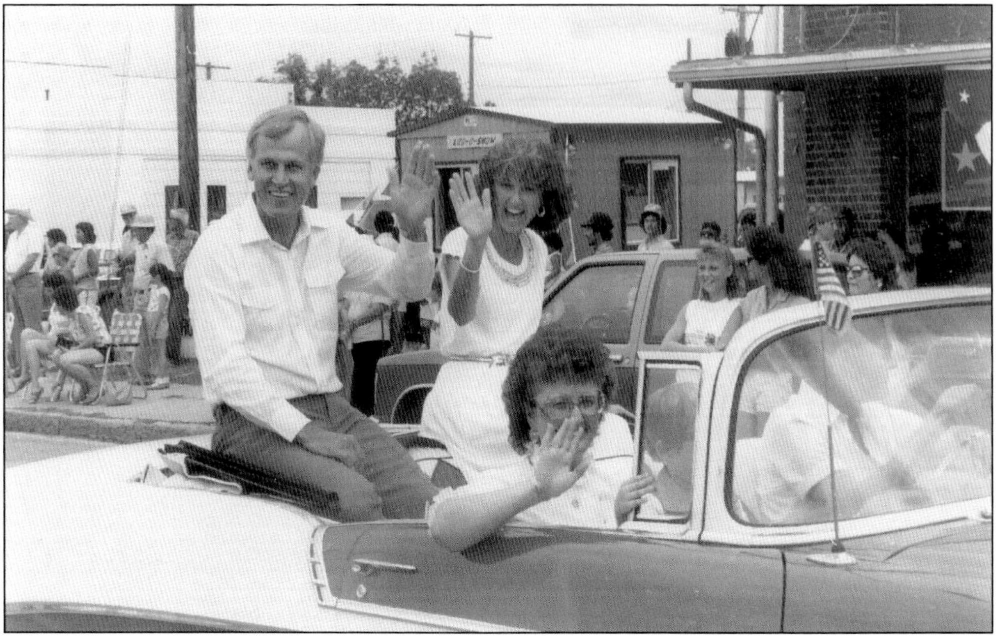

Stamford graduate Charles Stenholm, a descendant of Swedish pioneers and a successful cotton grower near Ericksdahl, was elected in 1978 to represent the 17th Texas Congressional District. Stenholm served in the House of Representatives until 2005. Stenholm (waving from car) strongly supported the Texas Cowboy Reunion. Another Stamford graduate, Robert Strauss, was the chairman of the Democratic National Committee from 1972 to 1977 and the US ambassador to Russia from 1991 until 1993.

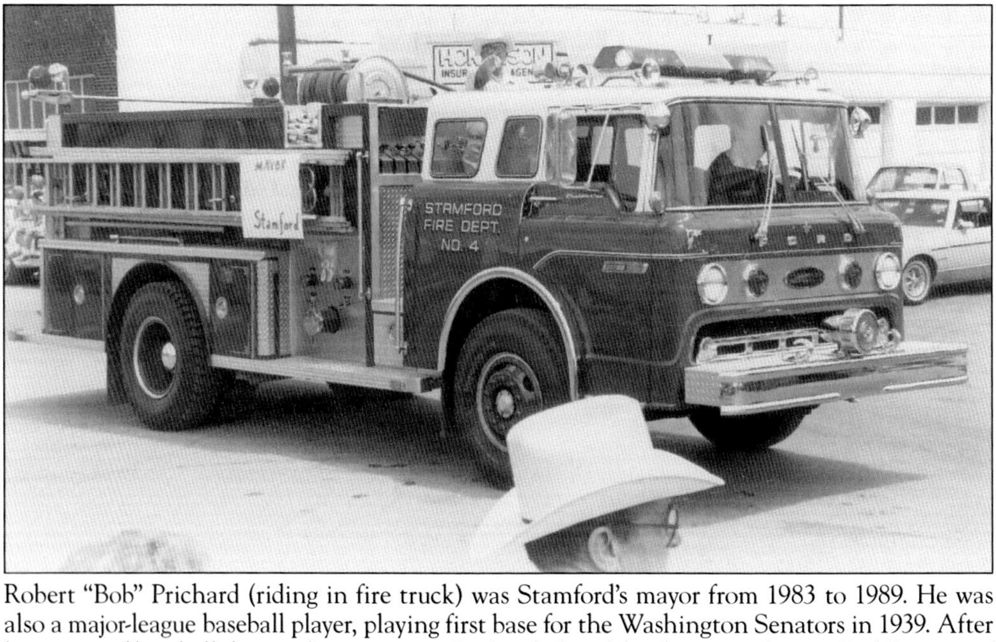

Robert "Bob" Prichard (riding in fire truck) was Stamford's mayor from 1983 to 1989. He was also a major-league baseball player, playing first base for the Washington Senators in 1939. After being out of baseball during the war years, Prichard played for the minor-league Red Peppers of Paris, Texas, until 1949. Prichard moved to Stamford in 1958, where he owned and operated radio station KDWT until his death in 1991.

By 1986, the pioneer cowboys who began the reunion had passed away, but new generations stepped forward to continue the tradition. Here, old-timers register in the Roundup Hall before going next door to the Will Rogers Bunkhouse. The bunkhouse was built in the 1930s, partly with funds many ranches paid to have their brands carved in stone along the building's exterior.

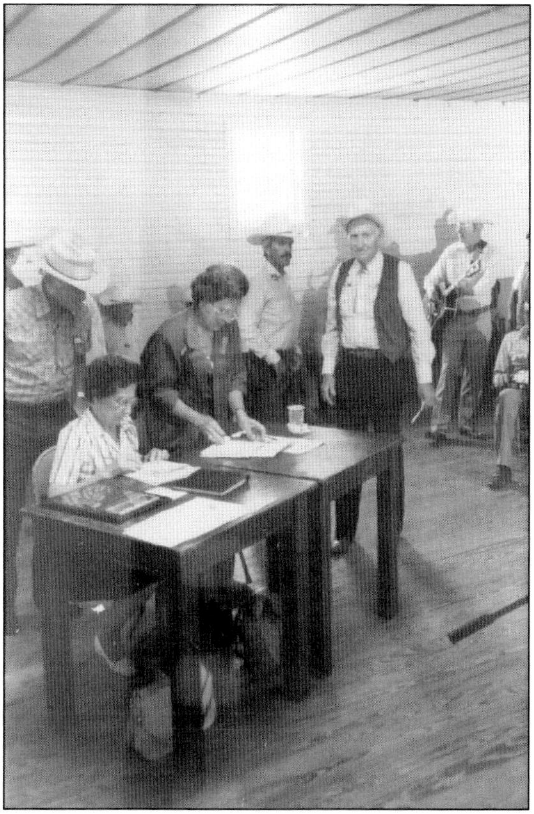

The Roundup Hall also hosted the annual Old Timers Fiddler's Contest. Later that evening, as they had for decades, couples took to the floor of the Roundup Hall to dance to the beat of country music. They danced on the same floor once used by square dancers twirling in colorful costumes and by teenagers jitterbugging to the music of Elvis Presley.

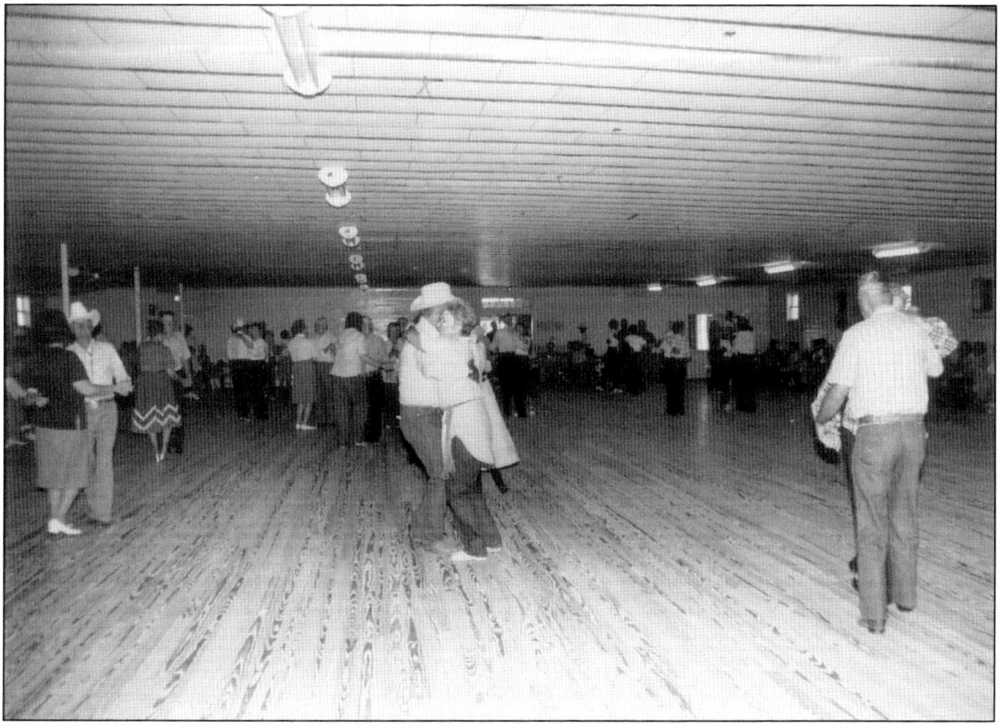

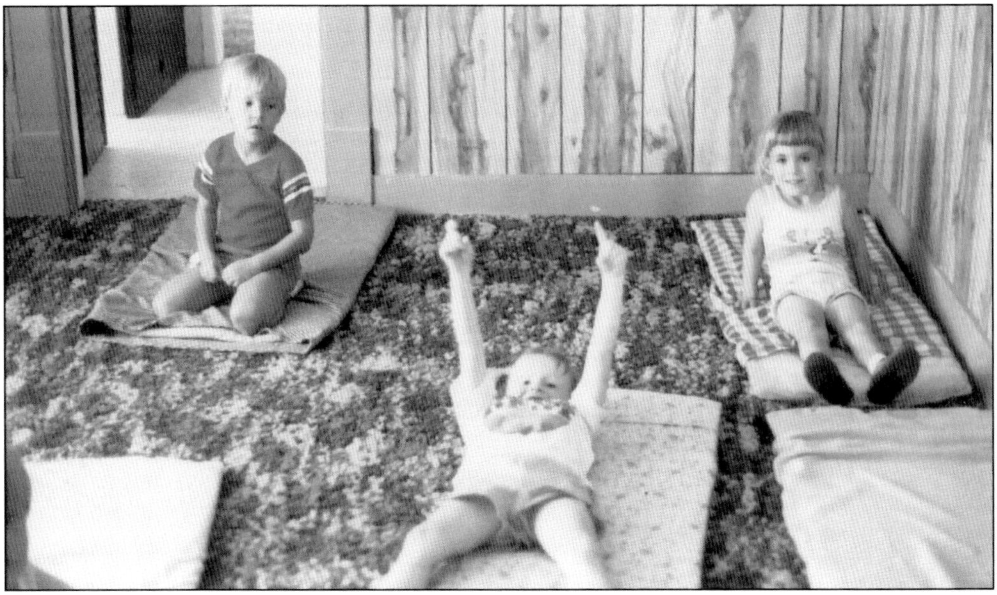

With its low crime rate, Stamford was shocked by the 1988 disappearance of seven-year-old Cortney Clayton (on pallet in center) a block from her home. A total of 300 searchers combed the area without success. The case received national attention. Seven months later, her remains were found in Shackelford County. Sandra Rhea, who taught Clayton in her day care center, recalled, "Cortney absorbed love like a sponge and gave her love as free as the sunshine."

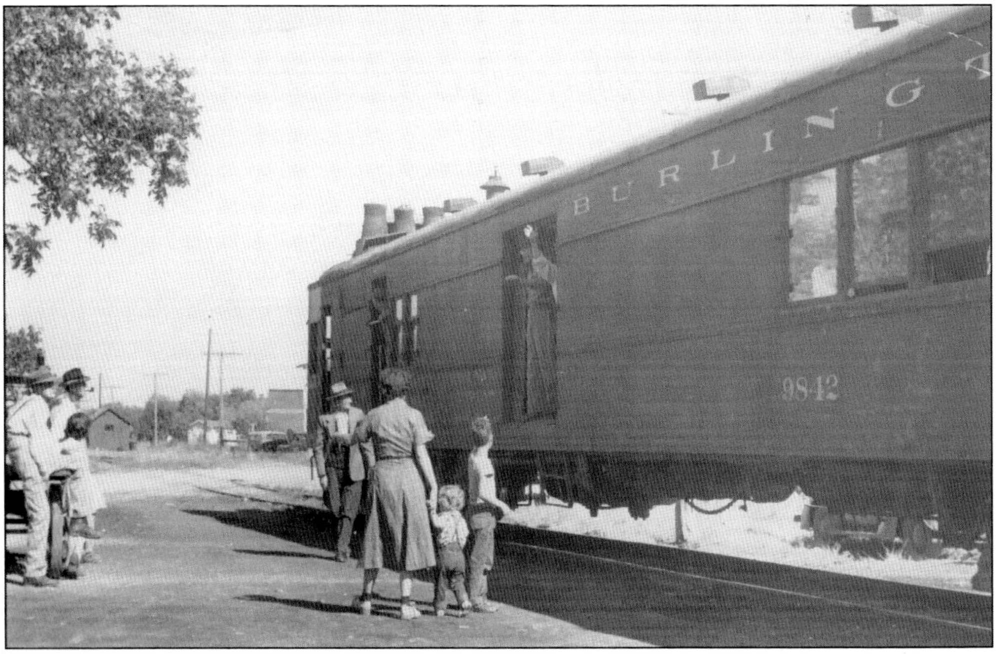

Railroad traffic in Stamford gradually declined. The Stamford & Northwestern ceased operations in 1967, and the Missouri-Kansas-Texas (MKT), the last owner of the old Texas Central line, ran its final passenger train to Stamford in 1967. Burlington had purchased the Wichita Valley Railway in 1905. For a few years, there were "doodlebugs"—passenger and freight train combinations. But by the mid-1990s, all were gone, along with the railroad lines themselves.

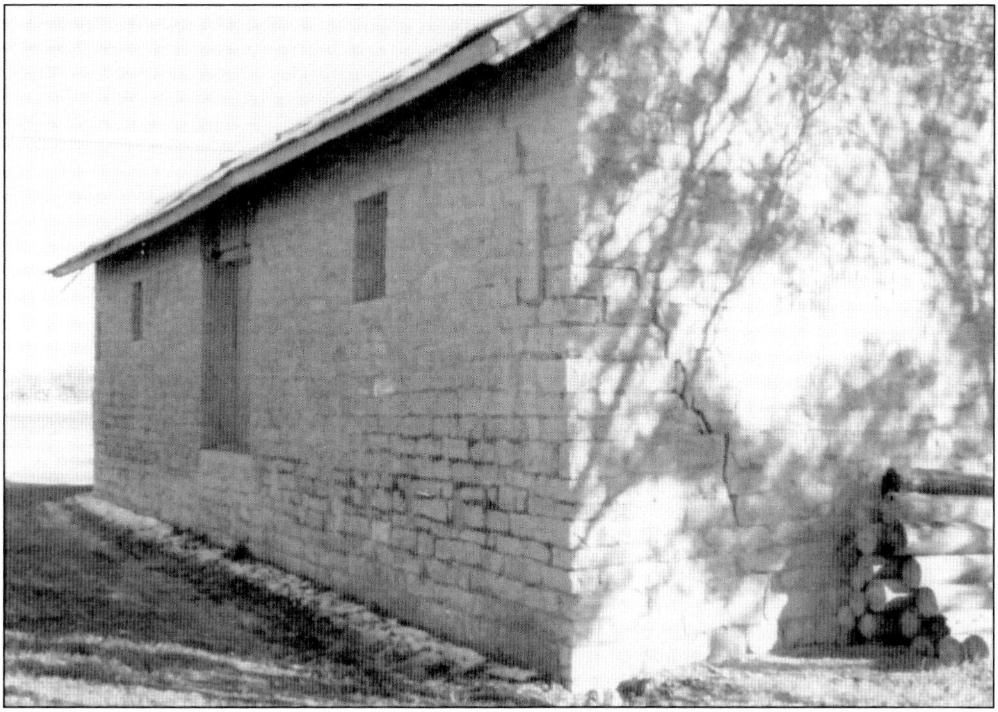

The Swenson Ranch Commissary is a last surviving relic along the railroad right-of-way. Built of Leuders stone around 1900, the commissary stood adjacent to the Texas Central tracks. Supplies were off-loaded from the trains and stored in the building until the foremen from the different SMS ranches could come to town to collect their supplies as well as a little news. (Photograph by James Collett.)

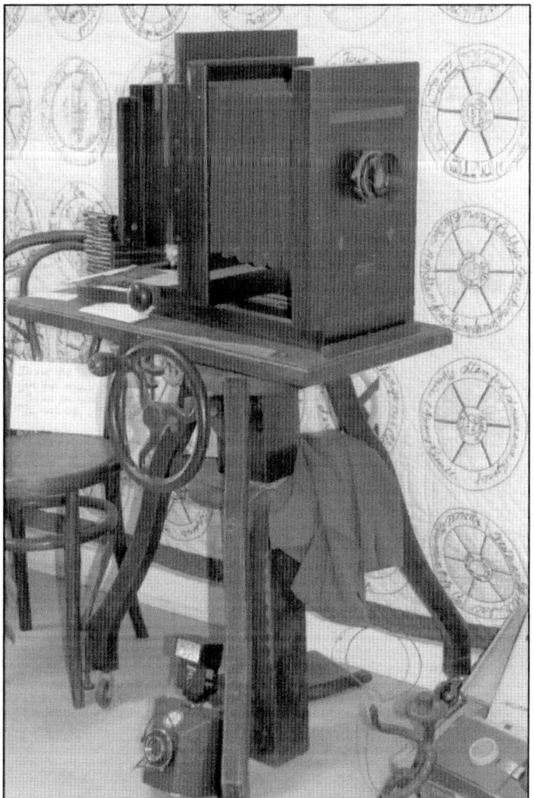

Photographer Tommie Rector successfully continued his father's business for 60 years before retiring. At age 98, he donated a vast collection of his work to the Cowboy Country Museum. Rector took only black-and-white photographs throughout his entire career, many on a Century Studio Camera (seen here) that he purchased in 1936. He also donated tintypes, glass negatives, and photographs taken by his father. (Photograph by James Collett.)

Stamford photographer Audra Arendall shot this storm through the gate at the old Texas Cowboy Reunion grounds before the 82nd Texas Cowboy Reunion in 2012. Thousands of spectators and contestants shared exciting moments in calf roping, wild cow milking, steer riding, team roping, and barrel racing. Professional rodeo cowboys were now allowed to participate, unlike in the original years. Old-timers met and swapped stories about earlier days in the cattle industry, and Western musicians played for dances at night. In 1932, Ray Rector wrote an article for the third reunion program entitled "How It Started." He closed with the statement, "We believe our organization will continue to grow until the last drive has been made, the last alkali bogs have been passed and the last great round-up will find us all together where cutting horses never get tired and where no night guards are needed." That reunion has not arrived yet, but the one in Stamford is still going strong. (Courtesy of the *Stamford Star.*)

Six

LEGACIES

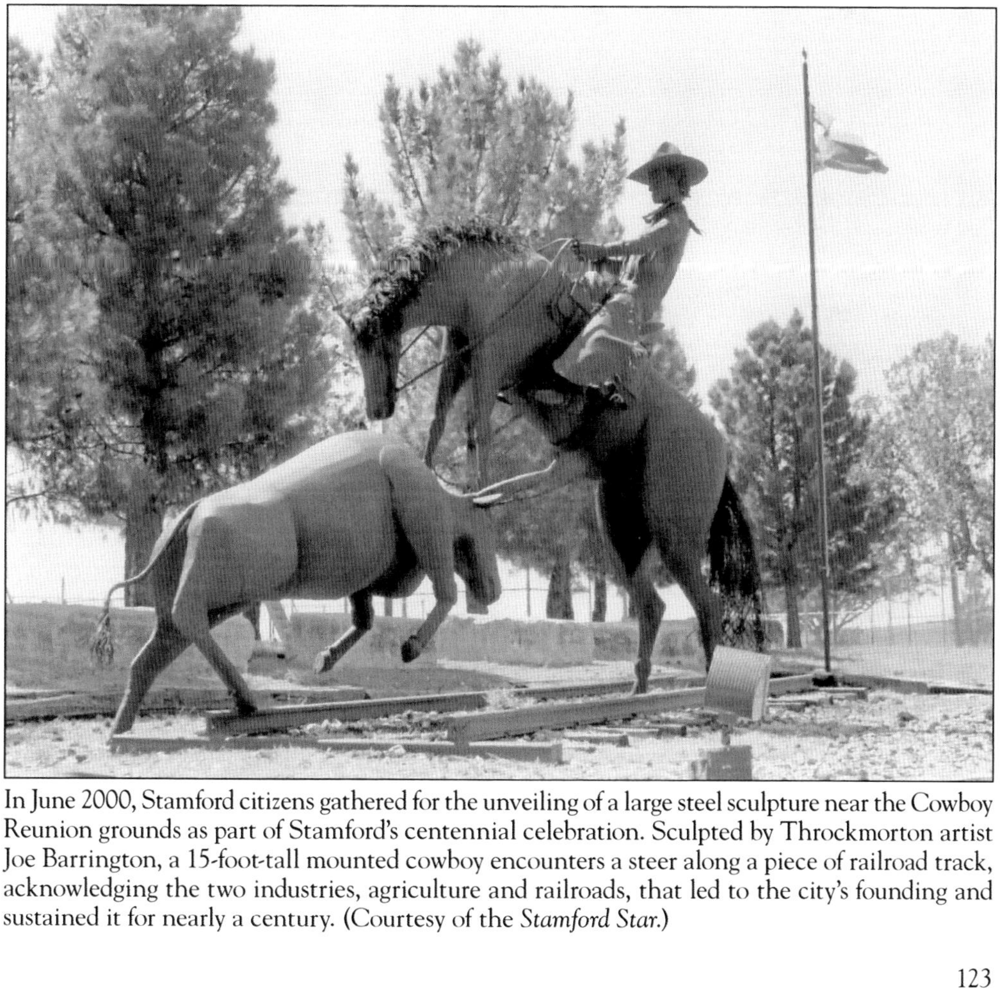

In June 2000, Stamford citizens gathered for the unveiling of a large steel sculpture near the Cowboy Reunion grounds as part of Stamford's centennial celebration. Sculpted by Throckmorton artist Joe Barrington, a 15-foot-tall mounted cowboy encounters a steer along a piece of railroad track, acknowledging the two industries, agriculture and railroads, that led to the city's founding and sustained it for nearly a century. (Courtesy of the *Stamford Star*.)

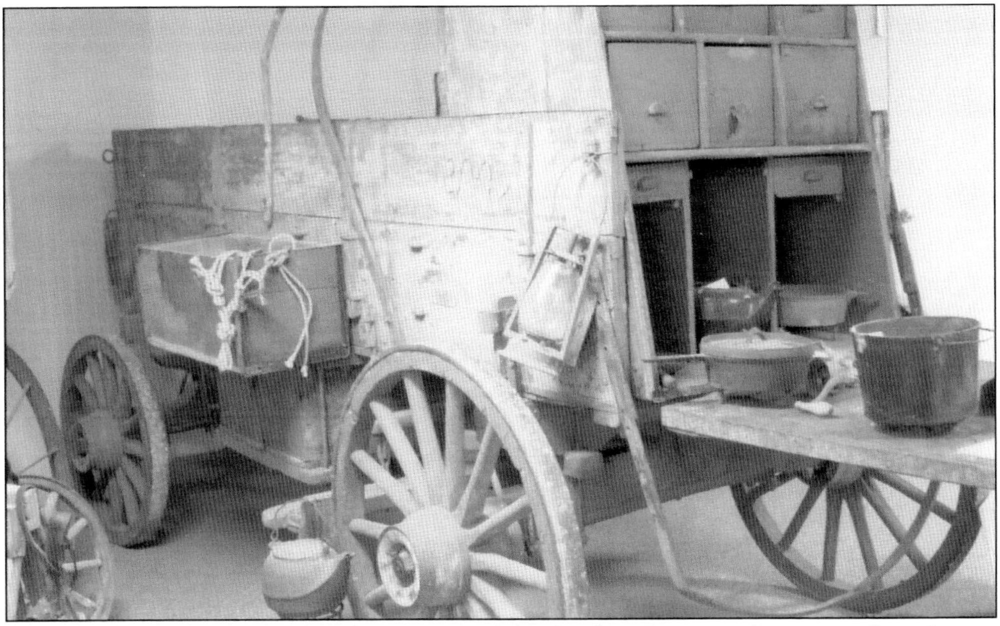

The SMS chuck wagon is a prized possession of the Cowboy Country Museum, with its famous ranch brand carved into the sideboards. The Stamford Inn closed as a hotel in the 1960s, becoming a private club and then a nursing home before being abandoned in the early 1980s. It survives only as a dilapidated ruin. The Swenson Land and Cattle Company is still managed from across the street. (Photograph by James Collett.)

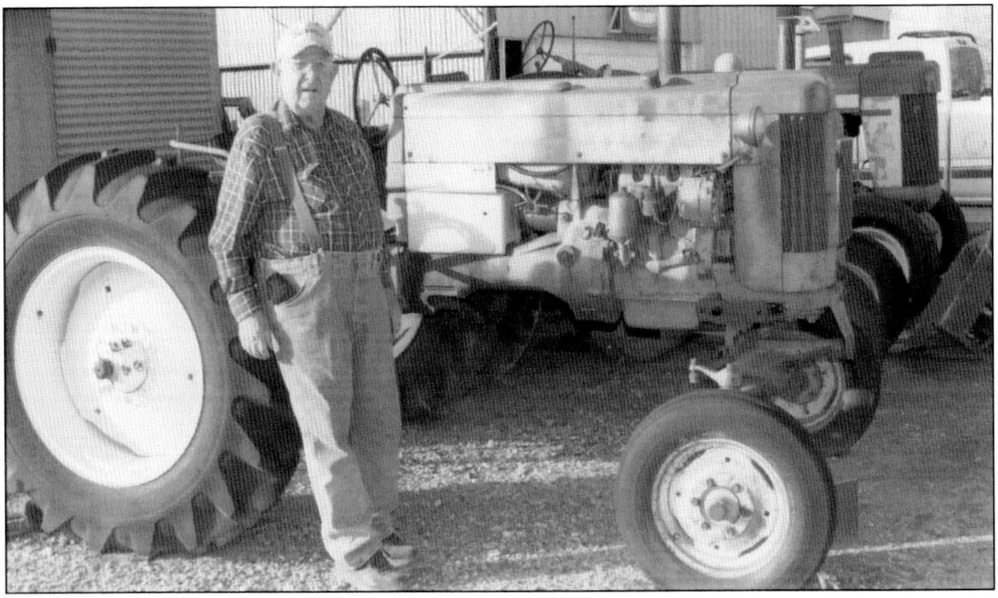

Oran Brigham lived in Tuxedo for more than 45 years before moving to Stamford to farm and operate a small convenience store. In 1989, he began purchasing and restoring old tractors, mostly John Deere models, eventually acquiring the old Tuxedo School auditorium to house part of his collection. By 2011, Brigham had two buildings containing 45 fully restored tractors, with many others, like this John Deere Model 40 from 1940, awaiting their turn. (Photograph by James Collett.)

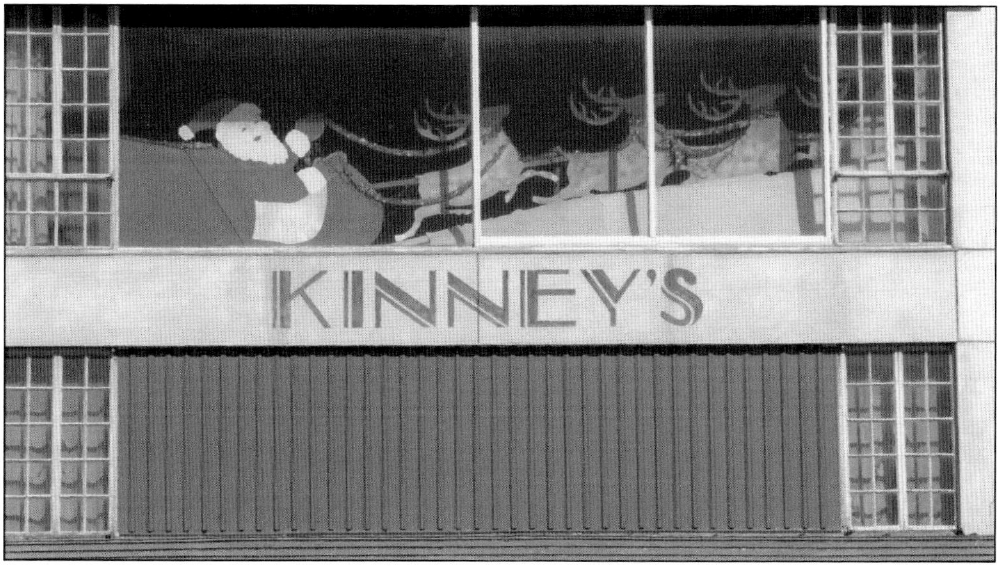

In 2010, Kinney Furniture, the oldest remaining home-owned Stamford business, closed its doors. It had served the region for generations, but the ease of modern travel and delivery finally spelled its end. Many worried about another tradition disappearing. For 70 years, the store had displayed a reindeer and sleigh in the upper-story window. That Christmas season, Santa still flew above the square each night. (Photograph by James Collett.)

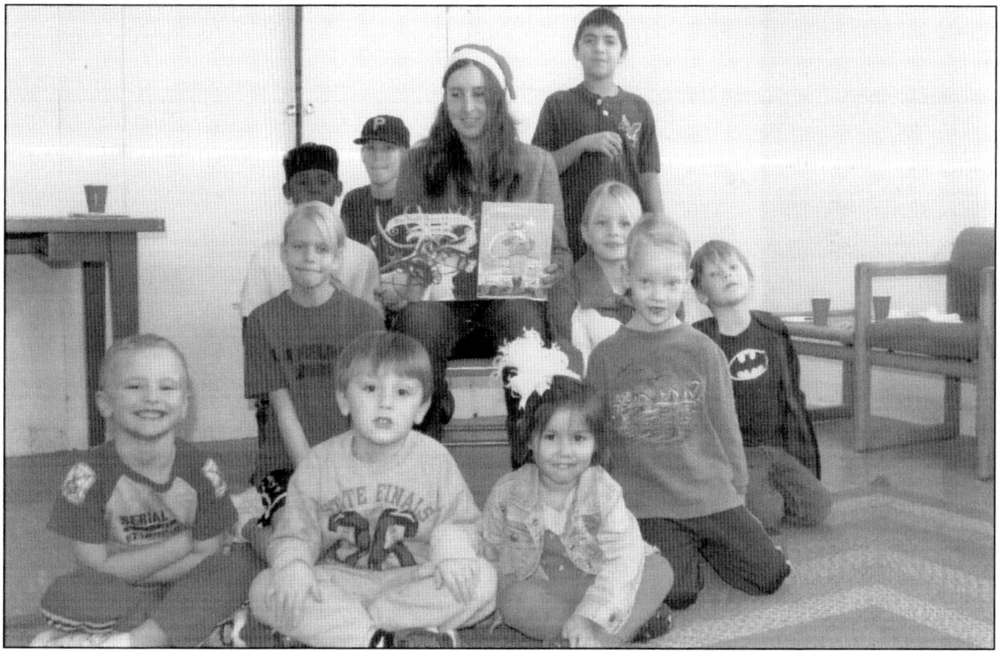

In December 2011, librarian Lucile Frazier (center) read several Christmas books to local children, including, from left to right, (first row) Seth Hall, Tristan Reilly, Krailyn Becker, Matthew Knowles, and Keith Knowles; (second row) Debra Knowles and Dyna Knowles; (third row) R.J. Smith, Caleb Young, and (standing) Alex Pardo. As it has for more than a century, the Stamford Carnegie library continues Carnegie's dream of a free public library available to all. (Courtesy of the *Stamford Star*.)

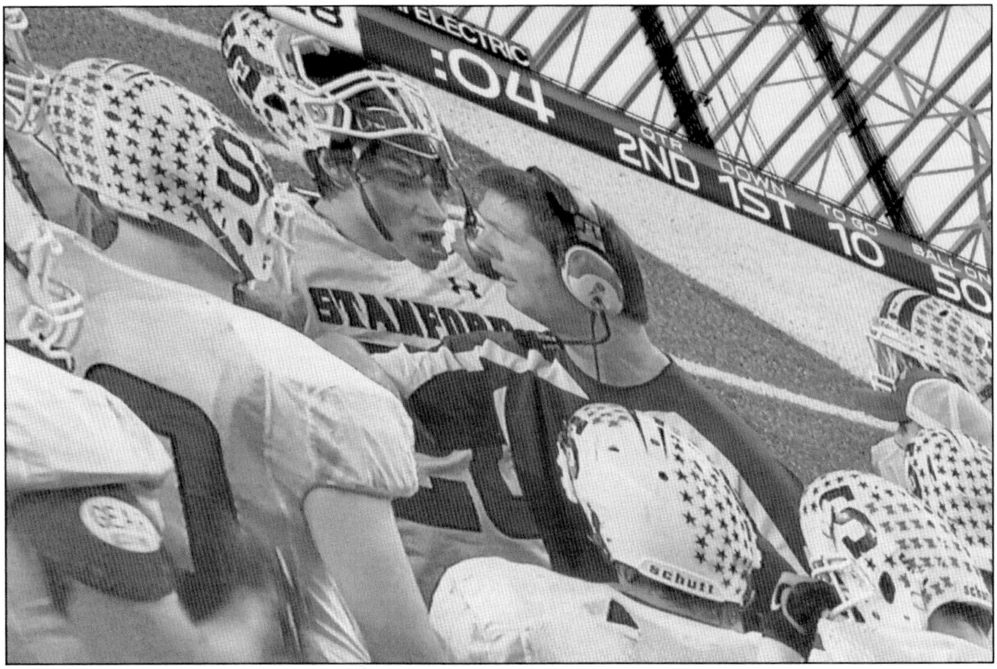

In December 2011, the Stamford Bulldog football team advanced to the class 1-A state championship game, its first since 1959. The team faced the Mason Cowpunchers in Cowboy Stadium, the world's largest domed structure and the home of the Dallas Cowboys. The high-definition "jumbotron" gave fans a front-row seat to watch coach Wayne Hutchinson instructing the team while player Jesse Ramos listens intently. Mason defeated Stamford 62-40 to win its first state championship. The following year, the Bulldogs returned to Dallas to win their first state championship in over 50 years. (Courtesy of the *Stamford American*.)

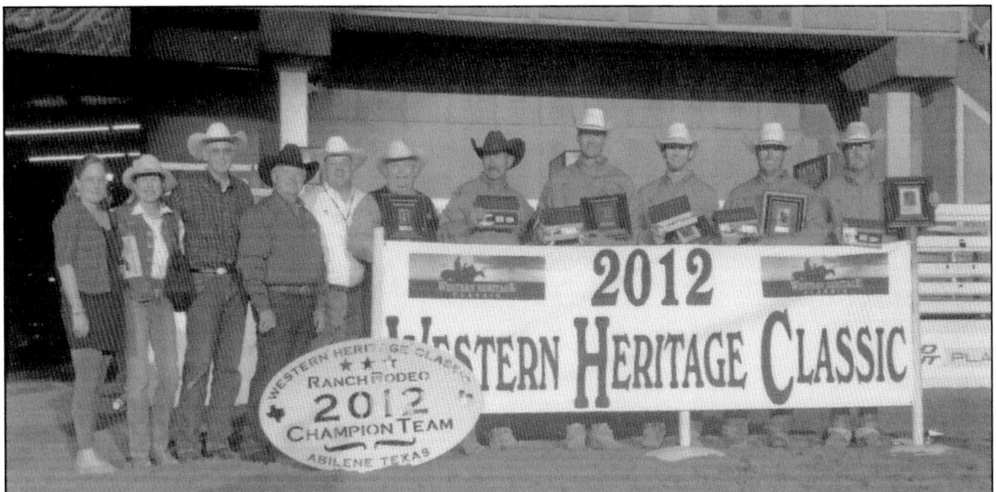

In 2012, Swenson Land and Cattle Company won the champion team title at the 28th Annual Western Heritage Classic Ranch Rodeo in Abilene. The Classic involves team competition in authentic ranch activities to determine the best working ranch. The winning team included, from left to right, Dennis Braden (behind sign, in black vest), Monty Jones, Clint Jones, Caleb Rice, Carrol Jack Lewis, and Mark Voss. (Courtesy of Fly Thomas, photographer.)

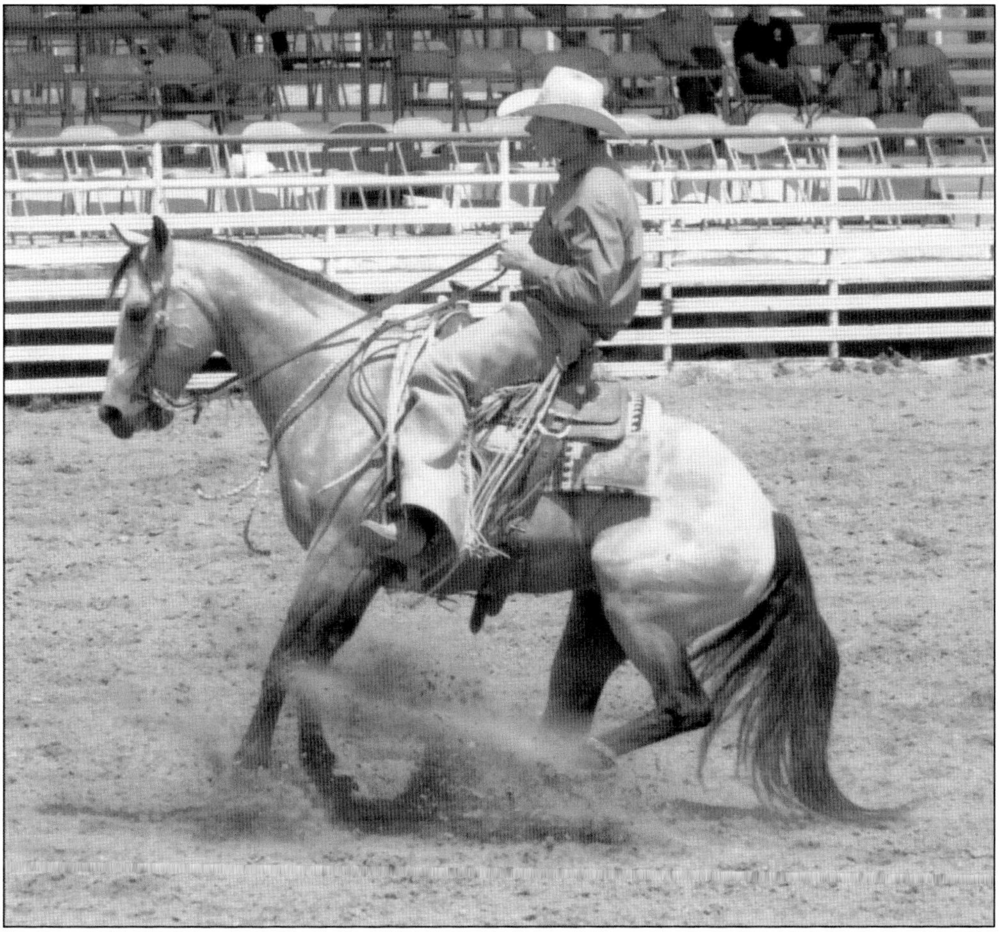

In July 2011, Zinn Lindsey, a 17-year-old from Aspermont, Texas, competed in the ranch horse competition at the Texas Cowboy Reunion. Lindsey was already a youth champion in this competition, where horse and rider work together in a timed event to complete a set of tasks, including a reining pattern of turns and stops (seen here), before working a cow's movement and finally roping a cow. Lindsey is the great-grandson of Cleo Shipman and the great-great-nephew of John Selmon. Named Zinn for his paternal ancestors, Clara and Emma Zinn, Lindsey competed against riders with years more experience who rode for famous ranches—the SMS, Pitchfork, and Matador—and placed second. His story is one of many in Stamford, where families like Rector, Kinney, and Selmon and organizations like Penick Hardware, the Stamford Inn, West Texas Utilities, and the Swenson Land and Cattle Company have produced rich legacies carried into a new century by Stamford descendants in this city on the West Texas prairie. (Photograph by James Collett.)

Discover Thousands of Local History Books Featuring Millions of Vintage Images

Arcadia Publishing, the leading local history publisher in the United States, is committed to making history accessible and meaningful through publishing books that celebrate and preserve the heritage of America's people and places.

Find more books like this at
www.arcadiapublishing.com

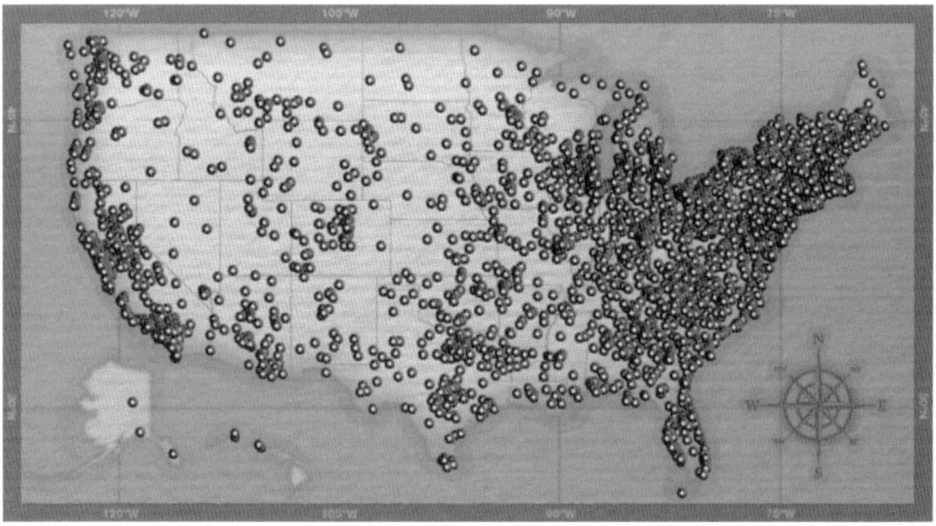

Search for your hometown history, your old stomping grounds, and even your favorite sports team.

Consistent with our mission to preserve history on a local level, this book was printed in South Carolina on American-made paper and manufactured entirely in the United States. Products carrying the accredited Forest Stewardship Council (FSC) label are printed on 100 percent FSC-certified paper.

MADE IN THE USA